VOID

Library of
Davidson College

Jean Price-Mars
and
Haiti

Jacques Carmeleau Antoine

Preface
by
Jean F. Brierre

THREE CONTINENTS PRESS, INC.
Washington, D. C.

972.94
A634j

© 1981 Jacques Carmeleau Antoine

First Edition/Three Continents Press, Inc.
1346 Connecticut Avenue, N. W.
Washington, D. C. 20036

ISBN: 0-914478-55-9 (Cased)
ISBN: 0-914478-56-7 (Paperback)

LC No: 80-80888

All rights reserved. No part of this book may be used or reproduced in any form or any manner whatsoever without written permission from the publisher, except for brief quotations in reviews and critical articles. For inquiries, write the publisher.

Cover Design by Tom Gladden

81-5888

Acknowledgments

I wish to express my gratitude to Dr. Mercer Cook, former United States Ambassador to the Republic of Senegal, and to Professor Maurice A. Lubin, from Haiti, professor of African literature at Howard University in Washington, D. C. My indebtedness to my two former colleagues at Howard University and friends of many years goes further. Mercer Cook, who has been my Good Samaritan ever since I left Haiti in 1945, was the originator of the idea of my writing the biography in 1969. He was then Chairman of the Department of Romance Languages at Howard, to which he had brought me three years earlier and had assigned me to teach a course on Haitian literature. He made the suggestion one morning as he told me the sad news he had just heard of the death of Price-Mars, two or three days after it had happened. As I accepted the challenge Mercer helped me all through the writing of the book with the generosity and thoroughness that characterise his personality, not only by his criticisms and suggestions, both general and detailed in respect of the book's composition, but also through the painstaking process of editing my Frenchified English from the first to the last page of the book.

Maurice Lubin, who was still in Haiti in 1969 when I began to write the biography, helped me no less generously and thoroughly in doing for me the leg-work in Port-au-Prince, going indefatigably to one library after another to look for the source materials I wanted to have for the biography. Not only did he succeed in finding them, he took the pain of typing out a monumental amount of research notes which he sent me, even faster than I had expected to receive them, belittling always his efforts and trouble in locating and preparing these materials for me. And because he had maintained a close relationship with Price-Mars during the latter's last decade of life, serving on occasions as his secretary, Maurice's own perception of the man was invaluable to me as I tried to capture the true personality of "the Uncle" who had lived almost one hundred years through so many different circumstances and the ups and downs of a Crusader-politician's life.

I have dedicated the book to both Mercer Cook and Maurice Lubin, not simply as a testimony of my appreciation for the help they gave me in the preparation and writing of the biography, but because they have labored on it along with me from the start, the three of us moved by the same admiration and affection we ardently share for the author of *Ainsi Parla l'Oncle* whose memory now belongs to the whole of mankind.

Jacques C. Antoine
Buenos Aires

For
Mercer Cook
and
Maurice A. Lubin

Jean Price-Mars

I will formulate the message of Jean Price-Mars in the following manner: "We are fighting the cowardly occupation of our territory by the American Marines. We will be free tomorrow. But once independence has been recovered, we have to begin the era of The Great Duty—purge ourselves of the last drop of slave blood in our veins, and according to Chekhov's phrase, burn the old robes which suffocate us and make us look ridiculous, the silly clothes we are decked out in, the paste jewels and the artifices of deceit. We must be ourselves, Haitian negroes, sons of titans who, alone and singlehandedly, broke off the chains of slavery."

Jean F. Brierre

Haiti

Contents

	Acknowledgments	*v*
	Preface by Jean F. Brierre	*3*
I	The Seed and the Soil	9
II	Sixty-Four Leagues of Darkness and Misery from the Capital	19
III	A Vow in the City of Light	29
IV	The Spirit of the Founders	39
V	Navigating on Troubled Waters	57
VI	A Poetic Call to Arms	69
VII	Triumph and Disaster	81
VIII	Race, People or Fatherland	93
IX	Ministering to Youth	107
X	The Country Doctor's Elixir	119
XI	Thus Spoke the Uncle	133
XII	The "Foolish Dreams"	147
XIII	Victory and Defeat, Again	165
XIV	To the Unknown Black	177

Footnotes	*193*
Bibliography	*209*
Index	*215*
Maps	
Map of Haiti	*x*
Map of Northern Caribbean Sea	*2*
Map of Port-au-Prince	*91*
Map of Commune de la Grande Rivière du Nord	*118*
Photographs	
Jean Price-Mars	*viii*
Anténor Firmin	*52*
Dantès Bellegarde	*52*
Georges Sylvain	*145*
Jacques Roumain	*159*
Léon Laleau	*164*
Jean Price-Mars and Family	*189*
Jean Price-Mars	*192*

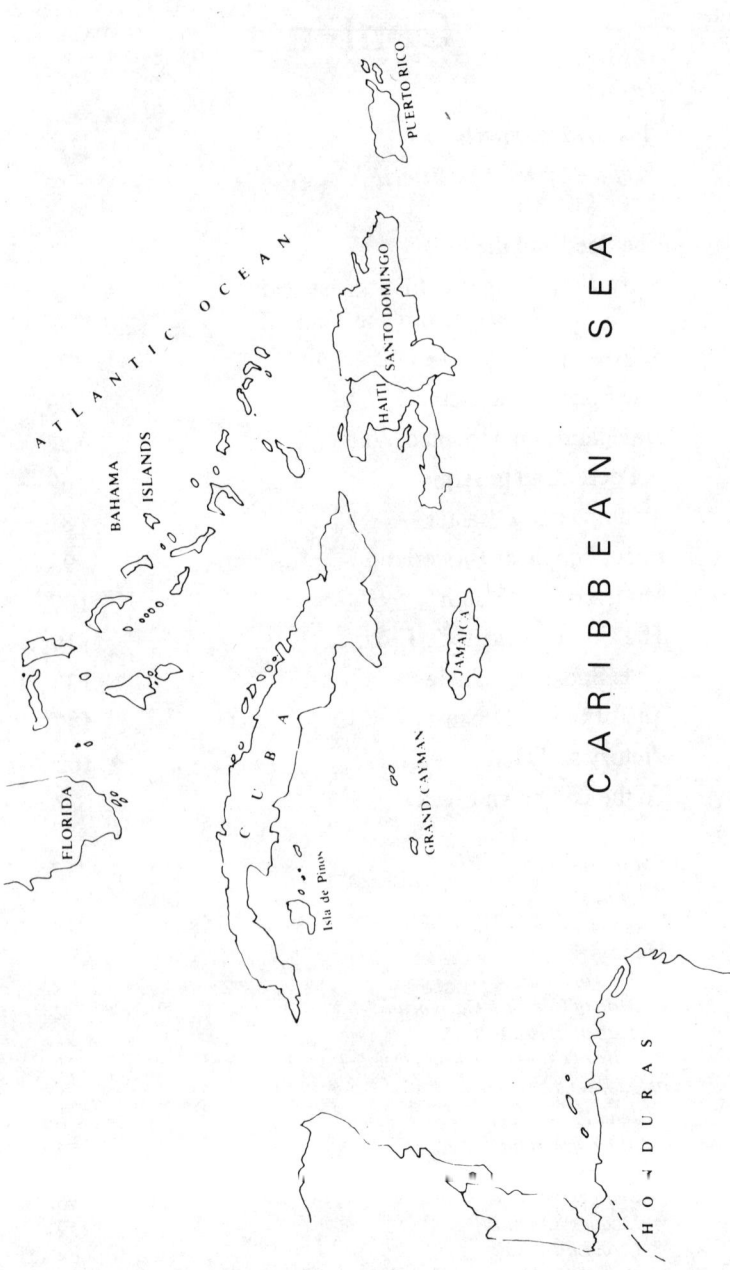

Northern Caribbean Sea

Preface

Between Legend and Truth

No one may choose his death, but each one has the opportunity to shape the path of his life through the underbrush of existing possibilities. It occurs to me, paradoxically, and without in the least wanting it, to square off life and death, as though one were not the natural conclusion of the other, death being the last phase and total, definitive eclipse of life.

Life starts to ooze death at the very moment of conception itself. The smallest tot faces old age and death at the moment of his birth. Siamese twins (death & life), together they track us, attending our highest joys and our seasonal brushes with confusion and despair. They plod on, the one the hidden nocturnal face of the other. Life inevitably engenders death, but it is death nevertheless which carves into the ice-chunk of terminal immobility the ineluctable immortality of temporal memory.

One lives fragmented in the eyes and in the ambiguous mirror of others. Everyone catches you up in his instant perceptions, through his various ocular deformities: near-sighted, far-sighted, or perhaps in a clear, unwavering gaze. You are a unique individual seen from different angles—profile, silhouette, straight-on—the mass of organized flesh which is your body.

Whether one wishes it or not, living means projecting some sort of image. There is a need to affirm one's physical and moral identity; a way, beyond one's bodily traits, one's stride, and one's expressions, of revealing oneself with a word, a look, a smile, a gesture—all those things which emphasize and make up a personality. There is also one's accent; a light glaringly harsh, or soft as a humid morning; the set of one's lips in anger or affirmation; an arm akimbo, or stiff as an exclamation point.

Gathered up in a set of fixed landmarks which the greediness of time cannot erode, in unwavering stances, the life of Jean Price-Mars is now, since his death on March 1, 1969, a definitive entity which some try to understand, and others try to dissect like Macabees, all in an effort to situate it properly in that fluid continuum called history.

None of Price-Mars' contemporaries, whether Seymour Pradel with his flair and dilletantism; Constantin Mayard with his endless sincerity; Pauleus Sannon with his good cheer, suavity, and eyes fatigued by historical research, or Sténio Vincent (that orator of emptiness) with the sybaritic crown awarded him in the reign of the man who precipitated Haiti's decline: none of them (save in a footnote in an anthology or elementary textbook), were worth the curious and intelligent attention of any of the historians and researchers of my generation.

None of them, not even Dantès Bellegarde, corrupted by the outmoded, bourgeois, French culture, was able to transmit the multi-dimensional message left by the man who will forever bear the sobriquet of "The Uncle."

That Jacques Antoine, wounded patriot, with his sharp intelligence, his lucid, objective mind, builds this monument of inestimable value to our celebrated forefather, Jean Price-Mars, amidst a mind-boggling collage of defeats, courage, glory, shame, treachery, ambiguity, opportunism, cowardice and precocious ambition that runs through our history testifies that the pedestal on which he places our hero is one of gratitude and collective fervor.

The backdrop of his childhood in the North of Haiti, at once pathetic and heroic, where certain generals and intellectuals were transformed into guerilla chiefs and vectors of calculated violence, but dominated nevertheless the statue of King Henry Christophe in all its grandeur, and his two-hundred year old Citadel; in a climate of ecumenical tolerance (with a Protestant father, Catholic grandmother, and with the Voodoo drums summoning him in the tropical night with their throbbing rhythms); with the family cult devoted to his grandfather Jean Belley, called Mars, first deputy from the colony of Saint Domingue to the French National Convention; with the geological accidents which mark the boundaries of his native village; the first textbook, the first bible...all these things made up the rites of initiation for this boy into the society of man.

On the first reading of this historical exegesis by Jacques Antoine, I had the impression that he had written a slice of the history of Haiti which already pregnant with Jean Price-Mars, would later swell into major events, crossing the dawn of the twentieth century, and continue with the unfurling of flags on January 1, 1904, a day of pomp and glory, the Centennial of Independence. I thought he would record Price-Mars' first adolescent footsteps, up to the point where his awakening would make this son of a well-known peasant from Grande Rivière du Nord the man predestined to liberate the conscience of an entire generation.

I know that linear time is still just time, and that it never really "crosses" anything, and that it is we, who, needing an illusory security, and who are harried by an unending hunger to remember the past, sacrifice real life by inscribing it in our chronicles without which we would not be in a "civilized" state.

At first, I had the impression that the real center of interest in this large book was not really Jean Price-Mars, he being but a pretext

Preface

chosen as a sometimes hazy example of tragedy, but history, methodically thought-out by a wary historian.

Re-reading the work—one must always re-read—showed me that the union of history with historiography, like biology with histology, can be felicitous.

Indeed, the stature of the man in question, with his self-esteem bound up with the true Haitian people, his unrivalled cultural activism, his exemplary humility which was not without its controlled anger, cries and barbs demands that his magi's profile, his sage words, his venerable kindness so similar to that of African teachers and elders in the shade of the palaver tree, ought not to be shown in a private studio for the "happy few," but on the vast screen of life lived differently by all its varied protagonists; the screen itself of *history,* beautiful, painful and tragic, of the Haitian people.

I have perhaps already said it, but I want to emphasize it further without in the least dimishing the honest historian's objective and almost neutral style, his vision of men and events, that I admire his pen which never spews bitter ink, scratches across the paper or tears the page.

Had I been able to write the same work, even if to do it I had only a slab of basalt, I would have, with a flint searing with a pre-historic and savage anger, carved, in all its pathetic truth the face of a unique and integral, black Haitian. In his time, he was the only leader, in the bosom of a perfectly assimilated elite, who was conscious and proud of his African origins.

I would have had another approach to the man, simply because I am not, and never could be, an historian like Jacques Antoine. It must be a question of culture and temperament because even in my old age, I am still deeply moved by an implacable anger.

I am fond neither of iconography, nor of monumentalism, but dear to me are Papa Ibra's seemingly simple pencils and ink which speak succinctly in blood and flesh of untouted courage which exhausts its strength, foundations and truth in the single certainty of being right today and tomorrow.

For today: No one dares contest the good initiated in *Ainsi Parla l'Oncle,* in which Price-Mars, in his uneven, not always well-disciplined style (which marks all his books) speaks of the African origins of the Haitian people and denounces, without playing the street-corner prophet or the rabble-rouser, the imbecilic bovaryism of the scholars and so-called elite of his time—bovaryism which earned them the arrogant remark of Wilhelm II, forerunner of Mr. Adolf Hitler: "That fistful of negroes barely tinted with French civilization."

Ainsi Parla l'Oncle appeared in 1928 at the height of the American occupation. The country was on edge. A wave of extreme nationalism had aroused all strata of society. Bands of peasants, armed only with gourds and machetes, were going off to protest the crushing taxes, to confront the North American monsters whose sons and grandsons, despite their napalm and bombers, would be defeated in Vietnam by bamboo arrows and rice bullets. It was the genocide of Marchaterre.[1]

Other politicians whose names it is unnecessary to mention here, thought that this genocide would have had echoes throughout the world.

With calm, an orator less flamboyant than the blustering Pierre Hudicourt, Price-Mars, whom the Ku Klux Klan had harrassed in the heart of the American bush, knew that the geographical dimensions of his country, and the audacity of its revolutionary origins relegated Haiti to be but a dot on the globe, and that no European state would forgive him for unfurling the flag of freedom in the very center of the slaving nations of the Americas, sluts of the world.

Nobody except a few intellectuals understood Price-Mars and his evangelical mission. I use the word "evangelical" in its absolutely profane meaning, intentionally avoiding the word "message."

It is thanks to him that the Indigenist Movement was born which would spawn a truly great generation of totally Haitian writers, from Jacques Roumain to Regnor Bernard, René Belance and Paul Laraque.

Price-Mars had the courage to study the Voodoo religion (for it is indeed one) which comes from Ife, Nigeria, and which arrived in the holds of the slave ships along with the deported Dahomean peoples.

This monotheistic religion which people confuse with sorcery and magic was first explained by Price-Mars. And because he was black and didn't speak in Greek decrees, they accused him of participating in Voodoo-like black masses. And simply because he enunciatd this truth: that magic and sorcery exist on the fringes of all the revealed religions. But when my mentor Jacques Roumain wrote on the "Sacrifice of the Assotor Drum," the most vocal paien to the Voodoo religion, they didn't accuse him of practicing it. That was because Jacques Roumain who, like Senghor, had Paul Rivet for his teacher, and who had the courage to renounce his heritage as the grandson of a President of the Republic, found favor in the eyes of the very elite whom he had scorned.

My mentor (Roumain—I would say in other circumstances why I call him thus) would perhaps not have been inscribed in the roll of unstanding Haitian citizens had he not known Price-Mars who wrote with such talent and friendship the preface to Roumain's *Enchanted Mountain*.

I will formulate the message of Jean Price-Mars in the following manner: "We are fighting the cowardly occupation of our territory by American Marines. We will be free tomorrow. But once Independance has been recovered, we will have to begin the era of The Great Duty—to purge ourselves of the last drop of slave blood

Preface

in our veins, and according to Chekov's phrase, burn the old robes which suffocate us and make us look ridiculous, the silly clothes we are decked-out in, the paste jewels and the artifices of deceit. We must be ourselves, Haitian negroes, sons of titans who alone and singlehandedly broke the chains of slavery.

The legend did not wait for Price-Mars' death to cover him sometimes with an aura of mysticism or haughty grandeur, sometimes with a corset which did nothing whatever to shield him, but which only served to repress the natural boundings of a heart forced into restraints.

He had begun to die well before 1966, on that morning when he understood that fate was slowly but surely burying his tools of knowledge, those beacons of discovery embodied in his sense of sight. The man I met, for the last time at the world-wide meeting of Africa and the Diaspora, the First World Festival of Negro Arts (at Dakar)—did he feel diminished by the everlasting sunset which the death of his eyes presaged? In the company of an aeropagus of learned men, writers, historians, sociologists, researchers, literati, did he feel that he was becoming useless and already marginal? Did he have the feeling that, while living, oblivion was already surrounding him? I do not know. But nothing is sadder than a smile which fails to light the face; than the almost staring eyes which barely distinguish vague forms in a fog which grows thicker with each passing day.

Already doomed to reside in a country which to this day stinks of blood and cadavres, a huge open-air slaughterhouse, now blindness forced him into a second, more shadowy exile, where the microbes of anguish and the vermine of introspection multiplied.

To his contemporaries who reproached him for his luke-warm response to the American occupier, I will answer that he was not one to man the barricades and strut across the stage. He thought that for the Haitian people, whose North American centurions had created a disaster in the quagmire of genocide, there should be a covenant of conviviality, a future full of light and justice.

To those who say he denied his home region of the North, I will say that cultural logic, the only one he respected, demanded that he be close to the center of the battle, which did not simply take place in the streets and on parade.

They accuse him of a neutrality born of calculations, dubious stratagems, ambiguous postures, lofty mandarin-like retreats, and a certain impermeability to anything which was neither history nor sociology.

On the other side, they would like to lock him up in a stifling chapel, smother him in incense as though in some cultist shrine, far from the iconoclastic crowds as if, disembodied from birth, he had not been subject to the weaknesses and errors inherent in the human condition.

It is between these two currents of legend and demystification that I place Jean Price-Mars.

For tomorrow: What does it matter that people have distorted his message? It stays alive in the heart of the real country. "The Uncle," already having become a legend, will die of chagrin, an internal exile, clothed in dignity, facing the shame of the last quarter century in Haiti. But his austere silence spoke more potently than any cry, for, like Simon Bolivar, steeped in disgust, he will have ploughed the seas.

Jean F. Brierre
Dakar, Senegal 1980

---

[1]Place in southern Haiti, close to Cayes, where several peasants died under the bullets of the U. S. Marines in 1929.

One

The Seed and the Soil

The year 1876 was a very good one for the peaceful and industrious Jean Eléomont Mars. Until then, he had devoted his time solely to his family and business in his Commune of Grande Rivière du Nord, far from the political turmoil of the nation's capital. That spring, however, Grande Rivière elected him to the House of Representatives and he made his first appearance on the political scene. The enthusiastic youth throughout the nation heralded the results of the general elections as the beginning of a new era of political freedom. And on October 15, Eléomont Mars had further cause to rejoice. He became the proud father of a boy, his first child after two years of marriage.

Traditionally, general elections were conducted under the vigilant eyes of the local military authorities who usually sent their kin to the capital as deputies. In some cases the successful candidates were handpicked in advance by the central government. Occasionally, the "elected" deputies had never set foot on the soil of the communes they represented. Apparently Eléomont Mars had been elected by the free choice of the townfolk because of his personal reputation and the prestige of his family. At that time, Grande Rivière du Nord was, and had been for many years, the political fief of the Sam family, of which Eléomont's wife was one of many offspring scattered throughout the Northern Province and the metropolis, Cap-Haitien.

Eléomont's mother-in-law, Mrs. Elizabeth Godart, was a first cousin of General Tirésias Simon Sam, one of the most prominent military men on the Republic's political scene for a decade since the Salnave Revolution. He had been a member of the Committee of Public Safety that Salnave's partisans had set up at Cap-Haitien following the hero welcome the city had given Salnave in May 1865.[1] At the time of Price-Mars' birth, a sister of General Simon Sam was living at Grande Rivière du Nord; she was the wife of General Séide Télémaque, Commanding Officer of the county, the most important of the strategic positions in the Northern Province.

When Eléomont Mars was elected deputy, the Domingue Administration had lost the confidence of the Haitian people because of the heavy financial burden it had put on the country by negotiating various loans from foreign investors. These loans worked almost solely to the advantage of an arrogant and aggressive group of local businessmen and military officers who had gathered around Vice President Septimus Marius, a nephew of General Domingue and the real leader of the government.

As early as May 1875, while the rumor of revolution was being whispered about Port-au-Prince, the government ordered a number of arrests, including that of General Boisrond-Canal.[2] But he was warned soon enough to gain asylum in the American consulate at the capital. In this atmosphere, the government had its hands full and could hardly have militarily controlled elections in line with the practice established by the nation's first President, Alexandre Pétion, in 1806.

Two political parties emerged from the helplessness of the Domingue regime: the Liberal Party, under the leadership of Jean-Pierre Boyer Bazelais, and the National Party under Demesvar Delorme. Boyer-Bazelais was the scion of a prominent family in the capital, the grandson of the second president of the Republic. Delorme, a celebrated writer and a great orator, was born in Cap-Haitien.

There was little ostensible difference between the programs of the two parties: both proclaimed their allegiance to the republican form of government, their determination to respect the law and in general to follow the democratic process; both promised to bring order to the State's finances, to develop agriculture and expand industry and trade. Likewise, they both stressed their firm resolve to extend public instruction to all strata of Haitian society.[3]

Despite this apparent agreement on campaign issues, the parties were profoundly divided by an underground current of suspicion of a problem dating from colonial times: the Color Question. For the majority of the Liberal Party's adherents were the offspring of the former colony's class of freemen, most of them mulattoes, whereas the overwhelming majority of the National Party came from the people or pretended to be the true friends of the Haitian masses.

In reality, however, since independence Haiti had remained a military establishment whose generals had continued the colonial tradition of political ambition. Thus, except for President Boyer's twenty-year dictatorship, the country had gone from one general to another and from one Constitution to another in an attempt to satisfy with words the powerless intellectuals of the nation.

Deputy Eléomont Mars had married Fortuna Delcour Michel in 1874. During that year General Michel Domingue was elected President under a Constitution providing an eight-year term of office. But on October 15, 1876, when Eléomont's son was born, there was a new president. General Boisrond-Canal was elected on

July 17 after an infuriated populace, shouting in the streets that Domingue and Marius were stealing the people's money, had overthrown the government. Domingue was wounded in the arm and Marius was killed in the streets while, on the latter's order, the Republic's gold reserves—the product of a recent foreign loan—were being transferred from the State's bank to a ship in Port-au-Prince. The money was presumably on its way to Les Cayes, the chief city of the Southern Province, to which Septimus Marius had decided to move the seat of government for its security.

Fostering the illusion of the intellectuals that a new era of political freedom had been born with the elections of 1876, the House of Representatives elected as its president, Hannibal Price, who had been banished from the country by the Domingue government.[4] Like Boyer Bazelais, Hannibal Price was a staunch liberal. He was also a brilliant and forceful orator. Although a mulatto from Jacmel, he had much in common with his black colleague from Grande Rivière du Nord whom he had probably met at some time during his tenure as President of the Commercial Court of Cap-Haitien. Both men had been farmers, exporting coffee beans, mahogany and hardwood. Moreover, and perhaps more importantly, both were Protestants, members of a minority religion in an officially Catholic country. Price's grandfather, a former British marine of Wesleyan faith, had come to Haiti on a religious mission, had married a Haitian woman, and had died in the country.

Eléomont Mars' Protestantism could be traced to the migration of several American Negro Baptists to Haiti between 1823 and 1845.[5] The first of these was Thomas Paul of Massachusetts who arrived in Cap-Haitien in December 1823, distributed many Bibles and baptized a small group of believers in the Bay of Cap-Haitien. In 1849 another American Negro, Samuel Waring, came to the Northern Province and set himself up in the coffee business at Dondon, some ten miles south of Grande Rivière du Nord. After founding the first permanent Baptist church there, he went on to establish another in Grande Rivière and others as well in various towns and villages of the Northern Province. By the time of Price-Mars' birth, the Baptist churches in Grande Rivière du Nord, Dondon and Cap-Haitien, to which Waring eventually moved and later died, were solidly based and vying with the Catholic Church for new converts.[6] Eléomont Mars was one of the products of this Evangelical proselytizing. Whatever the cause of his respect and affection for Hannibal Price, he paid him the compliment of naming his son *Price*.

Price-Mars' birthplace, as well as the county in which it is located, got its name from the river that crosses the region on its way to the Bay of Cap-Haitien. From colonial times, the region has been regarded as one of the most fertile in the area as well as one of the most spectacular topographically. For all Haitians, Grande Rivière du Nord stands primarily as the Cradle of Haitian Freedom. Both Eléomont Mars' family and that of his wife took deep pride in some of the historic events that occurred there—perhaps even deeper pride for them than for other Haitians because their family names were connected with the circumstances that had made Grande Rivière a spiritual shrine in the heart of the Haitian nation.

These historic events remained vibrant in the memory of Price-Mars throughout his life. In 1918, the year during which Haiti practically lost her national sovereignty when the made-in-Washington Constitution was imposed on her, Price-Mars wrote an article recalling the memory of his grandmother. The article is entitled "Pan," the nickname by which he called her when he was a child. The caption under that title reads: "To the memory of Marie Elizabeth P. Godart, a descendant of the Black freeman who followed Ogé and Chavannes to the scaffold in order to establish social equality on the bloody soil of Saint-Domingue."[7] She belonged, he said, "to that rugged and laborious race of the ancestors who had been brought up on the epic songs of the wars for independence, and in whom the spirit of sacrifice had been exalted, along with an unconquerable faith in better days for their offspring."[8]

The reference to Ogé, Chavannes and the "Black freemen" deserves explanation. On August 4, 1789, the French Constituent Assembly passed an unprecedented Declaration of the Rights of Man and of the Citizen. But the colonial authorities in Haiti, then Saint-Domingue, and the white planters there were in no mood to apply it to the freemen of color. At the time numerous young freemen were in Paris studying, sent there by their parents because no organized schools existed in Saint-Domingue. Their fathers, all of them farmers, had become quite wealthy and by their efforts had contributed to the prosperity of the colony which had become the source of two-thirds of the total French colonial product. These young freemen in Paris immediately became involved in the proceedings of the National Assembly in the French capital through the Society of the Friends of the Blacks, established there under the leadership of Henri Grégoire, former bishop of Blois and a member of the National Assembly.[9] Among them was a mulatto, Vincent Ogé, who eventually decided to return to Saint-Domingue and to use force, if necessary, to persuade the colonial authorities and white planters to implement the will of the National Assembly.

Back in the colony, Ogé went at once to Grande Rivière du Nord and, with the assistance of Jean-Baptiste Chavannes, a black freeman, succeeded in raising a group of volunteers who armed themselves and attacked Cap-Français, now Cap-Haitien, the seat of the colonial government. They were easily defeated. Some were arrested, while Ogé and Chavannes took refuge in the Spanish part of the island. Captured by the Spanish, they were handed over to the French authorities who put them to death on February 23, 1791. Among those executed was Godart, the black freeman of Grande Rivière. According to a long tradition in the family of Price-Mars' grandmother, that Godart was their direct progenitor.

On his father's side, Price-Mars had no less memorable historical lineage. This he recalled with great pride in 1931 when he was a senator and represented the Haitian Parliament at the commemoration in France of the first centennial of the death of Henri Grégoire. Speaking before Grégoire's statue and in the midst of a huge throng of people who had come from various parts of the world—Negroes, Jews, Irish, whose ancestors were befriended and whose human rights were defended by Grégoire—Price-Mars asked the following rhetorical question:

> "But, Gentlemen, by what exceptional stroke of good fortune does it so happen that the privilege of representing the Haitian parliament [here today] falls upon a direct descendant of the first black deputy Saint-Domingue sent to the National Convention and in whose presence that distinguished Assembly proclaimed the abolition of slavery at its memorable session of February 4, 1794?" [10]

This humanitarian measure had been anticipated in Haiti on August 29, 1793 by French Commissioner Sonthonax, who proclaimed at Cap-Français the emancipation of the slaves and urged the colony: "Have the courage to want to be a people and you will soon raise yourselves to the level of the European nations." Less than one month later, Polverel, French Commissioner in the Western Province, followed suit. But he did so in a way that made emancipation of the slaves in that province a voluntary and official act on the part of the slave-owners, for he did not believe that the Commissioners had received from the French Government the power to make such sweeping decisions as those that Sonthonax had taken in the North. On September 22, Polverel summoned the people of Port-au-Prince to the main square of the city and invited the slaveholders to join him on the "Altar of the Fatherland" where he made them—white settlers, black and mulatto freemen—sign a register to relinquish their rights of ownership over the slaves. Then, as Sonthonax had done in the North, Polverel declared the new freedmen "French citizens with all the rights attached to the status of French citizenry."

These measures were furiously attacked in Paris. The French Constitution of September 21, 1792, that established France as a Republic, had given Saint-Domingue the right to send deputies to the National Convention which was both the legislative and the administrative body of the French Government. With the civil war ended in the colony, Sonthonax hurried to have three deputies elected in the North and charged them with the mission of requesting the National Convention to approve his proclamation abolishing slavery. The three deputies represented the three racial sections of the colony: one was white, one was black, one a mulatto.

On their way to France, the Saint-Domingue deputies stopped at Philadelphia to change ships to proceed to Europe. No sooner had they landed in the American capital than they were met by some French royalist exiles, who ransacked their luggage and attempted to assassinate them. One of these exiles, either knowing beforehand or discovering in the black deputy's papers that he was a military officer, said to him with contempt and anger: "You rascal! How dare you presume to command white soldiers?" He held a knife at the deputy's throat. But he let him go unharmed after the latter, who had retained all his composure, responded vehemently and proudly: "I have been a soldier for twenty-five years without reproach; and if one can protect white men and save their lives, one can just as well command them." [11]

On February 4, 1794, when eventually the Saint-Domingue delegation went to the National Assembly to take up the specific object of their mission, they were greeted by a tumultuous ovation. The black and mulatto deputies were invited to the rostrum to receive the President's "fraternal embrace." The High Assembly, which had declared in December 1792 that "it considered itself called to give liberty to the human race," not only approved on that very day the measures taken in Saint-Domingue, but went on to proclaim the abolition of slavery in all French colonies. A portrait of the black deputy in his official costume as a Representative of the French people—a painting by Girodet—is to be found in the Museum of Versailles.

This black deputy, the first to be admitted to the High Assembly, was brought to Saint-Domingue as a slave from Senegal at the age of ten, but had bought his freedom while in his teens. He had been a freedman for thirty-six years and had served as a soldier not only in the colony, but also on the American continent, fighting at Savannah along with eight hundred freemen from Saint-Domingue who, in 1779, volunteered to join the American patriots in their war for independence. He was profoundly conscious of his dignity as a human being, the more so because he had proved his worth in singular circumstances. Exemplifying qualities that would characterize Price-Mars, he would surely have shared his descendant's fondness for the quotation from Renan that introduced the aforementioned article, "Pan": "To live is to give his flower, then his fruit: what more?" The black deputy was none other than the commanding officer of Sonthonax' Honor Guard: Jean-Baptiste Mars, alias Belley, whom the Eléomont Mars family traditionally regarded as their direct ancestor.

Dr. Price-Mars refers time and again to Grande Rivière du Nord in his works, whether writing about historic events, social conditions, political happenings, or religious or folkloric aspects of the Haitian people. Enchanted by the scenery of Grande Rivière, he wrote:

> Visibly, nowhere else in Haiti except in this picturesque plot of land has Nature been more prodigal and more generous in providing a most splendid background. On the north, against the line of the horizon, as on the south, the west and the east, the mountains, nearby or faraway, present to the eyes the dazzling colors of their garments which change capriciously with the play of light . . . All these mountains meet and crowd together in apparent disorder, but seemingly to dam the river.[12]

At the time of Price-Mars' birth Grande Rivière du Nord still enjoyed the great popularity it had acquired during colonial days because of its impressive setting and the fertility of its soil. Later he proudly reminded his readers that the commune, which was the colony's first parish, also had retained the semi-urban, semi-rural aspects that its agricultural and commercial activities had given it during the colonial period. The French settlers of the past had readily taken advantage of the natural blessings of Grande Rivière and had made the whole region one of the most prosperous agricultural settlements in the colony, though the town which lies in the valley was often flooded by the river.

The feast of Saint Rose, the "Creole saint" to whom the town was dedicated, took place a month and a half after Price-Mars' birthday. The faithful firmly believed that Saint Rose had on three occasions, between 1772 and 1780, prevented their lands from being washed away and their lives from being destroyed by the river.[13] Visitors in great numbers descended from the surrounding villages, not only for the celebration of the Saint's Day but throughout the year, because the town served as the marketplace for the entire mountainous region. In colonial times a Catholic priest had referred to it as a "slough of sin," and certainly its inhabitants in 1876 were less devoutly Catholic than the grandmother whom Price-Mars pictured in front of the high altar, "contemplative, enraptured, carried away."[14]

They were, and still are, like all Haitian peasants, either boastful, or quiet, or more frequently quick to display their emotions. The men and women in Haiti's rural districts generally are orderly people and, as Leyburn has noted in his scholarly study, *The Haitian People,* they "are polite whether to each other or to strangers; this courtesy extends to hospitality: a stranger is almost sure to be offered shelter and food wherever he stops."[15] It is no less certain, however, that such merry-making as the former white masters permitted became more uninhibited in the market-town after independence, with generous imbibing of tafia, exciting cock-fights, and African or Creole dances either in the open for sheer exhilaration or undercover in Voodoo ceremonies.

Voodoo has always dominated Haitian life, despite the relatively large number of Catholic priests, sisters and brothers whom President Geffrard's Concordat of 1860 with the Vatican brought to Haiti. The rural people as a whole, like their African ancestors, found spiritual inspiration in it. Modified in Haiti, the African cult nowadays presents a syncretism of both the Christian faith and Animist beliefs one finds throughout the so-called Dark Continent. Such Catholic practices as wearing scapularies, reciting prayers, even in Latin, the burning of candles, as well as the holding of novenas and requiem masses, have found their place in the ritual that the *houngan,* the Voodoo priest, prescribes to his flock. Price-Mars was to write:

> They [these practices] could easily harmonize with the most intimate tendencies of Voodoo. Then a slow transformation struck at the very foundations of the ancient faith. And now it no longer rests solely on the latent or manifest spiritual power possessed by every being and phenomenon of our universe. It no longer implores the natural forces, endowed with conscience and will power, but teaches that the world is ruled by a Supreme Being who delegates his power to intermediary spirits to which one must pay homage and reverence. It maintains also that men are made not only of flesh and bone and . . . that they have a soul, which after death . . . needs the aid of the living to fulfill the other unknown, unsuspected condition of its supraterrestrial existence. For if the living should fail in this task, the soul would not only be tormented in heaven, but would come down to torment the living.[16]

Confusing Voodoo with superstition, President Boyer branded it as a crime in his Penal Code. Despite the more severe, and at times bloody, repression of the Voodoo cult, from the days of Toussaint until recently, the rural populations have clung to their *loas* (Afro-Haitian deities) the more strongly because they believe that their soul must "Return to Guinea" and that the *loas* are the only supernatural powers capable of facilitating the final voyage or of preventing their souls from going to happy reunion with the souls of their ancestors "in Africa."

On the other hand, the urban youth who had enthusiastically hailed the new Legislature of 1876 as the prologue to a new chapter of political freedom, were young men, many of whom had benefited from President Geffrard's educational program which went hand in hand with his religious concern for the rural populations. A mulatto, he was the posthumous son of General Nicolas Geffrard, a hero of Haiti's war for independence and a signer of the Act of Independence. President Geffrard undertook to raise the intellectual level of the urban youth by sending them abroad to study, particularly in France. He established lycées at Jacmel and Gonaives, the City of Independence, and created at the capital schools of music, painting and navigation, while setting up numerous primary schools throughout the Republic. His Minister of Education was Elie Dubois, whose name still stands as one of the greatest among those who have occupied that office.[17]

Nevertheless, throughout the eight years of his presidency the General-President was confronted with revolts in practically all parts of the country. At the capital, his daughter was assassinated in her home at the hands of political enemies. Geffrard resigned from the presidency in March 1867, and the following year Haiti split into three "Republics," as had happened in 1806 after the assassination of Dessalines.

The greatest blow the country ever received occurred during Geffrard's administration and it had to do with Voodoo. In 1863, only thirteen years before Price-Mars' birth, a case of cannibalism connected with Voodoo took place in a rural community, some twenty miles from Port-au-Prince. President Geffrard believed in summary execution of conspirators and revolutionaries, but ordered an open trial of the persons accused in order to demonstrate the exceptional character of the crime. Eventually two men and two women of a peasant family, the Pellés, went on trial for having killed and eaten a young girl in the course of a Voodoo service. They were found guilty and executed on February 13, 1864.

The Pellé case was particularly disheartening to the educated elite who were ashamed of the deplorable event and of the wide publicity it received abroad. While continuing to extol the glory of their ancestral black heroes, educated Haitians, some consciously, others unconsciously, tried to change the image of the "Black Republic," and to present it—in line with their intellectual aspirations and their way of life—as a "cultural province of France." Furthermore, the educated Haitians were determined to maintain the friendliest possible relations with France because at that time Haiti's economic life depended on France, the only country in the world to grant her credit. Finally, the Haitians had become frantically upset by Spanish and American threats. Consequently, they looked to France as a shield, the only one that might protect Haiti's independence.

In 1861, the Spanish Admiral Rubalcava brought a fleet of seven Spanish men-of-war into the bay of Port-au-Prince and forced President Geffrard, under threat of bombardment, to end his assistance to Dominican patriots attempting to prevent a Spanish reconquest of their land. Geffrard viewed this Spanish acton as a menace to Haitian sovereignty. Four years later, after Spain abandoned that territory, despairing of ever being able to subdue the Dominicans, the United States, under President Ulysses S. Grant, moved to annex the Dominican Republic. The Haitians were even more fearful of the United States because it had remained a racist nation despite the lofty tenets of its Declaration of Independence. They were also well aware that Lincoln's Emancipation Proclamation and the Fourteenth Amendment to the Constitution had done relatively little to uproot that racism.

Such were the thoughts that preoccupied Haitians at the time of Price-Mars' birth. As he matured, these preoccupations beset his own mind and took root as the nineteen year long American Occupation of his homeland began in 1915.

In 1918, when the United States imposed a new Constitution on Haiti, Price-Mars, taking his inspiration from the memory of his grandmother who belonged to "that rugged and laborious race of the ancestors," wrote:

> This land has not been lost for the generations it produced; nothing of what we are now doing will be lost for those who follow us: the dead do not die; not a gesture nor a thought, a sin, a tear or an atom of the acquired conscience will be lost in the depth of the soil; the most insignificant action on our part will raise our ancestors, not from the tombs where they do not stir, but from the bottom of our souls where they live forever."[18]

Two

Sixty-Four Leagues of Darkness and Misery From the Capital

Ti-Price[1] was six years old when his mother died, a victim of the smallpox epidemic of 1881-1883. The disease also took away two other young children his mother had from a previous union. There were no physicians in the whole county of Grande Rivière du Nord, or for that matter, throughout the rural regions of the Republic. In the cities there were a few physicians but generally they treated the urban patients exclusively. Even in Port-au-Prince it was the *houngan,* more often than not, who dealt with the health problems of the common people.[2]

Ti-Price, who was gravely stricken himself, survived although his father had lost all hope of saving him. He was saved, nevertheless, thanks to the devoted and untiring care of his grandmother, Pan. Stunned by his misfortune, the widowed Deputy became austere, "an austerity composed of mysticism and resigned fatalism."[3] Pan, who married Fénelon Louis Blot the year the epidemic started, took Ti-Price to her home and, from that moment until her death, made herself his Guardian Angel, all the more passionately because her sensibility had been intensified by the loss of her daughter and the two grandchildren, and by her fear that Ti-Price might also be taken away.

As a first cousin of the important General Tirésias Simon Sam, she had high ambitions for her grandson and hoped to make him a "model of virtue." Price-Mars later wrote: "She believed it necessary to impart to him at home a taste for work and respect for honor, to enable him to discover by himself not only intellectual discipline, but also the principles of a noble, proud life through character development and extensive knowledge."[4]

By the time the epidemic started in 1881, there was another President in the National Palace. General Louis-Félicité Salomon[5] had taken over on the night of October 3, 1879, after Boisrond-Canal had resigned following two days of fighting in the streets of the capital between governmental troops and the "liberal" partisans of Boyer-Bazelais. And in 1883, when the epidemic ceased its murderous work, Civil War again broke out, this time pitching "liberals" against "nationals."

Deputy Eléomont Mars did not return to the capital after the passing of his wife. What was going on in Port-au-Prince—civil war and political intrigue—could not provide solace in his bereavement or zest for public life. Moreover, his personal security might have been jeopardized because of his friendship for Hannibal Price, who was then in exile in Panama. Eléomont abandoned politics completely. Though he had grown morose after his wife's death, he devoted much time to the education of his son and to meditation on the Bible, in which he taught Ti-Price to read. Price-Mars described him as "rather a solemn man, affirming with Calvinist intransigence the excellence and infallibility of the Bible, the Book of Books."[6] Meanwhile, Mrs. Godart's attachment to the Catholic Church was so strong that one critic has portrayed her as a "bigoted woman."[7]

Usually in communities such as Grande Rivière, with divided religious allegiance, confrontation arises and soon the religious arguments flow out of the churches and temples into the streets or public parks. But Ti-Price never heard a religious argument either at home or at the house of his grandmother. Although both his father and grandmother had strong religious convictions, they were nevertheless tolerant of other people's views. As a matter of fact, Mrs. Godart proved that she was not "bigoted" when she took Fénelon Louis Blot as her second husband, for he was a Protestant and, even worse, an active Freemason.

The Catholic Church has always been, throughout the country, a fierce adversary of Freemasonry because the latter's members are held to be atheists. At that time, however, most masons were Catholics in traditionally—if only officially—Catholic Haiti. The lodges were political meeting places where men could gather to drink, plot against the government, and eventually set the date for action while offering the usual toast "To the Glory of the Architect of the Universe!" Thus Grande Rivière du Nord, like any other locality interested in politics, had a Masonic Temple affiliated with the Grand Orient of Haiti which had its headquarters in the Nation's capital. And Fénelon Louis Blot was a "venerable" of the Grande Rivière Temple, whose members called themselves "The Commanders of Mount-Thabor."[8]

The religious dichotomy around Ti-Price was tempered by the conciliatory spirit demonstrated by both his father and grandmother. As Price-Mars subsequently wrote: "They agreed that the child should follow his grandmother's religion until reaching the age to decide for himself. He was taught to honor with esteem and respect all sincere manifestations of piety. Probably it was this liberal conception of the most serious problem in human life that later made him tend . . . toward compromise and conciliation."[9]

Although Voodoo had been declared illegal, it remained, as we have already noted, the religion which the great majority of Haitians actually practiced. Their confidence in the powers of the *houngan* was strengthened by the knowledge that some of the Catholics and Protestants often slipped off to consult the Voodoo priests thought to possess supernatural powers not enjoyed by Catholic or Protestant clergy: the power to provide a "charm" to insure the success of a business venture; the power to prepare a *ouanga* to help political ambitions to materialize; the power to cast a spell on someone to make him or her irresistible. Men of governmental stature, especially the generals or other army officers who risk battle or assassination, sought a "point" to render them invulnerable.[10]

In the beginning Ti-Price took great interest in his father's biblical teaching, for the boy was full of intellectual curiosity. But as he grew older, he felt deeply isolated, kept at home while other children of the town attended the parish school where they enjoyed the company of other youngsters who frolicked together in the school yard. Eléomont Mars understood the situation perfectly, but having grown morbidly attached to the boy as a result of his wife's passing, he could not let Ti-Price out of his sight. As a compromise, he started a school at home and gathered around his son some of the children of their immediate neighborhood.

The father was of average schooling but liked to read. Using the impressive mountainous setting of Grande Rivière du Nord, he taught his son geography. He was no less interested in teaching his son human relations, and for that he used the *Fables* of La Fontaine, substituting local animals for those of the French author or using Haitian folkloric characters, such as Bouki and Ti-Malice, when human beings were involved. His instruction was in the Creole language, not only to impress the boy's mind more deeply, but also to help him gain the habit of relating his thoughts to the realities of his own environment. There were thus many tales to be told about the land and its people. Out of the humble teaching of Eléomont Mars was to stem, many years later, his son's creation of the Society of Haitian History and Geography, along with his passion for the Haitian countryside and for all its people.

When Ti-Price was about twelve years of age, his grandmother decided to send him to Cap-Haitien to attend the Henri Grégoire Collège (secondary school). It was there that Ti-Price actually saw for the first time a volume of La Fontaine's fables; he was amazed to discover that his father's stories in Creole were not of local origin. And if, as a consequence, the animals in his father's tales were soon superseded by those of La Fontaine, the local characters—Bouki, Ti-Malice and others—became dearer to his heart and mind.

Life at Grégoire Collège was not very pleasant for Ti-Price. Discipline was harsh under the school's principal, M. Manigat. Besides, Ti-Price's father had apprenticed the lad to a master tailor, hoping perhaps to revive a tradition established by Christophe, whom Ti-Price's godmother, Mrs. Arthemise Lacoste, had known personally.[11]

In all probability, Eléomont Mars wanted his son to settle down to a simple life at Grande Rivière and continue his business as planter and exporter. As a matter of fact, he was not too enthusiastic about his son's going away for an education. Mrs. Godart, however, had other plans for her grandson, plans she thought inspired by divine intervention. With placid irony, Eléomont "tried to temper the old woman's enthusiasm, pointing to the difficulties, the shortcomings of an education too narrow in its means and too ambitious in its goals for the final result not to be uncertainty and frustration."[12]. But Mrs. Godart was adamant.

At the time Ti-Price went to Cap-Haitien, dissatisfaction with the Salomon Government was rife. Although an octogenarian at the end of his presidential term, Salomon had the Constitution of 1879 amended, for it forbade immediate re-election and he wanted to stay in office. Among the many malcontents—liberals and nationals alike—was General Séide Télémaque, the Commanding Officer of Grande Rivière county. He moved to Cap-Haitien and sparked a revolution on August 5, 1888. But before he could get to Port-au-Prince with his army to storm the National Palace in the traditional manner, General Boisrond-Canal took up arms and forced President Salomon to flee and board a ship for France. General Télémaque reached the capital on August 18 to find that a provisional government was already being organized by the former president, who nominated Télémaque Minister of War. Boisrond-Canal's candidate for the presidency was François Légitime, a former Minister of Agriculture, then in exile on the British island of Saint Thomas. Télémaque, however, would not consent to Boisrond-Canal's scheme and, on the night of September 18, the two factions battled the issue in the streets of the capital. Télémaque was killed in the encounter. Immediately the North, Northwest, and the Artibonite set up a new government under the name "Republic of the North," while the deputies of the Western and Southern provinces elected Légitime President of the Republic of Haiti on December 16, 1888. Among those who constituted the Northern government were Fénelon Louis Blot and Anténor Firmin,[13] an ardent partisan of Boyer-Bazelais.

For nine months the nation remained plunged in civil war. Eventually the Légitime Government collapsed and General Florvil Hyppolite, President of the Northern Government, was elected to the Presidency of the Republic. Firmin became Minister of Finance and Foreign Relations. His presence in the Cabinet did much to strengthen the confidence of the Haitian people who were again getting a military government. He had thrilled the educated youth by

such passages in his book as the following:
> In Haiti, as elsewhere, the Black race needs liberty, a real, effective, civil and political freedom for its genius to unfold and bloom. If slavery horrifies the Blacks, despotism should equally horrify them. For despotism is nothing else but moral slavery; it permits freedom of motion to feet and hands but it enchains and pinions the human soul while causing the mind to smolder. It is indispensable to be aware of the fact that it is the soul, that is to say the power of the intellect and the spirit which working internally performs the transformation, the redemption and the progress of all races under the impulse of a free, enlightened will, unfettered by tyrannical coercion.[14]

To make things look even better, Hyppolite appointed Hannibal Price as Haitian Minister to Washington.

The expectations at the end of the civil strife proved to be illusory. In May 1891, after an attempted revolt in Port-au-Prince, the President rounded up a large number of suspects and ordered many executions without trial. He also demanded that all able-bodied men spend each night in their neighborhood military outposts. From that moment until the end of his presidency, the General revealed himself to be a bloody tyrant.

The following year, after Ti-Price had graduated from the Grégoire Collège, his grandmother decided to enroll him in the Lycée Pétion to complete his education in the capital. This lycée had received new luster from the Salomon regime, which had brought in a special contingent of French professors, primarily for that establishment. Eléomont's less glamorous ideas concerning his son's education were abandoned—irretrievably. The intellectual and political success of Anténor Firmin proved conclusively to Mrs. Godart and her grandson that with education, hard work, and good luck, anything was possible. Once again Providence seemed to cooperate in "Pan's" plans. In 1892, when Ti-Price graduated from Grégoire Collège, General Tirésias Simon Sam was serving in Port-au-Prince as Minister of War.

Grande Rivière du Nord was quite remote from the capital. A law enacted in 1821 had fixed the legal distance between the town of Grande Rivière and the city of Port-au-Prince at sixty-four leagues, about 320 miles. Through the years few people had ever covered that distance by land, except soldiers participating in revolutions, for the territory is rough and mountainous. Legal and administrative papers sent by land took months to reach their destination, if they ever did. One had to travel through forests and across dangerous paths on mountain flanks. Few people dreamed about going to Port-au-Prince other than those who were involved in revolutions. Consequently, most youngsters of the rural areas were destined to rot in their respective communities without any kind of social protection, living in utter poverty among their people, the eventual prey of epidemics such as that of 1881-1883.

On the other hand, military masters of places like Grande Rivière du Nord were irresistably attracted by Port-au-Prince, the seat of the presidency. It was not considered foolish or criminal to think revolution in the country. Indeed, revolution was the only thing relevant to the state of affairs existing throughout the Republic, and it sometimes proved successful for an individual or a small clique. Grande Rivière du Nord had seen two of its native sons succeed at it: General Philippe Guerrier in 1844, and General Jean-Baptiste Riché in 1846, both of whom were completely illiterate.

Both Guerrier and Riché were in their eighties when they died; Price-Mars was ninety-three. There have been fairly numerous cases of Grande Rivière inhabitants who have lived to be a hundred. This exceptional longevity seems to come from the vigorous, healthy life led there and from the region's topography and climate. On the surrounding mountains, the thermometer sometimes drops to almost 48 degrees Fahrenheit (9 degrees c.) and the region has an average rainfall of only 2.439 centimeters.

Ti-Price's grandmother enjoyed a ripe old age and did not die until 1910. Although she lived in such idyllic surroundings and was related to the politically and militarily powerful of the time, she profoundly felt the plight of the common people; this feeling became more intense after the epidemic had ravaged her own family. Thus she wanted Ti-Price to develop according to an ideal of grandeur and nobility. "She wanted him to become a model of virtue, this grandson, this belated product of an era fertile in cowardliness and spinelessness, an era stained by the sterility and violent efforts of a people seeking political stability in bloody rivalry for power and ... forgetting the notion of social solidarity and the sentiment of national duty. She wanted to make of him a man different from the other men she knew."[15]

So, at the age of fifteen, Ti-Price was shipped off to Port-au-Prince. Conditioned as he was by his grandmother's "foolish dreams," it was a determined, eager young man who entered the Lycée Pétion in October 1892. He spent no time brooding about being confined behind the walls of the institution as a boarding student, for he soon found a way to escape on weekends. From other classmates he learned that Protestants could obtain permission, as Catholics did, to attend religious services in the city. At that time, he identified himself as a Protestant, but in reality he was in the throes of an inner conflict as to the choice he would make between the Baptist cult and the Catholic Church. Eventually he emerged from that crisis with his own brand of religion: "something special, neither Catholic nor Protestant, but a Christianism that recognized truth in all religions, without specifying any particular form of worship."[16] Though he sought and obtained permission to attend Baptist services, he spent more time roaming about the city than in church. There were unusual things to be seen: the president's hideaway, *Mon Repos,* in the southern outskirts of the city where he would occasionally join other youngsters for a picnic; and in the center of town there was the huge iron market made in France and covering an entire city block. Still more exciting, perhaps, was the splendid traditional parade of the National Army on Sundays, with the General-President personally reviewing the troops.

This military display had less appeal for a French writer who published in 1891 a book entitled *Au Pays des Généraux.* The author, C. Texier, predicating his arguments on his firm belief that the white race is superior to all others and the black race inherently inferior, revealed the purpose of his book in the following sentences:

> For all impartial and informed minds on Haitian life, the fall of Salomon was the prelude to several years of internecine dissension which has brought the country to such a state of poverty and weakness that, like an over-ripe fruit, it will be ready to fall at the feet of any nation that may wish to pick it up. Which nation will it be? France? Categorically I reply no, without fear that facts will prove me wrong. England? I do not think so. The United States? This is likely, for this licentious people, sinking into fetishism and laziness, there must be an energetic, even a brutal, master.[17]

As a matter of fact, even before this prediction was made, the United States undertook to absorb Haiti in its sphere of interest by linking her in the chain of its continental defense. It so happened that an American admiral, Bancroft Gherardi, arrived in Haiti early in 1891 with instructions to secure the lease of the Môle Saint-Nicolas, on the northwestern coast, for the establishment of a coaling station for the United States Navy. Accompanied by a fleet of seven men-of-war, Gherardi was so determined to succeed in his mission that he wrote the American Secretary of State that he would gladly seize the coveted territory if the Haitian President, General Hyppolite, by an chance, was blind to the "Manifest Destiny" of the Môle.[18]

Since the publication the preceding year of Admiral Alfred T. Mahan's *The Influence of Sea Power Upon History, 1660-1873,* the thought of United States naval expansion had become obsessive and aggressive in the minds of the Admirals in Washington. The same year this book was published, Admiral Gherardi had undertaken naval studies in Caribbean waters and had become convinced that Haiti should be under U. S. control, as the following remarks in his reports attest:

> The strategic value of this island from a naval point of view is invaluable, and this increases in direct proportion to the millions

which American citizens are investing in the Nicaragua Canal. The United States cannot afford to allow any doubt to rest in the mind of any Haytian as to our fixed determination to allow no one to gain a foothold on, or to establish a protectorate over their island. It should also be make clear to them that the United States has no desire to annex it. It would not, at the present moment, be advisable to make any effort to get possession of the Môle Saint-Nicolas, but I have no doubt that in the near future it can be done.[19]

The Gherardi mission aroused frantic apprehension in all Haitians, including, of course, young Price-Mars who had been nurtured by both his father and grandmother in the pride of Haitian independence. The American minister in Port-au-Prince at that time was Frederick Douglass, the Negro abolitionist. Thoroughly incensed by Gherardi's naval diplomacy, Douglass underscored the reaction of the Haitian people and his own disapproval of the Admiral's views in his reports to the Department of State:

> I think it clearly my duty to state to you that the presence in this harbor ... of five of our war vessels and the knowledge that others are soon to join them, coupled with a general vague information that negotiations are pending ... concerning some matter in regard to which the Haitian people are unduly and perhaps unreasonably sensitive, has created a feeling of apprehension, anxiety, and even of alarm beyond anything of the kind I have ever before personally known to exist here.[20]

At the Haitian Foreign Office, Anténor Firmin skillfully dragged out a three-month parley with the American admiral for the lease and eventually told the doughty Gherardi that Haiti "could not enter negotiations without appearing to yield to foreign pressure and to compromise, *de facto,* [her] existence as an independent people."

Douglass was promptly made the scapegoat for Gherardi's failure and had to resign his diplomatic post. While certain New York newspapers published bellicose editorials against President Hyppolite, some prominent American businessmen formed a syndicate to furnish the "sinews of war" to overthrow Hyppolite and replace him with General François Manigat, then in exile in Kingston, Jamaica. They spent nearly half a million dollars to fit out a modern man-of-war to attack Port-au-Prince. On March 23, 1891, the New York *Herald,* echoing C. Texier, asserted "to let Haiti alone is to allow her to follow her own path back to barbarism."[21] The *Herald* knew the facts of the conspiracy but did not divulge them. They were ferretted out by the Haitian Legation, then located in New York, and were disclosed to the American people by the Haitian Minister, Hannibal Price.[22]

In reaction to such writings as the *Herald's,* Texier's, as well as another volume, *Haiti or the Black Republic,*[23] published three years earlier, Hannibal Price wrote *The Rehabilitation of the Black*

Race by the Republic of Haiti. This book, along with that of Firmin, would constitute a springboard for Price-Mars as he subsequently penned his own defense of Haiti and the Black race.

The Gherardi Incident had indeed created an impassioned surge of patriotism among the Haitians, the more so because the year 1891 marked the centennial of the Slave Revolt. Although Firmin had successfully warded off Washington's designs on the Môle, he was forced to resign under attacks for having consented even to talk about the possibility of leasing a part of the "glorious black fatherland." And it was while reshaping his Cabinet that President Hyppolite had named General Tirésias Simon Sam War Minister.

The appointment of a relative to this high post was a source of pride to Ti-Price and the family as the youngster arrived in Port-au-Prince to continue his education. The internal and external politics of the Black Republic strengthened his enthusiasm for learning and spurred him to greater efforts to achieve the ambitions his grandmother had planted deep in his soul. Writing in 1967, he said:

> My grandmother coddled my frail childhood, embellished my boyhood with foolish dreams. She initiated and fostered my studies both at the collège and the lycée. At the end of my secondary school education, she was again the one who kindled my desire for professional training... The supreme ambition of my grandmother was to make me someone who would be worthy of consideration, useful to his country and to his race.[24]

In July 1885, he was awarded his baccalaureate and immediately enrolled in the National School of Medicine. Eight months later President Hyppolite died of a heart attack and General Tirésias Simon Sam took over the reins of government. He did so without any political commotion, for he was known to be of temperate disposition. With a cousin in the presidential palace, new doors opened for Ti-Price. He was now twenty years of age, intellectually alert, bursting with ambition and particularly eager for literary success. He readily joined the city's young intellectuals who had gathered the year before around *La Jeune Haiti,* a review founded in 1894 by the poet Justin Lhérisson along with two other youths the same age as Ti-Price: Mirabeau Drice and Seymour Pradel.

Ti-Price's decision to enter the Medical School may have come from his family's tragic experience during the smallpox epidemic, or perhaps as a result of his admiration for Dr. Léon Audain, a respected physician and forceful publicist, who also served as a self-appointed mentor of the young intellectuals. However, Ti-Price longed most of all for journalistic success. In 1898 he created *Le Journal des Etudiants,* with a first issue appearing on January 15 under his editorship. His lead article criticized the Military Hospital in Port-au-Prince. It created quite a stir among his student friends and in the Government as well, for he advocated a thorough reorganization of the hospital, which he declared "abominable." The Military Hospital, which Dr. Louis Audain, father of Dr. Léon Audain, had directed in 1869, was created for soldiers and their families. In fact, it served the entire indigent population of the city, since all their men were compelled to bear arms. Even the poorest people considered a visit to the Military Hospital "the last drop of humiliation,"[44] and preferred to continue to depend on the *houngan* for health care.[45]

But if Ti-Price's own circle praised his article, he was to hear— and painfully—another opinion from Dr. Léon Audain, who advised him to let his thoughts mature a bit before undertaking any other writing.[27] Dr. Audain's remark dampened Ti-Price's enthusiasm to such an extent that he stopped writing altogether. Nevertheless, that article stands as Dr. Jean Price-Mars' first act of "social solidarity" on behalf of the common people of Haiti and as the first step toward a career unmatched in the annals of Haitian letters.

Three

A Vow In The City Of Light

Ti-Price found himself in the thick of politics as a result of his cousin's ascent to the Presidency. Another cousin of the general, Vilbrun Guillaume, who had been Deputy from Grande Rivière since 1890, had taken Ti-Price into his home in the capital when the lad was a student at the Lycée Pétion. Vilbrun had little formal education. He had left school at the age of seventeen to go to work because his mother, then a widow, was poor and he did not want to be a burden for her.[1] As a deputy, he needed help, and Ti-Price served as his secretary and confidant. A big brother relationship existed between the two, although Vilbrun was seventeen years older than Ti-Price.[2]

Needless to say, Vilbrun admired his younger cousin who had completed the program of studies at Grégoire Collège at precisely the same age that Vilbrun had left school. As a drop-out, Vilbrun applauded the enthusiasm with which Ti-Price was pursuing his education at the Lycée Pétion. In 1893 Vilbrun's political fortunes soared to the important post of President of the House of Representatives. Ti-Price moved deeper and deeper into political affairs and deeper and deeper into the affection of his cousin Vilbrun as the latter's secretary and confidant.

In 1898, when Ti-Price founded the *Journal des Etudiants* at the Medical School, Vilbrun had already become Minister for War and Navy, following withdrawal of Firmin from the Cabinet. This opened the way for the Government to implement the law of December 21, 1897 providing for consolidation of the State's debts.

Ti-Price's disappointment when Dr. Léon Audain disapproved of his article in the *Journal des Etudiants* was great, but tempered considerably by the importance he had acquired in the capital on the intellectual and political fronts. Dr. Audain made it a point to take an interest in the young man's medical studies, and in 1899, when President Tirésias Simon Sam granted Ti-Price a scholarship to complete his medical training in Paris, Dr. Audain also went to the French capital to undertake some studies of his own. While there, he naturally continued to counsel Ti-Price. Along with the scholarship, which revitalized the latter's ambitions, the President accorded his young cousin diplomatic status by naming him Secretary of the

Haitian Legation in the "City of Light."

In 1899 relations between Haiti and France were most cordial and, in some respects, particularly rewarding for Haiti. The previous year the Haitian Government and the French Cable Company had contracted to secure rapid means of communication between Haiti and the rest of the world. To be sure, Ti-Price, like any other educated Haitian, looked to France as the champion of "all the most beautiful concepts, especially those which make man sacred to man without distinction based on class, race or color... [concepts] which infuse into the soul an indefectible notion of liberty, justice and personal dignity,"[3] as Anténor Firmin will say for all of them in his so-called "Political Testament."

Ti-Price settled in the Latin Quarter, the center of student life, his heart full of ambition, his mind captivated by "dreams of glory."[4] He realized that he carried a heavy burden on his shoulders: the hopes of his father and grandmother who had raised him in the fear of the Lord and in the observance of His Commandments.[5] On reaching Paris, "he felt apprehensive and bewildered to find himself in that fantastic city, alone to resist all kinds of temptations: of easy and impure love, of feverish and factitious activity in which one is thrown by Parisian life either toward pleasure or work."[6] From time to time he was shocked to see various Haitian students wasting "precious time" in beer gardens or other places of distraction. From afar his grandmother remained his guardian angel, writing: "Be careful not to become involved in some adventure of which you may later be ashamed." His stepbrother, Probus Blot, who was exactly the same age and had also come to Paris chose to live the life of a poet, not to say of a Bohemian, in the extravagant and gay fashion of the 1890's.

As already noted, Ti-Price was only mildly attracted by medical studies. Fresh from the enthusiastic group of *La Jeune Haiti* and still aflame with literary ambition, he could not have arrived in Paris at a more propitious moment. The literary giants of the day were Zola, de Maupassant and Anatole France; Toulouse-Lautrec, Georges Seurat, Cézanne, Henri Rousseau and Matisse were the influential painters; Auguste Rodin, the major sculptor; Saint-Saens, Debussy and Ravel, the giants in music. Paul Bourget, with his realistic understanding of human problems and his faith in the power of morality, was another of Ti-Price's favorites.

In Paris Ti-Price met Windsor Bellegarde and Mirabeau Drice, two of the three co founders of *La Jeune Haiti*. Both had been admitted to Paris' Ecole Normale Supérieure, which was then considered one of the most intense centers of French intellectuality. He also encountered Pauléus Sannon, who had been sent to Paris to study medicine but had changed his mind at the end of the third year to specialize in history. During the preceding year a new review, *La Ronde,* had appeared in Port-au-Prince, with Dantès Bellegarde,

Windsor's brother, as one of its founders. The review's director, Pétion Gérôme, exhorted Haitian youth to an intellectual and social revolution:

> To discharge the task which is ours, we must get out of the (prevailing) moral lethargy which turns young men of twenty into downcast old men. Let us undertake our work briskly so not to give to those who will come after us the opportunity of applying to us the Hebrew proverb: "Our fathers having eaten the grapes green have thus set their sons' teeths on edge." May this generation shake off the dust of its disillusions and face the future with greater assurance. Let us have faith! Let us act! [7]

Every generation of educated Haitian youth has been deeply concerned with the progress of the Fatherland, its human and social progress. All have felt that Haiti must justify by the work and the achievements of her citizens her unprecedented membership in the concert of civilized nations. The black nation had emerged from slavery with an annoying doubt in the hearts of many citizens about the potential of the Negro, a doubt planted in them by the white racists of the colony. The very year that Haiti gained independence, one of Dessalines' secretaries, Chanlatte, felt compelled to express that doubt in writing: "Is our black or yellow complexion an impediment to our progress in the arts and in virtue, or does it prevent courageous effort on our part?"[8]

Since the acquisition of that independence the country has known many bloody revolutions, while the nation's masses have remained illiterate, exploited by their military and political leaders with the collusion of the Republic's intellectual and social élite.

In a short story "His Ideal," written about this time, Ti-Price tells his state of mind on political and social matters under the name of Paul Dufailly: "Filled with contemporary social theories, his mind was open to all the discussions that captivated the minds of philosophers and statesmen of that century end. He wanted to reform society he felt was rotten in its foundation so as to have a better distribution of wealth, a better labor organization, and why not? Happiness for all. He was specially the friend of the humble, of the wretched people of the world."[9]

Although Ti-Price enjoyed diplomatic status, he lived in Paris among other Haitian students, many of whom were roughing it in the city, particularly during the cold Parisian winter. He shared a modest apartment with another Haitian student, Maurice Dorval, on the Montagne Saint-Geneviève in the Latin Quarter. At the time, Ti-Price had a somewhat inflated opinion of himself, an obvious result of his parents' constant adulation, to say nothing of his blood relationship with Haiti's all-powerful Chief of State. He revealed his painful self-consciousness in the same short story:

> Paul Dufailly was pleasing without knowing it and, above all

without wishing to be so. He had aristocratic tastes but was not vain about clothes . . . He was a man of the world without being mundane . . . In literature as in art he had theories that he tried to impose on others. He wanted to bring everything into the frame of true reality, forgetting perhaps that art and literature do not thrive solely on reality, but also on conventions capable of consolidating acquired truths. The profession he had chosen had developed a bent for observation. Accustomed to subjecting everything to the test of experience, he carried this spirit of observation everywhere and in everything. At social affairs he would try to scrutinize the individual consciences of people with whom he came in contact, always believing that he was about to ferret the secret of the enigma called the human heart. Besides, he was of an extremely sensitive temperament and had inherited from his mother an instinctive credulity and humaneness which he tried to hide under a conventional skepticism.

Ti-Price liked to discuss literature, to comment on the new novels and to analyze the writers' styles. One is not surprised to find the name of the author of *A Cruel Enigma* heading the list of authors he preferred: "Paul Bourget, Marcel Prévost, Daniel Lesueur, Pierre Louys, Zola, Anatole France, and all the others." He named them in that order in his short story entitled "Son Idéal."

Despite this absorbing interest in letters, he started his medical studies in Paris with great earnestness, hardly allowing himself time for his meals, and sleeping only three hours each night. Eventually he felt the effects of overexertion and slowed down a bit on his work at Medical School. In another short story, "Les Corbeaux" (The Ravens), he presents himself under the name of Gérard Lachault. Here Ti-Price describes himself, this time in the company of his friend, Maurice Dorval: "Both were sober and very reserved; they rarely went to the beer garden of the Quartier. They had a few select friends whom they visited two or three times a week. The rest of the time they remained in their apartment, chatting or reading . . . They shared the same ambitions. The social cause of the wretched had conquered their hearts.[10] When Dorval died two years later, he had lost all faith in Haiti, doubting that "an era of social justice could ever emerge from a land stained with slave blood."[11]

One can conjecture that the friends of Ti-Price and Dorval visited included Dr. Léon Audain, Windsor Bellegarde, Mirabeau Drice and Pauléus Sannon. They would discuss the literary scene in Haiti or the Affaire Dreyfus which then impassioned not only France but the entire world. There were many other Haitian students then in Paris and most of them took positions violently on the side of Alfred Dreyfus during the campaign (1897-99) led by French novelist Emile Zola. At that time Jean Jaurès, a Deputy in the French Chamber, was fiercely attacking the French bourgeoisie for its exploitation of peasants and workers. He too defended Dreyfus against the charge of treason. His fiery orations as a Socialist could hardly have failed to impress Haitian students who, like Ti-Price, had come from a rural community: "While the Christian bell tolls vainly . . . the rhythms of ancient thought and Oriental dreams, the tocsin of distress and ruin . . . is awakening the peasant for the first time to the noblest of thoughts and the highest of aspirations."

Ti-Price had been preoccupied with the "social claims of the wretched" since the experiences that had led him to write the article on the Haitian Military Hospital. In contrast to the deterioration of this institution, the Polyclinique-Péan, created in 1898 for members of the élite, had immediately become a splendid center of medicine, surgery and obstetrics under its founder, Dr. Léon Audain. Although Ti-Price had come from rural Haiti, he was nonetheless a member of the élite class which had joined hands with the Generals to exploit the peasants while mercilessly shedding their blood in civil wars to satisfy personal political ambitions.

And yet Ti-Price could not fail to see, given his bent for observation and his passion for analysis, the moral degradation of his cousin's administration. In June 1897, the Government's friends in the House of Representatives had tried to foment a ministerial crisis to remove Firmin from the Finance Ministry, but the people of Port-au-Prince gave the Cabinet such an ovation that President Tirésias dared not reshuffle it. Nevertheless, Firmin resigned his post in July because he found it impossible to work with the deputies. At the end of the year, the House voted the Government's project to consolidate Haiti's outstanding floating debt. This financial operation, purportedly aimed at reducing the country's financial burden, turned out to be a flagrant distribution of loot among the members of the Government and its cronies.

Meanwhile the salaries of public servants were reduced by twenty percent and were paid irregularly. They received payment in December for what was then called "un mois inconnu" to enable them to have a little something with which to celebrate Christmas Eve and Independence Day, January 1. Ti-Price's friends in Haiti and his parents might have been surprised to learn that he had been swayed by the thunderous rhetoric of Jaurès. But, as already noted, Price-Mars would do what most of his class never do—try to improve the lives of the masses. It was his moral conscience that had responded to Jaurès. In his short story, "Les Corbeaux," he tells that he and Maurice Dorval "never missed a public meeting where the booming voice of Jaurès, the ardent dialectics of a Viviani, would arouse the suffering multitude of the workers. And in their generous hearts, they, too, hoped the day would come when their own talents would allow them to change the fate of their good people of Haiti."

* * *

In 1900, as Paris was transformed into a dream for the Universal Exposition of French arts and industry, Ti-Price had to leave the city. He would have liked to remain in Paris at least long enough to view Auguste Rodin's display of some 200 figures, which constituted the artistic highlight of the Exposition. Ti-Price left France reluctantly, but his sadness had little to do with the Exposition.[12]

During his last days in Paris he had two painful experiences, one leaving him with a morbid fear about his health, the other molding his mind and heart forever. Beset by financial difficulties, the Haitian Government terminated the scholarships of Haitian students abroad, after having defaulted for three or four months on the monthly stipends. Most of the students hated to leave Paris, especially when the news from Port-au-Prince was so ominous. Many elected to stay. Ti-Price recounts their ordeal in "Les Corbeaux":

> The most clever ones [moved in with others] and slept by shifts. Those restrained by a sense of personal dignity did otherwise: they sold their books, their dearest possessions. Debts began to pile up as the things they could sell became more and more scarce. Their best suits soon went to the pawn shop. The money they got vanished in no time. The desperate appeals they made to their parents in faraway Haiti went unanswered. Over there, too, poverty had installed itself in many homes. Thus, no money came. And when there was nothing left to sell, they tightened their belts on empty stomachs and cheerfully went to the Faculties to pursue their studies if they could, but certainly to forget their hunger.

One winter day Maurice Dorval returned to the apartment with a fever, so cold he could hardly talk. There was neither coal nor wood in the flat. An occasional coughing spell interrupted Dorval's shivering.

"It's nothing," he said, making an effort to smile.

After he began to cough up some yellowish saliva, a physician was called to the apartment. Then came the terrifying diagnosis: Dorval had "granulie," a generalized form of tuberculosis which at that time rapidly became fatal. As Dorval kept complaining that he was thirsty and cold, Lachault, alias Ti-Price, kept running to the coal merchant, buying on credit. Finally spring returned. One beautiful, sunshiny day Dorval asked Ti-Price to open the window; as he tried to raise up on his bed to look outside, his eyes clouded and his head fell back on the pillow: he was dead.

As Ti-Price relates the circumstances following Dorval's death, they were most grotesque. The news "spread like wildfire throughout the neighborhood. Immediately all the merchants came and demanded their money. Lachault went to the Haitian Legation to ask for help. The Minister expressed sympathy and regretted that the

A Vow in the City of Light

Legation's assistance fund was depleted. But he would send an urgent cable to the Government for money. Though the telegraph cables were functioning, the money did not come. Haiti is so faraway when one is suffering . . . "

After four days of waiting in vain, Lachault persuaded an undertaker to send a coffin. As Lachault and a few friends who had come to the apartment were placing the body in the coffin, someone knocked on the door: "Open in the name of the Law!" It was a crier of the Seine Civil Tribunal accompanied by the coal merchant, who had come to attach the casket if the debt was not paid at once. Lachault became furious and attacked the coal merchant, creating a disturbance that attracted several other people who helped to chase away both the court's crier and the coal merchant. Fearing that they would soon return, this time with gendarmes, Lachault and his friends hastily carried the coffin with the corpse up the steep roads of Mont St. Geneviève to St. Etienne du Mont Church, where the parish priest consented to keep it temporarily.

Eventually Dorval's remains were brought back to Haiti. Ti-Price closes his story with the following apostrophe to the ghost of his friend: "You are resting now in the pink shade of the palm trees, in the midst of the white stones where the asphodel and royal balsamine grow, and where, on warm nights, the fearful spirits of your ancestors hover around . . . "

The other incident which marred even more profoundly Ti-Price's last days as a medical student was his encounter with Gustave Le Bon's book, *Psychological Laws of the Evolution of Peoples,* which first appeared in 1894. The French sociologist and anthropologist, editor of the *Bibliothèque de Philosophie Scientifique,* was already a well-known author. Ti-Price's interests were turning toward the social sciences. Taking time out from the Medical School, he went to study at the Museum of Natural History, the Trocadero Museum, the School of Anthropology. He also attended lectures on the social sciences at the Sorbonne and Collège de France. Naturally, he bought Gustave Le Bon's volume with great expectations.

Despite, or perhaps because of, his racial and historical background, Ti-Price would probably have agreed with Jefferson's dictum: "Every man has two fatherlands: his own and France." He was proud of being French by culture and Haitian by race, feeling as most educated Haitians do that it was the Blacks of Saint-Domingue who had forced France to implement the Declaration of the Rights of Man and of the Citizen, and in so doing, had caused France to become the Beacon of Humanity which Anténor Firmin had extolled in his so-called "Political Testament" in 1910. And Demesvar Delorme had done the same some forty years before in his own monumental volume of some 732 pages entitled *Les Théoriciens au Pouvoir.**

Ti-Price plunged into Le Bon's book, eager to learn from the renowned French sociologist and anthropologist the conditions in which people may attain full development of their potential. He clearly recognized the backwardness of the Black man, not only in Haiti but elsewhere, and he realized just as clearly the causes of that backwardness and his pride in being a Haitian. But his anticipated pleasure turned to anger as he read: "The primitive races are those among which one finds no trace of culture. Such are the Fuegians and Australian aborigines. The inferior races are represented by the Negroes. The in-between races are the Chinese, Japanese, Mongols and Semites. The superior races are the Indo-European people.

> These races are characterized by their definitive constitution as well as by their fixed psychological traits. As historical races slowly formed over thousands of years, they have become unchangeable because of the slowness of their formation.
> Thanks to the memory possessed by the most inferior beings—a privilege in nowise confined to man—it is doubtless possible for education to impart to an individual somewhat low down in the human scale the totality of the notions possessed by a European. A Negro or a Japanese may easily take a university degree or become a lawyer; the sort of varnish he thus acquires is however quite superficial, and has no influence on his mental constitution. What no education can give him, because they are created by heredity alone, are the forms of thought, the logic, and above all the character of the Western man.**

"Our Negro or our Japanese," Le Bon further affirms, "may accumulate all possible certificates without ever attaining to the level of the average European. It is easy to give him in ten years the culture of a well-educated Englishman. To make a real Englishman of him, that is to say a man acting as an Englishman would act in the different circumstances of life, a thousand years would scarcely be sufficient."**

Le Bon went on to condemn miscegenation, asserting that if a superior race mingles with an inferior race, the offspring are invariably inferior. Turning to history to support his theory, Le Bon added: "When the mixed-bloods by chance inherited a superior nation, as in Saint-Domingue, that civilization rapidly became decadent." These views, of course, had previously been expounded

---

*Dantès Bellegarde, *Ecrivains Haitiens,* Port-au-Prince, 1947, pp. 88-89.

**This translation is taken from the English version of Le Bon's book, published under the title *The Psychology of Peoples,* Stechert Reprints, New New York, 1924, p. 37.

A Vow in the City of Light

by Gobineau in his "Essay on the Inequality of the Human Races (1853-1855), which Anténor Firmin had attacked in his own work.

Undoubtedly Ti-Price remembered the incident that had occurred at Port-au-Prince in 1897, when the German Emperor echoed Le Bon's words to add insult to the injury he had inflicted on the Government of Tirésias Simon Sam. On December 6 of that year, two German warships, the Charlotte and the Stein, entered the Bay of Port-au-Prince to protest the sentencing by a Haitian court of a German living in Haiti. General Tirésias Simon Sam was forced to fly a white flag atop the Presidential Palace, and to pay an indemnity of $20,000 to Emile Lüders, the German national, even though by arrangement with the U. S. legation in Port-au-Prince, Lüders had been pardoned by the Haitian Government and allowed to leave the country.

The Haitian Government capitulated before the threat, after the United States refused to invoke the Monroe Doctrine and intervene, as urged by its own Minister to Haiti, William F. Powell, a Negro. Powell dared write Secretary of State Sherman: "This is the first time in my life I have ever had cause to be ashamed of being an American."[13] Commenting in Berlin on this event, the German Kaiser said: "My boys have brought to their senses those Haitian Negroes with a thin veneer of French civilization . . . "[14]

While the Haitian President, who had but four hours to accept the Kaiser's ultimatum, awaited Washington's decision, Pierre Frédérique, then editor of the newspaper *L'Impartial*, paraded through the streets of the capital, dressed in a flaming red suit, calling on the people to join him in urging the Government to resist Germany's armed aggression. He was promptly sent off to jail.

Ti-Price, who had been in Port-au-Prince at the time, had thus lived through that humiliation of his country and his race. Reopening the wound, Le Bon's words were a call to battle—a battle that would dominate his life. Years later he recalled his feeling on reading Le Bon:

> To pretend that Haitians have inherited Saint-Domingue's civilization and degraded it to a pitiful decadence; to pretend, by some hocus pocus, that an atrocious war lasting fourteen years, marked by bloody battles, after which a community of human beings, treated as animals, have reconquered by will-power the dignity of their persons and the right to govern themselves; to pretend that all this happened merely by chance and to try to scoff in that manner at the effort of a nation fighting against the world to defend its rights, is this not piling up sophistry upon aberration to support an *a priori* thesis? Is it not building a structure of errors, of apparent logical construction, to crush a portion of mankind under the charge of an irremediable inferiority?[15]

Then and there, in the City of Light, Ti-Price took this oath: "I rebelled against the unfairness and the insolence of such a judgment, and I vowed to join the glorious battle* for the triumph of scientific truth, for the exaltation of human truth, for the diffusion of the plain, unvarnished truth."[16]

---

* During that year 1900, the posthumous book of Hannibal Price, *Of the Rehabilitation of the Black Race by the Republic of Haiti*, appeared in Port-au-Prince. The author had this to say in its avant-propos: "I felt the need of raising my voice to defend my country so viciously slandered, to show and prove to other peoples that the words they have heard about Haiti are words of hatred and not words of History, and more less those of philanthropy." Price who had died in exile in Brooklyn, New York in 1893, had come back to haunt the minds of Haitian youth with this challenge, contained in his book: "This nation certainly has a mission from Heaven to discharge in the world, which it cannot betray without incurring God's wrath. This mission is the complete destruction of racial prejudice by making the progress of Haiti unmistakable."

Four

The Spirit of the Founders

The Government's decision to terminate the scholarships of Haitian students abroad in 1900, did not directly affect Ti-Price. Instead, he left Paris because of a political maneuver by President Tirésias Simon Sam. The latter's capitulation before the armed German threat in the *Affaire Lüders* had made him very unpopular throughout the country. In the eyes of the Haitians, such an act was unforgivable[1] just as it had been in the Môle St. Nicolas incident with Admiral Gherardi. Although Firmin, the leader of the Haitian intelligentsia, had rebuffed the haughty United States Admiral through diplomacy, public opinion nevertheless demanded his resignation from the Haitian Foreign Office for having consented even for a moment to consider the alienation of a part of Haitian territory. Since Dessalines' Constitution of 1805, Haitians had regarded the national domain as all the more "sacred" because their national pride had been coupled with another powerful sentiment that Haitian author Beauvais Lespinasse had expressed, some twenty years before Hannibal Price: "Haiti, eldest daughter of Africa, considers her history and her civilization as the first page of the rehabilitation of her race."[2]

President Tirésias Simon Sam knew that his already discredited government had become even more unpopular after the financial transactions of the "Consolidation." Unlike most of his predecessors who wanted to remain in power for life, in 1900 he had seized a providential opportunity to pass the reins of the State to one of his close collaborators. At that time the man the President and his friends feared most was Anténor Firmin, who had weathered the popular outcry of 1891, to become once again the idol of the country's young intellectuals.

The death of General François Manigat, Haitian Minister in Paris, was the unexpected blessing. The President immediately appointed Firmin to that diplomatic post, sending him to a glamorous exile as he had previously done with General Manigat.[3] It was common knowledge that Manigat would never give up his presidential aspirations. In fact, he had even had a marble bust of himself made, which he hoped to place among those of former Haitian Chiefs of State at the review grounds in Port-au-Prince.[4]

To kill two birds with one stone, the President sent along with Firmin the poet Massillon Coicou as Secretary of the Legation in Paris. Coicou was then President of the Association for the Celebration of the Centennial of Haiti's Independence and was quite active on the Port-au-Prince scene. As an enthusiastic partisan of Firmin, he was also to be feared. As a result of this move, Ti-Price was transferred to the Berlin Legation.

Despite the Emile Lüders incident, Ti-Price suffered no indignities in Berlin on account of his color or nationality. On the contrary, he reported that whenever he went to restaurants, for example, the waiters would address him as "Excellency." In Berlin he found not a general but an intellectual at the head of the Legation, Dalbemar Jean-Joseph. The latter was a prominent lawyer and jurist who had been Director of the Haitian National School of Law and had written extensively on the country's political and judicial institutions. He was also the author of a book on the subject of Haitian-Dominican Frontiers and may have prompted Ti-Price's research on relations between those two neighboring countries. At any rate, Price-Mars' most important contribution in the field of history, *The Republic of Haiti and the Dominican Republic* (1953), is dedicated to several persons, among them Nord Jean-Joseph, son of the former Minister to Berlin.

At that time Germany was engaged in fierce competition with France for business and trade with Haiti. In 1888, the German Government had sent to Haiti as its Consul Dr. Heinrich Goering, father of Hitler's Air Marshal. During his five years in Haiti, Dr. Goering successfully developed commercial relations between the two nations.[5] Many Germans had since settled there as importers, exporters or bankers. Firmin himself had learned the German language, as many other Haitians had done, for the Germans practically ruled Haiti's commercial and financial markets during the 1890's and their influence was still very strong when Ti-Price went to Berlin.

About a year after he arrived in Germany, an impassioned discussion started publicly in Port-au-Prince as to the date on which President Tirésias' term would expire. On electing him to the Presidency, the National Assembly had declared that his mandate would run until May 15, 1903. The Opposition, however, argued that, since the President had been elected on March 13, 1896, his term had *constitutionally* begun on May 15 of that year and should terminate *constitutionally* on May 15, 1902. Eventually the President announced that he would leave office on May 12, 1902. On that date the National Assembly convened to elect his successor, who would have been Minister of Public Works Cincinnatus Leconte, had not the people of Port-au-Prince intervened to disband the National Assembly under gun-fire.

A provisional government was then established with former President Boisrond-Canal as its head. As the call went out for a new general elections, Firmin immediately returned to Haiti and announced his candidacy for a seat in the House of Representatives, while campaigning at the same time for the Presidency of the Republic.

"An ardent, educated youth, full of faith in the future of the country," writes J. C. Dorsainvil, "campaigned for a public figure who enjoyed their complete confidence. Firmin was an outstanding writer and an upright administrator who reacted vigorously against abuses and twice corrected Haiti's financial situation."[6] Firmin soon discovered, however, that he had not the slightest chance of success so long as Boisrond-Canal was pulling the political strings.[7] Moreover, the other generals were hardly ready to relinquish their power to a civilian. They banded together against Firmin in the most effective demonstration they ever gave of their *esprit de corps.*

General Nord Alexis, the Provisional Government's Minister of War, personally took command of government troops in Cap-Haitian. He had grown old waiting for his turn to move into the National Palace. Now, at eighty-four, this would be his last chance. Thirty-five years before, Firmin had stood in his way.[8] Now General Nord had the upper hand and could settle that old score. He drove Firmin and his supporters out of Cap-Haitian. Firmin then went to Gonaives where he was enthusiastically elected Deputy, but proceeded into exile on the nearby island of St. Thomas. For General Nord had taken his army to Port-au-Prince and was proclaimed President by his troops on December 17, 1902. The National Assembly ratified this pronunciamento three days later.

Soon after Nord Alexis occupied the National Palace, Ti-Price was recalled from his post in Berlin. He did not return immediately to Port-au-Prince, possibly because one of the first acts of the new government was to appoint a Commission to investigate the affairs of the Tirésias administration, especially the transactions of the so-called "Consolidation." Ti-Price moved back to Paris and resumed the study of his new field of interest, sociology and anthropology, dividing his time between the Sorbonne, the School of Political Science and the Collège de France.

The following year Ti-Price returned to Haiti to run for the House of Representatives and "tried to elevate the contest to a real discussion of ideas."[9] The practical men of the community regarded his as a fool. "His candidacy was rejected by a coalition of all the interests he so fiercely opposed. He lost."[10] The happy winner of the election at Grande Rivière du Nord was the poet Probus Blot.

Despite the election of General Nord Alexis as Chief Executive, the country remained divided. Throughout the year preceding the celebration of the Centennial, a controversy raged among the Haitian intellectuals. Dr. Rosalvo Bobo, a journalist of Cap-Haitien, published a pamphlet, *A Propos du Centenaire,* in which he called the Haitians a "pseudo people." And he added: "In order to become truly a people, we need to have the first of all blessings, Freedom . . . I am at once confused and revolted at the thought that in the system under which we live, with Blacks enslaved by other Blacks, the worst off among the slaves are you, I, the whole group of intellectuals, because we are the ones most responsible for the shameful continuance of that system." In a previous article, Bobo had suggested that the best way to commemorate the Centennial was "to drape the entire country in mourning while the whole nation meditates over its past errors."

However, the Centennial celebration took place as planned. It began May 18, 1903 on the grounds of the National Palace with festivities to commemorate the creation of the Haitian flag. The people of the capital were convened by a salvo of one hundred cannon shots. President Nord Alexis, who claimed the privilege of defraying all the expenses of the celebration from his personal fund, recalled in moving tones how Dessalines had torn the white stripe from the French flag and then joined the blue and the red stripes to make the Haitian flag, symbolizing the Union of the Blacks and the Mulattoes.

Although "Unity" was also the theme of the January 1 celebration, an insurrection broke out in Port-au-Prince while the President was in Gonaives, the Nation's birthplace where he had gone for the momentous event. There the Palace of the Centennial had been erected on the very spot where the Act of Independence was signed on January 1 one century earlier. Government troops in the capital promptly stamped out the upheaval. But upon his return, the President rounded up a number of persons who had been accused of participating in the conspiracy or were presumed to be enemies of the Government, and they were mercilessly put to death without trial. As a result, many people who feared they might be implicated, sought refuge in foreign consulates, or vanished en route to voluntary exile in the Dominican Republic or on some British island in the Caribbean.

Ti-Price's defeat at the polls had elevated him in the esteem of the youth of Grande Rivière, and he came out of his retreat as the enlightened son of the community on the Glorious Day while cannons boomed all over Haiti. He attuned his voice to both national and governmental sentiment as he spoke during the festivities that took place at Cormiers, Dessalines' birthplace. His speech was immediately printed in Cap-Haitien and published in book form under the title *Les Fêtes de Cormiers.*

The President was known to revere the heroes of Haiti's War

The Spirit of the Founders

for Independence. In fact, he had married a niece of King Christophe who was also the daughter of General Jean-Louis Pierrot, a veteran of that war. The talk of "Dr. Price-Mars" as the youth of Grande Rivière called him, must have pleased President Nord Alexis a great deal. A strong military relationship existed between the Chief Executive and Price Mars' family. During the Civil War of 1888 that followed the death of Seide Télémaque, General Nord Alexis had established his headquarters at Grande Rivière du Nord. He was then Military Commander of the Northern Province, and as such had appointed Vilbrun Guillaume Military Commander of Dondon, the key position in the defense of Grande Rivière.

Early indications that Price-Mars enjoyed the new President's favor came when Nord Alexis named him and Dr. Léon Audain to represent Haiti at the Louisiana Purchase Centennial Exposition in 1904.[11] The Chief of Cabinet, Camille Gabriel, a relatively young man, may have been partly responsible for the appointment. He admired well-educated youth and usually took pride in helping them to find a place in the government. Price-Mars may even have been instrumental in getting Dr. Léon Audain selected, if only by suggesting the latter's name to the President or Camille Gabriel when he made his own bid for the assignment.

Dr. Audain, whom we have already met several times, had already put himself in a favorable light the previous year during the controversy over the Centennial Celebration. He had published a paper, *Some unpublished fragments of our contemporary history,* in which he castigated his compatriots for drawing a color line that had so often contributed to the country's civil wars. He named outstanding public figures and promising young men who had fallen victim to hatred motivated by the color question. Dr. Audain was a mulatto and the friendship that united him with Price-Mars was known to all the capital's intellectuals. Moreover, the mulatto and the black, both highly cultured, were excellent examples of what President Nord Alexis had in mind when he had called at Gonaives for union and solidarity among all the sons of the Haitian fatherland.

One can easily imagine Price-Mars' state of mind as he arrived in the United States after the Celebration in Haiti and his own speech about Dessalines at Cormiers. Drums and cymbals were still beating in his heart while trumpets sang the glory of Haiti's heroes. What a contrast with St. Louis where the Louisiana Purchase Exposition took place! He looked at the dejected Black men and women in the streets of that city. An incident occurred that not only reminded him of Haiti's heroes but also made him fear for the future of the Haitian people.

One day I was in the Haitian section of the St. Louis Exposition in my official capacity as a Commissioner of the Republic. At a certain moment I saw headed in my direction through the alleys of the Forestry Building two young Blacks, led by a brown-skinned man and surrounded by an excited crowd that was subjecting them to all sorts of indignities. The Blacks remained unmoved and looked stupid as they went along without paying attention. They were thin, backward, and had only a piece of cloth around their bodies from the waist halfway down to their thighs. Suddenly, when they arrived at the spot where I stood, they stopped and stared with amazement. Then they were convulsed with wild laughter as they began to point at me to call the crowd's attention to me. Finally, as they began to walk again, I could not help but follow them out of curiosity, and I arrived at one of the ends of the Exposition grounds where Yankee kindness had penned them up for the diversion of the strollers. In and around a few huts, there were some thirty Blacks dressed as I have just described. They had been brought there from the Philippine mountains. The two Blacks I had followed spoke to them and they loudly expressed some feeling toward me that I have not yet comprehended. In such cases one should not reach hasty conclusions, but it seems to me that I detected in the reaction of my congeners stupefaction, misgivings and a great deal of scorn. All of them were shouting, making contortions, pointing at me and laughing. When I decided to go on, all of them made a gesture, as if to reject me. I confess that the most miserable participant in that strange scene was neither a black Filipino nor an onlooker. What was going on in the mind of those primitive people? Maybe they considered me as one of their own who had rejected the faith of the ancestors since I was dressed like the white people and gave the impression that I understood the white man's language and seemed to be on good terms with them, the masters.[12]

Painfully Price-Mars recalled the works Hannibal Price had written in *The Rehabilitation of the Black Man by the Republic of Haiti:* "I am from Haiti, the Mecca, the Judea of the Black Race, the land where one finds the sacred fields of Vertières, of La Crête à Pierrot, of La Ravine à Couleuvres, of Le Tombeau-des-Indigènes, and hundreds of others to which every man with African blood in his veins should go in pilgrimage at least once in his lifetime, because it is there that the Negro had made himself a man; it is there that, on breaking his chains, he irrevocably condemned slavery in the New World."[13]

Price-Mars, who had reverently repeated those glorious names of battles in his talk at Cormiers, felt exceedingly proud of being a Haitian and a tinge of pity for both Black Filipinos and Black Americans. In general, at that time Haitians knew practically nothing about the Negro's struggles in the United States, their slave revolts before Lincoln's Emancipation Proclamation, their participation in the Civil War. Haitians knew even less about Filipinos.

Thus, more often than not, while they sympathized with Negro Americans about the treatment meted out by white America, they looked down on them, mistakenly believing that American Blacks had accepted their lot. Haitians had attributed the emancipation of U. S. slaves entirely to white abolitionists and the one Black American they venerated: Frederick Douglass. Inscribing a copy of his book on the Haitian-Dominican frontiers to Douglass, Dalbemar Jean-Joseph, Price-Mars' former chief in Berlin, wrote: "This package I have the honor of sending you, goes also as a tribute to the eminent man you are, for having raised the banner of our Race to such heights."[14] By the same token, a group of Haitian students in Port-au-Prince, in September 1894, while Price-Mars was enrolled at the Lycée Pétion, sent a letter to Douglass expressing sentiments usually reserved for their own national heroes:

> Born Haitians and accustomed since childhood to venerate the memory of men who by their work, their spirit and their talents have earned the admiration of nations . . . we cannot, despite the timidity that restrains our youthful enthusiasm, refrain from addressing to you these feeble words to express our love for the immense task you have undertaken with body and soul and which has succeeded only because of your knowledge and indomitable perseverance. After reading your book, *My Bondage and My Freedom,* and considering the sacrifices you have made for the cause of your Brothers, we have exclaimed: On the façade of the Pantheon of our history, we see the name of Douglass emblazoned—glorious and immense name that symbolizes the abolition of slavery and the rehabilitation of the African race . . . [15]

Conversely, the vast majority of Negro-Americans knew very little about Haiti. In fact, Hannibal Price said that he was prompted to write his book because of constant inquiries from distinguished American Negroes while he was serving as Haitian Minister to the United States. These men wanted to know the truth about Haiti, which the white press was picturing as reverting to the state of an African tribe. In 1904, Mr. Ebenezer D.C. Bassett, another Black former U. S. Minister to Haiti, found it necessary to defend Haiti in an article published in *Voice of the Negro* and entitled "Should Haiti be Annexed?"

The encounter with the Filipinos on the Exposition grounds seemed another argument in support of Le Bon's thesis. Price-Mars was most distressed. His mind had been obsessed with the thought of progress for Haiti ever since his article about the Military Hospital. In Paris, Berlin and now in St. Louis, he had been able to compare the white man's progress with the relative backwardness and lethargy of his fellow Blacks. Moreover, the white man was constantly forging further ahead. For example, the St. Louis Exposition prominently displayed a hundred or so automobiles, one of which had come all the way from New York under its own power.

Observing the progress the United States had made since its conquest of electricity, Price-Mars became uneasy, remembering both the brazen attempt to take the Môle St. Nicolas in 1891, and the warning given the Haitian people in Rosalvo Bobo's pamphlet, *A Propos du Centenaire:* "Today is no longer the old yesterday. At this hour we must move more rapidly. We no longer lack elements or progress. The small nations must spontaneously follow the trend. If not, they will be crushed."

The insurrectional movement that marred the Centennial celebration a few months earlier had definitely shown that color division among the Haitians was still alive. Hannibal Price had died but his book, particularly at that time, was mercilessly pricking the Haitian's conscience as it asked: What use have we made of the liberty and independence acquired at so dear a cost? What causes have hampered or quickened Haiti's steps on the road to Progress? And the posthumous author tells the story of an old soldier of the War for Independence who would repeat over and again: "This country will be lost, the white people will take it back, if Blacks and Mulattoes do not put an end to their disunity."*

Apparently it was during his stay in St. Louis that Price-Mars appreciated more fully than ever the thoughts that concluded Hannibal Price's book: that the most important matter before the nation was to educate the Haitian people so as to remove false ideas from their minds and, from their hearts, base sentiments which have obstructed Haiti's progress on the road to Civilization.* As he mused over all this in his room at the Douglass Hotel in St. Louis, he renewed his determination to work for the betterment of Haiti and the Black Race. He even took for himself a new name as a "manifesto" of his resolve that his compatriots should enjoy domestic peace and solidarity. On August 19, 1904, he wrote Booker T. Washington, expressing the desire to come to Tuskegee. For the first time he hyphenated the Christian name he had received from the mulatto author and the name of his Black father. He signed his letter: *Price-Mars.***

* * *

On his return to Haiti, Price-Mars did not rush to divulge his impressions of the United States, except to a few trusted friends,

---

* Dantès Bellegarde: "The posthumous book of Hannibal Price made a profound impression on the educated youth of 1900, because it approaches with sincerity and courage the essential problems of Haitian society." *Ecrivains Haitiens,* Port-au-Prince, 1947, p. 97.

** The Booker T. Washington Papers, U. S. Library of Congress, Washington, D. C.

such as Pauléus Sannon. He dared not publish them in newspapers for he knew that what he had to say, about Negro-Americans in particular, would not help his plans for the immediate future. The citizens of the "Cultural Province of France," to whom he would have to speak probably would not approve, and they were all-powerful around President Nord Alexis. He also knew that he was specially vulnerable at that time because of his "blood" relationship with ex-President Tirésias Simon Sam. During the month of December when he returned home, adversaries of the Government, presumably those who had favored the Consolidation, undertook to hoard the small Haitian coins in an attempt to paralyze trade among the more impecunious portion of the citizenry to cause starvation and eventual disorder. In reaction to this, on Christmas Day, which fell on Sunday, various sentences were pronounced by the Criminal Court at Port-au-Prince against several of the Consolidars, both foreigners and Haitians standing trial in person or *in absentia.*

Among the foreigners were three Frenchmen: a director of the National Bank of Haiti, a sub-director and a bank clerk; a German capitalist who was the custodian of the bank bonds, and an American involved in illegal transactions in the bonds. The Haitians were all kin, relatives or friends of the former President.[16]

Speaking on January 1, 1905 at the National Palace, President Nord Alexis had this to say:

> At the Gonaives commemoration of the hundredth anniversary of our independence, I reminded you of our past mistakes, of the misfortunes they engendered, and of the delay that our internal troubles had caused the onward march of our society. However ruinous our international disorders may be, never have they obstructed the progress of the Republic with as many obstacles as the passions and prejudices to which we have been exposed for one hundred years. But nothing up to now has shaken your hope for the future—nothing, it seems has been able to stifle the vital strength of Haitian nationality, though you had to exert twenty times more effort than any other people to prove yourselves worthy of sovereignty . . . It is from your confidence that I draw the necessary energy for the discharge of my task. It is to Union today that I invite you in the name of our ancestors to treasure their ideals; it is to Union that you will have to turn to ensure peace and progress and national strength, so you may bequeath intact this land to those who will come after you.

Later that year Firmin published in Paris a volume entitled *Mr. Roosevelt and Haiti,* in which he expressed ideas very similar to those of President Nord Alexis: "If Haitians should fail to look back on their past and should fail to grasp the necessity of changing their habits to abandon all the prejudices among themselves that have delayed our national development, the best help that might come to Haiti from the exterior will be of no avail . . . Our destiny, in the final analysis, must be our own work." And he reminded his compatriots: "the United States is watching us."

All Haitians at that time were profoundly conscious of Haiti's precarious international situation, the more so since President Theodore Roosevelt had threatened the whole Western Hemisphere with his "Big Stick" and had perpetrated his brazen foray into Columbian territory to grab the land the United States wanted in order to build the Panama Canal. President Nord Alexis, who considered himself the personification of the Haitian Nation, was obsessed by fear that the "Vultures of Imperialism" were only waiting for Haiti to die from the wounds of her civil wars. He gradually became a tyrant and at times a cruel one. As a result, the country fell under the constant watch of the police. J. Montague Simpson, a British subject from Jamaica, who visited Haiti that year, remarked: "A policeman would sooner go without his pay for a day than his club for an hour, as he also put it to striking use in his daily rounds and common tasks."[17]

On returning from St. Louis, Price-Mars had gone straight to Grande-Rivière du Nord to campaign once more to represent his birthplace in the House of Representatives. Whether he had the blessing of the President personally or that of Camille Gabriel, he had no trouble this time in getting himself elected. Perhaps the townsfolk had realized by then that the lad they had known as Ti-Price had become a man of competence and character.

At the House of Representatives Price-Mars associated with a progressive group that comprised, among others, his old friend, Windsor Bellegarde, along with Louis-Edouard Pouget and Fleury Féquière. Pouget had served before him as Secretary to the Haitian Legation in Berlin.[18] Fequière was an educator whose name became prominent in 1906 after the publication of his book, *Haitian Education.* This was a volume of some 500 pages which stirred up heated discussion on the subject of "A choice of discipline": Was it realistic now to continue to follow French thinking in education or was it not wiser to adopt Anglo-Saxon methods?[19]

While the debate over a "choice of discipline" was going on, Price-Mars, secure in his new position as Deputy, decided to disclose his impressions of the United States. He chose to speak at the Alliance Française in Port-au-Prince on "The Equality of Human Races, according to a recent work by Jean Finot." Although addressing citizens of the "Cultural Province of France," who made up the larger part of his audience, he was really speaking to the men and women of the "Black Republic" about their "brothers" in the United States. He deplored, of course, the degraded status the white man had accorded the Negro there. But he had brought back a large measure of humility concerning his Haitian citizenship after his visit to Tuskegee Institute. There he had seen the Negro-Americans' determination and struggle to improve their lot in the United States. In fact, he had become their brother, not really because of a common color, but because of their courageous progressive spirit despite the adverse circumstances that confronted them in their daily life. He told his audience that the Negro-Americans, whom they had practically ignored, were on the road to progress:

> As for me, I cannot deny that the racial question in the United States had troubled me before I had the privilege of knowing that country. I wanted to see with my own eyes what was going on in that strange milieu. I affronted all the ignominies of racial prejudice.

He went on to mention that Negro-Americans had thirty-eight universities, the most outstanding of which were Howard and Fisk. "The first, during the forty years of its existence, has conferred degrees on more than 2,000 students, including 300 clergymen, 700 physicians, 200 lawyers. Fisk University has awarded 400 diplomas in 1904 to physicians, teachers, clergyman, engineers, etc."

> Our congeners have talented poets and musicians, such as Paul Laurence Dunbar, [Bob] Cole, the Johnson Brothers, etc. (The latter have written a series of delightful poems which they have set to music themselves. I heard them throughout the country.) They have eminent historians and sociologists, such as W. E. Burghart Du Bois, mathematicians of high standing, like Dr. Blyden. Finally, they have produced the most powerful American orator of our time, Booker T. Washington.[20]

Price-Mars had first met and interviewed the distinguished Negro educator in 1903 when Mr. Washington visited Paris while on a European lecture tour. At that time Booker Washington was certainly the most influential Negro in the United States, adviser to presidents and philanthropists, author of a best-seller, *Up from Slavery*, which Price-Mars had probably read in the French translation. But it was his program of practical education that Price-Mars wanted to examine at Tuskegee. Perhaps it could be beneficial to Haiti.

Consequently, after attending the official functions of the Exposition in St. Louis, he travelled through the Black Belt, a frightening experience in 1904 for a Haitian diplomat who had just spent four years in Paris and Berlin. "I was once practically put in a cattle-car," he said. "I was often insulted in street-cars. I endured all these vexations so I could more closely and more effectively analyze the complex aspects of the racial problem."[21] The highlight of his trip, however, was the two weeks he spent at Tuskegee as the guest of Booker T. Washington. "One cannot form from a distance," he enthused, "a comprehensive idea of the social scope of Booker T. Washington's work, which is to prepare for all branches of industry skilled workers who, not only will be able to make an honorable living for themselves, but also, by their discipline and training, will be in a position to exercise great influence in the gigantic struggle between Capital and Labor."[22] He saw in the Tuskegee educator the harbinger of the rehabilitation of the Black masses through collective and individual efforts.

Whether or not Price-Mars had a hand in the preparation of Fleury Féquière's book as a result of his close relationship with the author in the House of Representatives, the fact remains that it was more or less Booker Washington's philosophy of education that Féquière proposed in that volume. Under the subtitle, "Booker T. Washington and his Work," Féquière had this to say:

> Among all the . . . valid reasons for knowing the United States there is one that I will qualify as major: the fact that in that country there are some 12 millions of our congeners who are an integral part of the American community. Two of these appear in full focus: Frederick Douglass and Booker T. Washington. These two men, whose first steps in life were handicapped by the bonds of slavery, are two characters of living edification for their race.
>
> Booker T. Washington is the man for whom destiny had reserved the task of undertaking the education of his congeners . . . He began by preparing himself in the hard school of experience, conforming completely to the saying: "He who wants the end, wants the means." The end he wanted was to cultivate his mind so as to become fully aware of the problems that the recent Emancipation had posed for his own race . . . At Hampton Institute . . . Booker Washington tested his own worth and learned the wholesome influence that hard work can exert on the morale of a man who gives himself without reservation to his task. He trained himself through working and so he came to modify whatever may have been faulty and irrational in his conception of life.
>
> This man who has changed the mentality of his race, and has been able to transfer his renown to Tuskegee Institute where Black Americans learn the best of human values—this man deserves the high esteem and consideration of all, particularly of Haitians who cannot remain indifferent to the lot of any segment of the race.[23]

Price-Mars was no less charmed by the Negro-American women. In order perhaps not to hurt the sensitivity of his female listeners at the Alliance Française, he borrowed from Jules Huret's book, *De New-York à la Nouvelle-Orléans,* this flattering description of Negro-American women:

> And I saw some happy portents for the future. In the upper echelon of Black society, I met many men of character and talent and many women of great distinction. On these faces of women with amber complexion, a proud, almost haughty profile, ardent, melancholy eyes that seemed steeped in liquid mother-of-pearl, lips just fleshy enough to express sensibility, chin rising in a graceful curve . . . . head firmly attached to a lovely, downy neck, chest convex, waist narrow and supple, hand small and

distinguished, I discovered in full aesthetic evolution the human type to which I belong.²⁴

The same year, 1906, under Fleury Féquière's leadership, the House of Representatives created at Port-au-Prince the Vocational School for Girls, known as Ecole Elie Dubois. He also persuaded the House to pass a law to have the State Treasury assume financial responsibility for the School of Applied Sciences, which had been founded in the capital in 1902 by a group of private citizens, most of them Haitian engineers trained in Europe.

In discussing *The Prejudice of Races,* a book by French author Jean Finot, Price-Mars showed that he had acquired a commendable amount of personal knowledge in the field of anthropology since his eventful vow in Paris six years earlier. Although he praised Finot for the scientific probity and the solid organization of his book, as well as for the abundance of information it contained, Price-Mars actually made his review a display of his own knowledge in the field of anthropology. As he talks, one realizes that his mind is still burdened by Gustave Le Bon's attack on Haiti. In fact, he seizes with delight this opportunity to refute Le Bon's arguments by painting the life of colonial Saint-Domingue in the light of true history with its reverberations on the Haitian nation:

> It is generally admitted that since 1804, Haiti has been devoted to anarchy and decadence, that we have been unable to utilize the brilliant civilization of Saint-Domingue and that finally we have reverted to the level of the African tribe. This opinion is so firmly established that the most circumspect minds have found it difficult to eradicate. This is probably why Mr. Jean Finot, in his masterful book on race prejudice, has not dared to call for the revision of this summary condemnation by presenting evidence of our evolution along with that of our American brothers. I bitterly blame him for that. If he had tried to know us, I am sure he would have found legitimate justification of his opinion. First, our writers who have dealt with the question would have furnished him new evidence to bolster his arguments, and secondly, the works of our scientists would have strengthened his conviction that the development of Black brains is not indifferent to Humanity.²⁵

At the outset of his talk, Price-Mars had referred to the Haitian writers Anténor Firmin and Hannibal Price with great praise for the respective works. "But both books," he said, "despite their respective merit, despite the scientific probity of their documentation, have the fault—for certain minds—of having been written by Haitians, and thus may not be considered objective."²⁶

Warming up to his subject, Price-Mars presented a few historical facts to refute the detractors:

> Now if there is a manifestly erroneous opinion, if there is a historical heresy, it is the one that affirms the free and independent Haiti has inherited Saint-Domingue's civilization. The truth is, in

Anténor Firmin

Dantès Bellegarde

the former French colony there existed an organized society with the refinements and customs of 18th century French society, but it was exclusively and absolutely made up of whites, who had at their disposal, for the maintenance of their luxury and welfare, a large number of slaves whom they regarded as beasts of burden and chattels. Among these slaves, whose number, thanks to the morbid cruelty of the masters, constantly increased with importation from Africa, there existed no political bonds before their arrival in Haiti. Brought from various regions and from the long African coast, from tribes that were enemies and spoke different languages, these slaves found solidarity on Haitian soil only as a result of their common misery and the similar treatment of which they were all victims.

But then, when the hour of liberation came, the will of a genius—that of Toussaint-Louverture—knew how to bend, discipline and organize these heterogeneous elements to make them into a nation which broke its chains and demanded its rights to liberty. This immense, prodigious effort had, as its conscious or unconscious stimulus, the very cruel treatment to which the great mass of slaves had been subjected for so long.

The problem, then, was not to know what liberty was and how to organize it in a nation. The problem was simply to stop the misery caused by the excessive brutality of the masters.

Thus, the fourteen-year war that eventually brought about the independence of our country, was an atrocious war on both sides, a war of extermination without precedent in history. Lacking modern weapons, the insurgents used the torch. You recall the famous slogan that so accurately depicts our forefathers' state of mind: 'When the first cannon fires the alarm, the cities are to disappear and the nation to rise up in arms!'

It was after having thrown off the swaddling-clothes of Saint-Domingue in such a manner that Haiti established herself on a mountain of ruins. It was amid these disastrous circumstances that the new nation was born.[27]

Price-Mars acknowledged the fact that Haiti was underdeveloped economically. But as he saw it, the important question, considering the kind of criticism leveled at Haiti, was and still remains whether the Black man is capable of civilization. The facts, he said, reply favorably and conclusively to that question: the Blacks, who had been held outside of humanity until 1804, have since created a new political society which is holding its own in international exchanges. He pointed out that in 1789, when the French Revolution began, Saint-Domingue was at the peak of its economic development, producing 77 million pounds of coffee annually. Despite the devastation wrought throughout the country by the war for independence, Haiti in 1906 was the fourth largest coffee-producing country in the world, with an average production of 70 million pounds from a territory of some 830,700 square kilometers.

Moreover, when Haiti began her independent life she had only 480,000 citizens.

He confessed that he would personally consider such achievement rather slim if Haiti had contributed nothing else to civilized life. "No, what characterizes our evolution," he affirmed, "is the harmonious development of our mental faculties, the rapid conquest we have made in the intellectual domain . . . For there are no disciplines of the arts or science that have discouraged our minds. We have successively cultivated everything: music, poetry, painting, sociology, applied science, etc.

"If therefore a country can only be judged by its outstanding scholars and artists, how could we fail to mention that two volumes of selections from our writers of prose and poetry, published in 1904 on the occasion of our Centennial, received the French Academy's highest honors? Does not all this prove that the Negro brain is fit for intellectual endeavor?" To demolish completely Le Bon's theory of the hierarchy of races, Price-Mars pointed to the military success of the Japanese over the Russians in 1905.

Price-Mars was an honest scholar. He did not close his eyes on the tragedy and ugliness of the Haitian political and social system, which he knew only too well. "Are we Haitians without faults?" he asked. "Oh! Who can be a good man and yet not be saddened by the spectacle of corrupt public practices? Who can be a patriot and yet not weep over our recurrent civil wars, over the immorality of some of our public men, over our stubborn retention of practices that have already caused us so much suffering?

"What serious thinker can fail to be disturbed on seeing the gap widen in this country between the élite and the masses?

"Alas! Those are problems over which our philosophers and sociologists turn gray, without losing hope or courage. One cause of those problems which they denounce most forcefully and which has done the greatest harm to our young society is the theory of racial inequality. It has been so widely accepted that we too are inclined to admit the inferiority of the black race to the white race."[28]

When Price-Mars delivered that lecture, the country was again smoldering with revolutionary passion, either from the underground activities of certain members of the previous Administration, or from the expectation of a military coup led by Firmin similar to the one Boyer-Bazelais mounted in 1883. The "Liberals" were particularly impatient because of their contempt for Nord Alexis' police-state régime and for his personal lack of intellectual preparation.

Dantès Bellegarde, who was then an official at the Department of Public Instruction, published Price-Mars' speech in the *Official Bulletin,* as he had done for such scholarly works by other Haitian intellectuals. This caused great commotion at the National Palace where Price-Mars was accused of being a "Firminist." Nord Alexis formally ordered the Minister of Public Instruction to forbid in the future "the publication of any such writings as those of Léon Audain and Price-Mars." The *Bulletin* was not created to serve as a platform for those who are trying to achieve their ambitions," the President added.[29]

Dr. Léon Audain frequently spoke at the Haitian Society of Legislation,[30] discussing those aspects of Haitian society which, he felt, needed correction. The National Palace, which had welcomed the two men as its friends in 1904 when it sent them to the St. Louis Exposition as its representatives, was now dubbing them with the label reserved for its worst enemies, that of "Firminist."

One can be absolutely certain that Price-Mars was expressing a deep personal feeling when he asked in his lecture: "Who can be a patriot and yet not weep over our recurrent civil wars?" A trained and critical observer, and a man with a generous, sensitive spirit, he could not have failed to see, remember and regret what the casual Jamaican visitor, J. Montague Simpson, had noted: "There are standing monuments in Port-au-Prince which cause two different impressions, the one favorable, the other unfavorable: the walls of buildings which have been destroyed by fire. These exhibit the ability of the country's workmen, and the terrible results of political animosity."[31] And he had said earlier: "There are as honorable and conscientious men in Haiti as can be found in the best countries in the world, but the motto of the Republic—"L'Union fait la force" [In Union there is strength]—is sometimes lost to sight and dead to action."[32]

Price-Mars had mentioned the name of Firmin once in his lecture to call attention, naturally, to the latter's book. Unfortunately, the title of the lecture was too similar to that of Firmin's book and, according to Dantès Bellegarde, that was enough for the National Palace to tag the Firminist label on him. The conclusion of the speech refutes in advance the Government's accusation:

> Let us recognize that we are, all of us, men like all other men. Let us remember what we owe to our dear land, the *mater dolorosa*, and that our duty one to the other is to maintain solidarity as sons of the same fatherland.
>
> Finally, let us respect in everyone of us what constitutes the highest beauty in life, I mean, the eminent dignity of human nature.

Price-Mars had indeed expressed the Spirit of the Founders, Dessalines and Pétion, joint creators of the Haitian flag. Their union and unshaken solidarity in the fight against France had made Haitian independence possible. Like Nord Alexis and others, Price-Mars, who had dedicated himself to the preservation of that solidarity, was apprehensive lest Haitian disunity threaten the future of Black sovereignty over the Black Republic.

At this point, he was parting company with the citizens of the "Cultural Province of France," whose mentality had become obnoxious to him. He would remain their friend in the context of social life as he would remain faithful to French culture to the end of his life. But he had now declared the independence of his mind and spirit from both Dr. Léon Audain and French models. The insight he had gained during his visit to the United States, particularly from Booker T. Washington's experiment, had opened his eyes to new horizons of effort and constructive action in behalf of his "good people of Haiti."

Although Price-Mars may have known that others were plotting revolution, he envisaged in his lecture a peaceful revolution by lucid minds that would strive to introduce new methods of education to help young Haitians, boys and girls, urban and rural, to become tomorrow's industrious and useful citizens, in line with the process he had glimpsed at Tuskegee. And in closing his speech as he did, Price-Mars had pledged himself to a new undertaking that would occupy him for the next thirty-three years of his life. First, he would try to answer the question Chanlatte had posed in 1804: "Is our black or yellow complexion an impediment to our progress in the arts and in virtue, or does it prevent courageous efforts on our part?" Secondly, he would make an *Authentic Black Man* of himself, to refute the image of the Negro that Gustave Le Bon and other detractors of the Black Race had painted and had even forced into the minds of many Black men and women. In the spirit of Haiti's founders and under the inspiration of Booker T. Washington and other Black Americans, Price-Mars had just taken the first giant step on the road toward Black Consciousness.

Five

Navigating on Troubled Waters

As a Deputy in the House of Representatives, Price-Mars is primarily remembered for some verbal shots he fired at the Minister of Finance, Frédéric Marcelin, in discussions of economic measures. Marcelin, who had shouldered the heavy responsibility of dealing with the discouraging economic situation left by the previous government, was being mercilessly crucified, openly or by rumor, while some of the "consolidars" tried all sorts of maneuvers to derail President Nord Alexis' economic projects. Obviously, Price-Mars could not forget how Nord Alexis had tarnished the previous administration of his cousin. The mere sight of Marcelin, coming to the House to present and discuss economic remedies, immediately put him on edge. Even in his lecture at the Alliance Française he had depicted Marcelin as his special devil, referring to Haiti's economic situation since independence, Price-Mars did not hesitate to call the preceding year, 1905, "the most miserable" commercial year the country had ever known.

Frédéric Marcelin, who was an accomplished man of the world, would not let such an attitude on the part of Price-Mars deter him from being courteous toward the latter. On several occasions as he met Price-Mars on the street, he would stop his buggy and offer him a lift. To be sure, Price-Mars was one of those who wildly applauded Marcelin during that same year 1905, when he proposed a law to grant the poet Oswald Durand a pension equal to that of a President of the Republic. The poet, a former President of the House, had been acclaimed "National Bard" by the Deputies as well as by intellectuals throughout the nation. As Marcelin put it, Oswald Durand was the Chief of State of Haitian Intellectuality.

Marcelin himself was a brilliant writer; he had attracted the attention of the Haitian literary world with his first two novels: *Thémistocle-Epaminondas Labasterre* and *La Vengeance de Mama,* published respectively in 1901 and 1902. In all probability Price-Mars was referring to Marcelin in his talk at the Alliance Française when he said: "After quite a laborious period of imitation our literature has finally found its originality in satirizing our customs as well as in describing the ravishing beauty of our landscape. In some of the pages of our writers, whose depth is equalled only by the grace of their style, one feels at last . . . the thrill of great art."[1]

Years later, referring to Marcelin by name but not without observing that Marcelin, the writer, was superior to Marcelin, the public man, Price-Mars added:

> His works—novels, short stories, critical writings, political apologies, economic studies—are worthy of respect for their number as well as for their contents. He has put his personal touch on all aspects of Haitian life: a gloomy vision, a pessimistic philosophy of human nature. Thus, his cruel and merciless picture of our society results from a powerful sense of realism, an implacable concern for exactness. Yet the artist's sensibility comes through a quiver, despite his great effort to conceal it. It would be a mistake to believe this accomplished man of the world impervious to the suffering of all those puppets whose ugliness and weakness he had described . . . [2]

The novelist had given a true-to-fact portrayal of Haitian society at that time. The portraits he painted of his characters are unforgettable. The novel is all the more fascinating because it is written in harmonious prose at times bordering on poetry, particularly in the description of the Haitian landscape. Nevertheless, the episodes on Haitian political life are so disheartening that they easily seemed suspect to French critics. As a matter of fact, Frédéric Marcelin had actually started in Haitian literature the trend that would eventually develop under Price-Mars' leadership, first at home into "Indigenism" and "Africanism," then abroad as "Négritude." In defending his novels in 1903, Marcelin expressed the basic thoughts that Price-Mars would champion twenty-five years later in *Ainsi Parla l'Oncle,* which made him famous throughout the world. Marcelin wrote:

> . . . our literature in general must more and more seek its inspiration from our history, from the material or moral features of our people, from the physical beauty of our land. They must be exalted so that we may become attached to them. To a great extent, it is literature which makes the soul of a people. It is . . . the most educational, the most precious testimony of its genius and originality. We must direct our efforts to this task and toward this most desirable end.[3]

In regard to Haitian political life, Marcelin said that he had tried to reproduce it "photographically" in order to impress Haitian youth with its ugliness:

> We must cry out the truth to them, we must shout in their ears that politics, as now practiced, is leading them to death in poverty and shame, and militarism, as now conceived, is suicide in a bloody and unproductive despotism.[4]

Price-Mars' allusion to the critical economic situation may have been the principal cause of Nord Alexis' angry reaction to the speech at the Alliance Française. For such an allusion concurred with the Opposition's whispering campaign that because of the General's fear of foreign loans, Haiti was surely headed for complete ruin and would perhaps fall more rapidly under United States annexation.

On November 1, 1904, the American Minister William F. Powell, a Negro educator, reported to foreign press correspondents that the Haitian Government had granted a concession to two Americans, Louis Dalmas and Edward A. Blanton, Jr.:

> the most important concession ever granted to foreigners [to construct a railroad that] will penetrate the very heart of the Republic, traversing a region said to be rich in minerals, including copper, silver, gold, iron and lead, and a section of virgin forests, where one can find satin-wood, ebony, cedar, pitch pine, white walnut, and three kinds of mahogany. It will also reach a section represented as being rich in logwood and guaiac, which have not been marketable heretofore on account of the difficulty of reaching transportation by water. The railroad will also afford access to the cocoa belt. The terminus is to be Port-au-Prince, which will be reached by continuing the road from Hinche by way of Las Cahobas, Mirebalais and Arcahaie. When this is accomplished, there will be a continuous railway line through the interior to Gonaives and eventually to Cap-Haitien.[5]

On December 31, however, Minister Powell made no mention of any such project while speaking at the National Palace as Dean of the Diplomatic Corps. He contented himself with saying: "This Republic has gained for herself a page in the history of the world, and it remains for the sons of these men who have acquired it to preserve it, for the future of this country is in their hands; its prosperity and progress also."[6] Similarly, the following day, Haiti's Independence Day, President Nord Alexis did not refer either to the grandiose project of the railroad.

Haiti's financial situation was indeed deteriorating rapidly. In 1905, the government began to issue paper money and nickel coins. The exchange rate for U. S. currency, which was at 138.5 when Nord Alexis took office, soared to 400 per cent in 1907. And at that time the only important project the government had undertaken was the construction of the Roman Catholic Cathedral, the "Basilica of our Lady," which was being built in the Gothic style by a Belgian company. Yet all seemed to go well, as far as the political situation itself was concerned, under the iron fist of the old General-President. However, his mind remained plagued by the constant fear that Anténor Firmin might "return" as Boyer-Bazelais had done.

Ebullient partisans of the eminent writer, such as journalist Pierre Frédérique, affirmed that "God is great and Anténor Firmin his prophet."[7] For the most part, however, people in the capital, especially the wives and mothers, prayed that no revolution would occur.

In the immediate vicinity of the "Basilica" being erected, several city blocks still exhibited the ruins of Mulattoes' private residences and commercial establishments which Salomon Government's agents had burned down in the night of September 22, 1883, both in retaliation and as a warning to the "Liberals" at the capital, following Boyer-Bazelais' aggressive landing in the southern town of Miragoâne.

Meanwhile Price-Mars demonstrated keen political sagacity in the House of Representatives by remaining aloof from a controversy in 1907 that could have had regrettable consequences. The incident had to do with the validation of a pro-Government Deputy, Thomas A. Vilmenay, who had been elected during general elections held on April 14. A journalist, Vilmenay was known for his vitriolic pen. On April 16, the pro-tempore President of the House named a number of his colleagues to a committee to examine Mr. Vilmenay's credentials. Price-Mars was one of those designated, but he declined the honor "for reasons of convenience and personal delicacy." No sooner had the committee left the Hall than it returned with a favorable report which the pro-tempore President immediately submitted to the House. Two deputies, both close friends of Price-Mars, protested. Speaking first, Louis-Edouard Pouget argued that Vilmenay was not fit to serve in the House because he had been arrested as a counterfeiter in 1901 and, even though set free by a jury, he had been caught in the act of committing the crime.

Vilmenay took the floor to reply. Availing himself of the name of the President of the Republic, with dithyrambic praise for Nord Alexis, he warned the House: "Those who are dreaming of I know not what premature event in the frenzied emotion of their unhealthy ambitions and regard me as an adversary to get rid of, are wasting their efforts in these intrigues." This was an obvious allusion to widespread expectation among the "Liberals" that Firmin would soon return to take personal command of a coup to overthrow Nord Alexis.

Fleury Féquière intervened in the discussion, making the following statement:

> I shall not be long and it is not necessary after the judicious considerations presented by our colleague Pouget. But in a discussion of this importance and of this exceptional and delicate nature, an opportunity is available to everyone to produce the evidence . . . of his own morality and conscience . . . [8]

He went on to say that Vilmenay had been absolved by the jury in 1908, thanks to the oratory of his defense lawyer Michel Oreste, but today as Vilmenay came to the House requesting the "Dignus intrare" we shall unanimously reply: "Indignus." [9]

As Vilmenay again took the floor he declared that "formal

commitments taken vis à vis the Government" by many of the newly elected deputies were in fact a legislative mandate to support the Government. These words plunged most of the deputies into deep silence, but Pouget did not let himself be intimidated and said:

> If all of us have been nominated by the Government, the Government has then ignored the Nation's sovereignty and has confiscated the rights of the people in the last elections. Let us disband before the Sovereign People disband us.. Let us leave the whole place to Mr. Vilmenay. If on the contrary, we are the legal representatives of the Nation, elected by popular suffrage, let us turn out this man in a gesture of protest.[10]

Eventually, the House did just that, rejecting the report on Vilmenay by unanimous vote. Deputy Price-Mars was present when the vote was taken, but he had not said a word throughout the entire debate. He was, of course, keenly aware of the fact that the Consolidation affair was still a very live issue. Like most of his colleagues, he feared a confrontation with the vitriolic, irresponsible Vilmenay, but he had a more important reason for not giving the National palace another occasion to regard him as part of the Opposition. This reason was that his old friend, Pauléus Sannon, had been taken into the Government as Foreign Minister.

During the fall Price-Mars again lectured at the Alliance Française, but on a subject that offered little opportunity for anyone to accuse him of "Firminism." This time he spoke on "Esthetics and Races." He began by saying that in his previous talk he had demonstrated the inanity of the theory of the hierarchization of races, and had tried to prove, by the example of the Haitian people and the Negro Americans, that "the Black race, while assimilating the progress of modern civilization, is increasingly improving its mentality." But some fanatics of Darwinism had sought to find in the Negro, as Burneister did, the missing link between humans and monkeys. Thus they had compared the anatomy of the two species down to the most minute details. Some of these scientists had claimed that the Negro generally has long arms, often longer than his legs, so as to allow him from time to time to assume the posture of quadrupeds. The works of Hugo de Vries, Armand Gauthier, Metchnikoff and others have refuted these claims, and the research done by Ranke has shown that long arms are, on the contrary, more widespread among whites than among Negroes. All this went to prove, Price-Mars felt, "not a difference between Yellow, Black and White, but their probable common origin from the simian species."[11]

Price-Mars moreover felt that it should not be taken for granted "that an ethnic ranking system based on corporal beauty cannot be established." How does one assess plastic beauty in a human species? Is Beauty an innate idea? The Greek concept of Beauty, Price-Mars remarked constitutes "at the present moment a rather onerous heritage for us Negroes who cannot claim Greek ancestry and yet are applying Greek esthetic standards in our judgments." This is the result of education. Before we learn to think by ourselves, we are taught to think with the same formula others have used, so much so that our judgment develop within a mold that changes very, very slowly. "As for us Haitians," the lecturer stressed, "the education we receive brings us closer to a contemporary Frenchman than to our African ancestors, and the idea of asking ourselves what the latter might have thought on a given subject does not even enter our minds."

The esthetic criteria of the Greeks and many other ideas Haitians now have were suggested through education and borrowed from Western civilization. But their power is the more irresistible now because they have become the foundation of the collective Haitian personality.

One might perhaps think that Price-Mars was ready to reject Western civilization. Far from it! He added that the difference of opinion that the African ancestor might have from that of a present-day Haitian would only show "the distance covered through the process of the evolution of ideas . . . some African tribes have customs so different from Haitian mores which offend our taste so violently, that we instinctively repudiate them without thinking that they may have been those of our forefathers; and as you know, a modification of taste could very well be the result of a certain philosophy of life."

He went on to say that the Chinese and Japanese, who are old civilized peoples, also have standards of beauty which differ from those of the Western world. Therefore, the esthetic feeling is less objective than a law of physics; it varies according to peoples and races as well as to individuals, depending on their degree of education. In the appreciation of any plastic form there enters an intellectual element—taste, whose power is proportional to the individual's degree of culture. Price-Mars then gives us his own credo: "The thing *par excellence* will therefore be the cultivation of taste. It is this that the Greeks have bequeathed as the most meaningful example in the history of mankind. For three centuries, by political necessity as well as from a marvelous esthetic intuition, they have produced in the arts and in life the most beautiful plastic form that has ever existed." Similarly, he reminded his listeners that it was also on Greek soil that Philosophy had grown, "another splendid flower of the human genius."

Price-Mars pointed out how backward Greek art was in its beginnings with its poor copies of the Egyptian and Assyrian models the Phoenicians had brought them. However, the genius of their race enabled them to develop their own taste, which eventually allowed them to evolve from the images in polished wood to the splendid statues of Pallas Athena in gold and ivory. The Greeks sought to achieve in marble an idealized human form and proceeded to do so through a rigid selection, just as they also attempted in real life to fashion their youth in the gymnasium. In the final analysis, one realizes that the Greek race and Greek art are only products of evolution, determined by man's patience and spirit. Although one cannot rank races on the so-called classical beauty, the latter carries with it a suggestive lesson.

Price-Mars then proceeded to show that Blacks, too, are beautiful even under the Grecian canons of pulchritude. In various parts of Africa, one finds people presenting, except for skin color, body features quite similar to those of the Caucasian races. From the testimony of Moreau de St. Méry, the Africans who came to Saint-Domingue from Senegal were "tall, well-built, erect, and of an ebony blackness; they have long noses quite similar to those of whites;" from Cap-Vert, "they are tall with good features;" and from the Gold Coast, that furnished the largest number of slaves to the French colony, "they were well-built men."

Those Blacks, Price-Mars continued, constituted the foundation for the mixture of races in Haiti, with contributions from France, Spain and, to a lesser degree, from the native Indian population. He hailed this mixture as he described what he called the "Haitian race." This picture was no less flattering for the Haitian woman than the portrait he had previously drawn (with borrowed words) of Negro American women. He named all the different types of Haitian beauties: the Black, the Brown (or Griffon), the Mulatto with copper-like skin, or the quadroon.[12] Those types of women all share the same comeliness of form and features. With their male counterparts, they represent racial evolution in the development of their mentality as well as in their physical appearance. One could see them in the drawing rooms of Haiti's larger cities, where the ladies, clad in Paris gowns, "fill the eyes with joy." Unfortunately, the Haitian masses have been left behind at the very stage from which the evolution of the privileged urbanites had begun.

Price-Mars, with his own ebony skin, was well aware that his remarks would puzzle other Blacks and the Mulattoes in the lecture hall. The latter would laugh up their sleeves at the thought that he was trying to escape from his blackness, while the former—particularly Black intellectuals rabid on the color question—would condemn him for his crime of *lèse* Black Pride. Nevertheless, he concluded his talk with these words:

> Some among you may think that I have wasted my time in discussing such a topic. They may insinuate that all this is unimportant, and moreover, with respect to human action, the role played by many illustrious persons has been unrelated to their external beauty . . . On the other hand, one may repeat Pascal's

famous words: 'If Cleopatra's nose had been shorter, it might have changed the face of the world.' Yes, one may make either statement and still be right. But I shall enjoy the sympathy of those who agree with Mr. Edmond Paul, that the social question in this country may very well be a matter of esthetics.[13]

In this lecture Price-Mars again gave a fine display of the mind of an educated man. He felt the need to assert himself, to impress the Haitian intellectuals and charm the ladies. He loved them all and wanted to be the object of their admiration. And yet, as he started on the task of establishing his true personality, he did not compromise his own ethics and feelings. He spoke as he did because his visit to Tuskegee and his observation at home convinced him that those things had to be said. He had the courage to say them, though he knew beforehand that they were at odds with popular opinion. Like Montaigne's famous *Essays,* Price-Mars' study was himself. He spoke with the honesty of a true scholar, fulfilling the vow he had made in Paris "to reveal the plain, unvarnished truth." He was dreaming of educating the whole Haitian people, to change their mentality as he patiently educated himself, to refashion them lovingly but forcefully by means of his own personal modeling clay. That modeling clay may have looked black to others, but to him it was nothing less than the "human nature" from which he was determined to carve something as beautiful as a Grecian sculpture.

* * *

Since the National Palace officials were scrutinizing the words of everyone, trying to detect subversive thinking under the magnifying glass of their morbid suspicion, the mere fact that Price-Mars mentioned Edmond Paul in his speech could have disturbed them. But by that time, the great majority of Haiti's citizens, with the exception of some fanatic "Liberals" who now saw in Firmin Haiti's only change of progress, had come to realize from hindsight that Edmond Paul's military adventure with Boyer-Bazelais at Miragôane in 1883, was a disaster. For it had brought considerable material damage to the country while deepening the gap between Blacks and Mulattoes. Edmond Paul had died in Kingston, Jamaica in 1893.

Consciously or unconsciously, Price-Mars had only been flirting with the "Liberals," for he came from a family traditionally of the other camp. These "pompous terms of Liberals and Nationals," as Edmond Paul had seen—before the Miragôane adventure—had nothing to do with real political parties which bind their partisans to a definite program of action. In Haiti most of the educated people had liberal ideas and thus could gather among themselves around various literary journals and cultivate the Muses. Those who had actually fought battles with guns as "Liberals" or "Nationals," who had lost relatives or friends or property as a result of bloody confrontation between the two groups, more often than not remained faithful to their respective allegiances. In that respect and in his genuine concern for the "wretched people" of rural Haiti, Price-Mars was a "National" in his subconscious.

More often than not in Haiti political allegiance means political hatred which binds people for generations not only toward the person that had caused the hatred even after his death, but also toward his relatives with the same morbidity. In that respect Price-Mars has shown that he was, by far, no enemy of President Salomon whose memory has been anathema to Liberals and their offspring ever since the bloody confrontation at Miragôane. One of the friends Price-Mars held close to his heart since his student days in Paris was President Salomon's daughter, Ida, who was then also a student in the Paris.

Eventually the political tension erupted in January 1908. General Jean-Jumeau[14], who had gone into exile with Firmin, returned with a group of friends and surreptitiously landed at Gonaives; Firmin arrived a few days later. The General succeeded in reaching Marchand, Dessalines' former capital, but was defeated by government troops. He was taken prisoner and executed immediately, while a number of his men managed to escape and took asylum at the United States Consulate in St. Marc. Firmin himself went to the French Consulate at Gonaives. The Government demanded their release and Washington instructed its consul to comply with that request. No sooner were the refugees turned over to the Haitian authorities than they were executed without trial. The French Minister, Mr. Pierre Carteron, having learned the fate of these people, refused to bow to the Government's request. Under his protection, Firmin and the other refugees at the French consulate in Gonaives were able to take a boat to St. Thomas.

President Nord Alexis still had one year to go before his constitutional term ended on March 15, 1909. As the rumor spread that this nonagenarian wanted a second term, the poet Massillon Coicou, embittered by "a bloody vision of all Haiti's men of worth falling victim to an old man,"[15] decided to try to overthrow the General-President. As he began to hatch his conspiracy, he was denounced by a cousin, Jules Coicou, military commander of the capital. On the night of March 15, Massillon, two of his brothers and seven friends were arrested and executed.

The two incidents involving Firmin and Coicou may have made Nord Alexis feel the weight of his years, for he changed his mind about the second term. He may also have been influenced by pressure from his entourage. At any rate, he remained adamant about naming his successor: General Turenne Jean-Gilles, then military commander of the Northern Province. To clear the way for the latter, he decided to remove another potential candidate, General Antoine Simon, military commander of the Southern Province, by abruptly dismissing him on November 10.

General Antoine Simon reacted by mounting his horse at once at the head of his personal army. Midway between Les Cayes, his provincial capital, and Port-au-Prince, he was met by government troops which he defeated. On December 2, Nord Alexis left the country. Curiously enough, he left under the protection of the same French Minister, Pierre Carteron, who had saved Firmin from the General. Three days later Antoine Simon took possession of the National Palace amid a delirious ovation by all sectors of the capital's population.

The new President was practically devoid of formal education. He had raised himself from the duties of a rural sheriff to the Presidency by military power and a keen sense of the realities of Haitian life. For twenty-five years he had been the military commander of the Southern Province and had remained there while political turmoil intermittently engulfed the rest of the nation.

Price-Mars was one of the first beneficiaries of the new Government. His old friend, Pauléus Sannon, was sent to Washington as Haitian Minister and took Price-Mars along as Secretary of the Legation. Sannon, who was born in Les Cayes, was in all respects the Southern counterpart of Price-Mars in terms of intellect and his views on the racial question. Besides, he ardently shared Firmin's political thinking, as was evident from a book he published in 1905. That volume may have attracted Nord Alexis's attention to him if only to show that the government was not opposed to such ideas as the following: "It is necessary to repeat . . . that rights and political guaranties are not an empty sham that can be distorted by craftiness and ruse, or brutally violated; they are essential conditions that are unremovable from any civilized state."[16]

Simon's primary instructions were to see what might be the prospect of financial aid from the United States. The exchange rate for Haitian paper money had skyrocketed to nine hundred percent for one U. S. dollar by the time Nord Alexis was overthrown. The new government wanted a foreign loan to undertake important work in the economic field and to begin construction of the railroad. Eventually the Simon Government succeeded in obtaining a loan from France of some sixty million francs at five percent interest. Part of the loan was to serve for the withdrawal of Nord Alexis paper money and for warranty of a new Haitian currency in gold. A contract was also signed with the French group authorizing it to establish a Banque de la République d'Haiti to replace the Banque National d'Haiti, whose operations had been suspended by Nord Alexis as a result of the "Consolidation" affair.

had been suspended by Nord Alexis as a result of the "Consolidation" affair.

The United States intervened to request participation in the financial arrangement, arguing that the French deal was not to the best advantage of Haiti. Washington dropped its objection after the Simon Government agreed to sign another contract with American financiers for the establishment of a railroad between Port-au-Prince and Cap-Haitien. Influenced perhaps by the opposition to these contracts, expressed in the newspapers by Pierre Frédérique and Rosalvo Bobo, the Haitian parliament showed no inclination to approve them. In fact, approval did not come until the two journalists were incarcerated.

Although Price-Mars would retain his romantic turn of the mind into old age, he seemed to have become very shrewd since the time Dr. Léon Audain had advised him to let his thoughts mature. From now on he managed to associate himself with practically all the Governments of Haiti until his death on March 1, 1969. He was, of course, greatly helped by his increasing knowledge, his talent as lecturer and writer, as well as by circumstances and his unshaken moral conviction. But the fact remains that he seemed to catch in the wind the smell of the future.

Up to now Price-Mars had followed the thoughts of Firmin and Hannibal Price with filial devotion. In his last talk at the Alliance Française he even seemed to have wanted to retain the label of "Firminist" by openly concurring in an opinion of Edmond Paul, a Black "Liberal" whom Hannibal Price had called "the most sincere, the most ardent, the most devoted servant of his country and of his race."[17] But now, after Firmin had made the attempt and lost his bid for the Presidency, the Firminist label was useless. For Price-Mars, who had political ambitions, it might well have been an obstacle because he would surely need the sympathy of the Northern intellectuals. He knew that their idol had never been Firmin, but Demesvar Delorme.[18]

Remembering Price-Mars' first lecture at the Alliance Française, one might have thought that he wanted to return to the United States to help develop contact with Negro Americans, whose progress he had described in such glowing terms. Instead, a few months after he had reached his post in 1909, while his government was desperately searching for means of survival in the U.S.A. and elsewhere, he left Washington to go on a sentimental journey to Italy and Switzerland. He claimed to have gone to Italy on the trail of Hippolyte Taine, after reading the French historian's *Voyage to Italy*,[19] but confessed that "a trip to Italy had always tempted my ambition." It so happened that Italy and Switzerland, which Price-Mars decided so hurriedly to visit at this crucial moment in Haitian history, were precisely the two countries that Delorme had rendered popular in the Black Republic. Was it that Delorme's ghost* had risen in Price-Mars' mind as he pondered on Haiti's problems and his political future as well as on the calamity that Haiti again had an ignorant national leader?

Soon after Price-Mars returned from Europe to his post in Washington, he developed pneumonia and rushed back to Haiti. While convalescing in Grande Rivière du Nord, he lost his beloved grandmother. She died of exhaustion while nursing him back to health. As he put it:

> Her nightly vigils at the bedside of the patient, her mind preoccupied ... by the fear that his death was imminent, rapidly consumed all the substance of her own life ... One evening, while saying her prayers to the "just God" in an adjoining room, begging Him to take her instead ... one heard her let out the terrifying wail of a wounded beast. Grandmother had just collapsed in one fell swoop ... She was dead ... The eternal miracle of love had just been performed once again.[20]

Pan's death cast Price-Mars into an inferno of tormenting thoughts which he described as follows:

> To whom could he now offer the rich cluster of his magnificent hopes? Who could now pacify his heart as he faced the misery of this world and human maleficence? Here he was now, sad and alone, hating himself and feeling useless to others. He wanted to give himself wholeheartedly to some great concrete issue: race, people or fatherland, but wherever he looked as discovered ... the same uncoordinated human herd, pitiful and hungry for dreams, with its gregarious instincts and its uncontrollable impulsiveness. Everywhere he found only a dust of humanity waiting to be transformed into a state of cohesion.[21]

---

*Delorme died in Paris in 1901.

Six

A Poetic Call to Arms

General Nord Alexis, who was from the North and had participated in political maneuvers and military coups for at least fifty years prior to his coming to supreme power in 1902, obviously knew the danger inherent in the magnificent railroad project heralded by American Minister William Powell. For as it turned out, his successor's acceptance of that project brought down the government of the Southern general. "Many public men in the North of the Republic," writes J. C. Dorsainvil, "only saw in the railroad from Port-au-Prince a direct threat to their political preponderancy."[1] As a consequence of this feeling, while Price-Mars was still in the North, a revolution broke out in the town of Ouanaminthe, on the border between Haiti and the Dominican Republic.

President Simon personally went into the Northern Province and quelled the revolt. He allowed his troops to loot the town which they burned down afterward. But soon after the President had returned to the capital, the revolution again flared up in the North. And again General Simon went after the rebels. But this time only to see his army melt before his eyes, his soldiers deserting either from weariness or to the rebels. He then spurred up his horse back to Port-au-Prince, and eventually took a boat on August 2, 1911, for the island of St. Thomas. He arrived in time to see Firmin die there a little more than a month later.

The chief of the Revolution was General Cincinnatus Leconte, former Minister of Public Works in the Government of President Tirésias Simon Sam. He had taken refuge in the Dominican Republic after President Nord Alexis had appointed a Commission to investigate the affairs of the previous Administration. This investigation led to the trial of the illegal bond-holders. Leconte, who would have been elected to the Presidency to succeed Tirésias had not the people of Port-au-Prince disbanded the National Assembly, was convicted *in absentia* in the Consolidation Trial.

General Cincinnatus Leconte "unfurled"—to use the verb by which Haitians in the capital usually describe the event—a multitude of *cacos*[2] from the North and from the Haitian-Dominican frontier region. These men, wearing large straw hats with upturned brim and pieces of red cloth around their necks, fell on the capital like a horde of barbarians, threatening everyone with long machetes as they poured into the streets of Port-au-Prince.

Cincinnatus Leconte was thus elected on August 14, 1911. At first the people of the capital were lukewarm to his Administration, but he succeeded in controlling his *cacos,* sending most of them back to the North, to the great relief of the Port-au-Princians. By this measure and the business-like character of his Administration, he finally won their confidence. "True or false," wrote Dorsainvil, "the word got around that Leconte was perhaps the only one in the Government who wanted honesty in the Administration."[3]

Although President Leconte was not authoritarian, he nonetheless warned that he would not tolerate governmental abuses. In a circular-letter, published in *Le Moniteur* of December 2, 1911, he expressed his determination "to sacrifice many tested friendships and loyal sympathizers if, God forbid, you fail to meet your responsibilities. I expect all government employees to realize that they are now working for the reconstruction of the country."

Price-Mars reappeared on the capital's political scene with an article, "The Reform of Primary Instruction," which appeared in the July 5, 1912 edition of *Haiti littéraire et scientifique.* He presented his views at some length and informed his readers that he had interviewed the Minister of Public Instruction, Tertulien Guilbaud. The latter was a poet who had celebrated Haiti's Founders in a book of verse, *Fatherland,* published in 1885.

Basically, Guilbaud was an educator. He had taught mathematics at the capital's lycée and literature in Cap-Haitien. In his first report to President Leconte, the same month the President signed his circular-letter, Guilbaud described the situation of Haitian public instruction as follows:

> The state in which I found the national primary schools is, in truth, pitiful. To speak only of Port-au-Prince, and from that you will form an idea about the rest [of the country], there are in that city, independently of Catholic establishments, 19 schools, 10 for boys and 9 for girls. The total number of pupils in those schools is only about 520.[4]

Minister Guilbaud then worked out a plan to improve this situation. By July, when Price-Mars published his article, the Minister himself presented three projects of legislation dealing with public schools. But before these projects could be voted on, the National Palace blew up on August 8 at 3 a.m. killing President Leconte and some three hundred soldiers who constituted his Presidential Guard.

The National Assembly met the same day and elected General Tancrède Auguste President of the Republic. The new Chief Executive had served as Minister of the Interior in the Governments of both Hyppolite and Tirésias Simon Sam. He was known as a man who kept a tight grip and believed in firm control. Like Leconte, he had been convicted *in absentia* in the Consolidation Trial. After the overthrow of Antoine Simon, when he was able to come out of hiding, he had turned his interest from politics to private enterprise, exploiting a vast tract of land he owned in the Cul-de-Sac Plain near Port-au-Prince.

President Auguste retained most of Leconte's collaborators, declaring that he would continue the latter's "liberal, progressive policy." But a campaign of rumors spread against him in the capital and throughout the country in Creole, in French, and even in Latin: *Is fecit cui prodest* (The guilty man is the one who benefits from the crime).

Curiously enough, the Northern populations remained completely silent and calm, while the people of the capital lived in the throes of mortal apprehension, remembering the deluge of *cacos* Leconte had "unfurled" on the capital and interpreting the Northern silence as the forerunner of another military avalanche to avenge Leconte's death and install a new Chief of State.

In September and October the Parliament approved all the legislation Guilbaud had proposed in July. One project provided for the creation of three General Inspectors of schools. Guilbaud appointed Price-Mars to one of these posts and in December sent him on an inspection tour of the schools in the Northern Province.

During the same month of December President Auguste decided to visit the Northern Province in order to try to win the sympathy of the military commanders in that region. He needed their support to ensure the viability of his government. Apparently Price-Mars, who was in Cap-Haitien at the same time as the President, did not let the festivities honoring Auguste distract him from his administrative duties. In fact, when he went to inspect the city's Secondary School for Girls, he learned that the students had been given a holiday. This should not have surprised anyone familiar with Haitian customs. Nevertheless, in his report, he referred to it as a "disorder": "I accepted the reasons the Principal gave me to explain this disorder: namely, recess on account of welcoming festivities in honor of the President of the Republic."[5]

The observer had his eyes wide open during the Northern school inspection. At the National Lycée, he found "the building in bad shape and well below what one should expect in an establishment of such importance . . . it is far from corresponding to the idea one has of a modern school. Therefore I am taking the liberty of recommending . . . the construction of a new lycée building in line with the requirements of health and comfort." The higher level classes in literature were more or less in good order, but the intermediate science courses were unsatisfactory. The physiology and physics teachers "are manifestly unqualified for their tasks." Moreover, "the history courses are generally mediocre."

When Price-Mars returned to the Secondary School for Girls, he found only sixty-one students present, though the school had an enrollment of one hundred and three. Of one of the classes he wrote: "I did not find a single student who was able to show me the island of Haiti on the map. I could not help saying aloud: 'This is a disaster!' " The principal of the school was incompetent; she had no prestige and no authority over the teachers; she did not know what was going on in the school. Nor was the building kept tidy.

He also visited the schools in the country of Grande Rivière du Nord. At the primary school for boys in his home-town, he found only twenty-seven pupils of the sixty-five enrolled. The teaching methods were bad and the teachers most irregular. Returning to the school three days later, he found no teachers present. From the school register he learned that from "October 9 to December 10, out of thirty-nine working days, the two teachers who had daily assignments had been absent, Mr. Denis twenty times, Mr. Hyypolite sixteen times. I suspended them," he wrote. He appointed two other persons temporarily to prevent the closing of the school.

General Inspector Price-Mars found the most encouraging moments of his inspection tour in the schools under the direction of Catholic priests and sisters. Their school for boys in Cap-Haitien was "a model school," which had produced "all the good teachers of the vicinity." And the Inspector added, "If all the schools of our rural regions were like this one, there would be no problems of primary instruction to trouble the nation's conscience."

At the Catholic school in the Commune of Ranquite, Price-Mars was equally pleased: "I counted there 20 students; the higher division of the school is very interesting because of the practical method it uses. Elememtary notions of everything, even some notion of geometry, are given along with some instruction in Haitian literature. Georges Sylvain is not unknown as a fabulist and writer of prose. They also know that the French Academy has crowned the verses of Mr. Etzer Vilaire. Some practical teaching of civics as well as instruction in local and departmental geography is given to the students. One finds there promise of the greatest future."

At the Catholic school for girls in the town of Grande Rivière du Nord, the native son was carried away by joy: "I attended a class in Haitian history. Nowhere else have I found such a rational method of instruction that connects the study of history to that of geography. They were discussing the territorial divisions of the aboriginal people of the island. Very easily the students showed on the map the various "cacicas," explaining in their own language the difficult beginning of our national history. There was nothing bookish and one could, in a way, appreciate the individual effort of each student. If you consider that these children after returning to their homes only speak Creole in their relationship with their parents, you can realize the difficulty that has been overcome. The students offered a literary program in my honor during which I was able to judge their progress in diction. I hope, along with the Sister-Superior, that in two or three years, we shall have at Grande Rivière du Nord some candidates for the Elementary diploma. That will be a sort of revolution in the region. Even Cap-Haitien has not yet presented any candidate."

Generally after the visit to classrooms Price-Mars assembled the teachers to offer criticism or to suggest new methods of teaching. He even gathered in Cap-Haitien the inspectors of Fort Liberté, Trou, Grande Rivière du Nord, and Borgne and gave them a talk on Pedagogy. As for general observations, Price-Mars was convinced that the positions of General Inspectors and Provincial inspectors of schools were of great importance and necessity. He had received a most sympathetic welcome from the various populations he visited, and pointed out this fact: "We have also received the greatest courtesy from the military commanders. I cannot say as much about all the functionaries of Public Instruction."

Immediately after Price-Mars returned to the capital in January, 1913, he requested Minister Guilbaud for a month's leave and took a boat for France. Paris, one guesses, attracted him for all kinds of reasons. He was still single, liked to study, and obviously had come out in good shape from his bout with pneumonia although he continued to worry about his health.

On the other hand, President Tancrède Auguste returned to Port-au-Prince from his trip in the North only to fall prey to a languishing illness. The capital at once fell into an apprehensive wait as the rumors that the President had been poisoned in the North swept the whole country. In the midst of this national anguish the review *L'Essor* published in its issue of March 13 the following prose-poem under Price-Mars' signature:

The Mutilated Victories
O poet, hide your pain under words
that have a pompous melancholy as
the peasants of Thebaid did closing
up the holes of their huts with
painted coffin boards.
Flaubert

My friend, why did you flee from me?
Why have you hidden from me amidst the blaze of the day
the luminous glow of your eyes? Have you felt the heavy

immanence of the mystery enveloping the proud restraint
of our relations?
Maybe. For while in the fields of the North covered with
fertile grass, amidst the uproar of the cavalcades and
the martial notes of the trumpets, I felt growing in me
the insatiable desire for Triumph and Glory, my troubled
and apprehensive soul wanted to forget in the mirage of
the Dream the impossible temptation.

Then sprang up by my bed the image of a woman who
resembled you like a sister.

Wearing a helmet and as agile in her peplos as an ancient
Amazon, she showed me in the lordly beauty of an imperative
gesture the ascending road of Hope.
And I believed in her.

* * *

My friend, why did you flee from me? Have you heard, despite
the silence of my lips, the call of elective affinities?
Maybe. For when fatigue came from long horse-back trips and
I looked over there, at the top of the hills, for the oblivion
of the daily humble task in the serenity of the familiar
evenings, sleep hardly weighing on my eyelids, I saw a woman
who resembled you like a sister. She looked like that girl
of the bitter water whose fascinating beauty
has been immortalized by the divine bard. She spoke
to me of some obscure and sibylline things,
and her voice was so pure and so sweet
in the serenity of the familiar evenings that
I woke up feeling fine and more confident
in the wait for better days.

* * *

My friend, why did you flee from me? Have you given up
the mission of being kind among all the other souls that
are not touched by the beauty of human suffering? For alas!
when, under ardent fevers and innumerable pains, death
brushed against me during those long minutes of agony and
sadness, I felt my bruised heart flapping its wings as if
it were imprisoned by matter. I lost the hope of seeing
daylight again. But a woman came who resembled you
like a sister. She looked like the virgins of the legends
who bring back from the unfading regions the cheer
of laughter and the mysterious charm of life.
The unexpected miracle came to pass for me.
I was born again to the joy of living.

* * *

> So I went to your palace to thank you.
> O comforter sister, in that fairy palace where you have
> the implacable azure of the sky for dome and the emerald
> of trees for scenery, I found you inaccessible
> to my wishes and to my prayers!
>
> My soul, why did you flee from me?
> Why did you hide from me amidst the blaze of the day
> the luminous glow of your eyes?

The first impulse one has during and after reading the poem is to smile with commiseration at the thought that Price-Mars, who had so vehemently condemned "verbomanie" which he said "is one of the most wide-spread diseases" among Haitian intellectuals, had himself fallen prey to the disease. In one of his talks he described the disease after a French author as a "pathological tendency" which prompts a "certain category of individuals to speak, to create with words (also in writing says Price-Mars) situations devoid of objective reality or of which they only have borrowed and vague notions, never personal and often not even well assimilated."[6]

"The Mutilated Victories" is no "verbomanie" at all. It is a symbolic poem in the Rimbaud manner that would be categorized in the 1920's as *surrealist.* It carried the emotional tone of nightmare or insane hallucination that Rimbaud and the surrealists used in their verses, as Salvador Dali does in his paintings, to achieve the effects of dream-like unreality. In this sort of poetry or painting the writer or the artist tries to express deeply felt emotions. And in the case of "The Mutilated Victories" one gathers at first sight that Price-Mars is getting release from a great frustration.

This poem has puzzled its readers ever since its publication. So far critics have mentioned it only to indicate that Price-Mars was also a poet, even though primarily regarded as historian, sociologist, anthropologist, ethnographer and ethnologist. As a matter of fact, Henock Trouillot, his long time associate at the Haitian Society of History, Geography and Geology, after saying that Price-Mars was one of Haiti's most penetrating social writers, made this remark: "There are however some rare lines of Dr. Price-Mars which have the accent of a confidence. One has the impression that at that time he mingled with the Muses. Such is this most suggestive page of the "The Mutilated Victories." And to explain the poem, without explaining anything however, he referred to Price-Mars' bout with pneumonia, quoting from the middle of the first stanza ". . . while in the fields of the North" down to the "impossible temptation."[7]

Since Trouillot made his remark in 1956, Price-Mars has himself furnished the key to the enigma his poem posed for the casual readers. Consciously or unconsciously he did so in his book about

Vilbrun Guillaume which appeared in 1961. That key unlocks the secret of an experience that was for Price-Mars a moment of tremendous emotional impact.

The window to Price-Mars' troubled soul is first the caption from Flaubert's *St. Antoine's Temptation*. The main character of that book, the anachorite of Thebaid is remembered for having resisted many temptations. The poem does speak of "temptation," thus the word constitutes a major clue. Moreover, the caption has the word "melancholy" which is the feeling that pervades the whole poem.

The scholar, while speaking with the Muses, was not speaking however of literary preoccupations. He was speaking of the burning political moment in the country—"the blaze of the day." He was speaking of the "pompous melancholy" of the peasants of the North-"Thebaid" welcoming President Tancrède Auguste "amid the uproar of the cavalcades and the martial notes of the trumpets," while "closing up the holes of their huts (their hearts) with "coffin boards" that were painted with the blood of three hundred Northern soldiers who had died with President Cincinnatus Leconte in the National Palace explosion in Port-au-Prince.

What was Price-Mars' state of mind at that moment? He was a Northern man. The President who was visiting in the North was being accused throughout the country in the rumors of having caused the death of his predecessor by the explosion of the National Palace. President Auguste was a Mulatto and President Leconte a Black.

Price-Mars has never participated, at least openly, in the morbid Black intellectuals' feast of "eating Mulattoes," but he could not help being conscious of his blackness in a country which at times has been sorely and bloodily divided on the color question. As a matter of fact, the historian-sociologist has shown how it has functioned in Haitian society:

> ... in Saint-Domingue that which in many respects established the scale of power and privilege—skin color—became in Haitian politics an attractive secret symbol, about which nothing was ever said officially, but which was nevertheless a concealed, dangerous cause of cohesion or rejection: a reason for action. And skin color in this multicolored country determined the separation of classes, the capability or incompetence for public service, as well as the sign of harmony or dissension in the community . . . [8]

He was the more conscious of the color question because the great majority of Haiti's citizens are black, as he was, and were still being relegated to ignorance and poverty in the rural regions throughout the nation. Thus one is almost certain that the death of President Leconte, great-grandson of Dessalines, affected Price-Mars deeply. Dessalines, too, was assassinated at the gates of the capital. His Empire was immediately dissolved and a Republic established under General Pétion, a mulatto. Politicians in Port-au-Prince had made Leconte miss the Presidency in 1902, thus preventing the great-grandson of Dessalines from presiding over the ceremonies celebrating the Centennial of Haiti's Independence. However, Leconte had captured the high office with the help of his *cacos* in 1911, only to be violently destroyed while earnestly striving to "reconstruct the country."

This was the bitter parallel that overwhelmed Price-Mars' mind at the time of Leconte's death. Writing forty-eight years later in his book on Vilbrun Guillaume, which deals in part with events surrounding Leconte's tragedy, he even used the word "mutilated," a term that reappears in the title of his poem. The political success of the two titans—Dessalines and Leconte (as seen by Price-Mars)—and their violent deaths are obviously what he called "The Mutilated Victories."

> In the past, a Black man, Jean-Jacques Dessalines, was born . . . in the shadow of Cormiers, which overhangs the valley of Grande Rivière du Nord. Over a period of time he personified the fearless revolt of his kind who were submerged, as he was, in ignominious slavery. He gave them freedom and independence. Then, less than two years after the solemn proclamation of the day of glory and redemption, human stupidity plunged the fraternal hands of his fellow-soldiers into his blood in the odious treachery at Pont Rouge. His *mutilated* body was subjected to acts of outrage by the crowd. This was the baptismal blood of the era of independence.
>
> One hundred and eleven years later, another Black man, who had come from the same valley of Grande Rivière du Nord, was the twenty-fifth Chief who believed himself worthy to succeed the Founder of the Nation. He too was immolated by the same crowd.[9]

In the second paragraph, although Price-Mars is referring ostensibly to Vilbrun Guillaume, he is undoubtedly thinking of Cincinnatus Leconte. Throughout his book he eulogizes the latter while trying to exonerate the former. In evaluating Vilbrun, he finds little to praise, except perhaps his burning desire to become a great President in order to redeem a name that had been soiled by Consolidation Trial. He speaks of Vilbrun's lack of education, his "greatest frustration in life." Without the slightest attempt to defend Vilbrun, he even brings up the accusation that the latter was often under the influence of liquor in the National Palace. At one point Price-Mars asks a rhetorical question as to whether Vilbrun was justified in taking up arms to satisfy his political ambitions, and he answers, "Certainly not." "Was he able not to do so? Another dilemma."[10] He explains, however, that Vilbrun had no other alternative because he was constantly under suspicion.

Of the two men involved, the only one who could really "believe himself worthy to succeed the Founder of the Nation" was indeed Cincinnatus Leconte, and not only because of his blood relationship with Dessalines. Price-Mars refers to Leconte's death four times with full details and great feeling:

> Had they not seen Leconte undertake a series of reforms in the structure of the State, reforms which made him popular and caused the nation to mourn when he was criminally sacrificed in the explosion of the National Palace on August 8, 1912?[11]

He described that explosion as "a mysterious conspiracy that blew up the National Palace in which Leconte perished along with 300 soldiers of the presidential guard." Pointedly he added: "Tancrède Auguste succeeded him without delay . . . "[12] As to the parallel, Price-Mars' most significant remark referred to Leconte, not to Vilbrun: "During the twelve months [of his Administration], he raised great hopes which suffice to encircle his name in a halo of imperishable glory."[13]

The core of Price-Mars' poem has to do with the "foolish dreams" his grandmother had instilled in him. While inspecting schools in the North, he felt that the time had come for the overthrow of President Auguste and, moreover, that Fate had designated him to undertake what he deemed to be an act of historical revenge. This is his temptation as he senses "growing in [him] the insatiable desire for Triumph and Glory . . . in the mirage of the Dream." Only recently his grandmother had helped to save his life when he himself had lost hope: " . . . the unexpected miracle had come to pass for me. I was born again to the joy of living." In such conjunctures as those of that moment, the historian would hardly fail to draw another suggested parallel to his "foolish dreams."

Coincidentally, in 1913 Price-Mars was thirty-seven—the same age as Alexandre Pétion when he took over the Presidency following the assassination of Dessalines. The fact that Pétion had been a soldier since he was seventeen whereas he, Price-Mars, was only a scholar, would be unlikely to dampen his faith in himself. For he had been a soldier–and a mighty one, too–who loved him like a brother. Vilbrun Guillaume obviously admired his younger cousin who had acquired an exceptional education and was well on the way to recognition as an outstanding intellectual. Before Vilbrun was forced to abandon school, he too had dreamed of acquiring a superior education. The son of a soldier* and a soldier himself, Vilbrun for some time had been nursing an ambition to capture the Presidency, and Price-Mars knew it.

Shortly after Vilbrun had been released from prison—where he only spent a few months after his conviction** in the Consolidation affair—Price-Mars paid him a visit on his farm at Paroy in the Limonade Plain, near Grande Rivière du Nord. In the course of their

---

*General Vilbrun Guillaume Sam died fighting for Salnave.
**Imprisonment for life, with hard labor.

"familiar" conversation, Vilbrun told him in a "sibylline" way—an adjective which also occurs in the poem: "Now I shall demonstrate my ability as an Army chief." He did not say as a Chief of State. But Price-Mars was not fooled. "I understood his thought without asking for an explanation; [I understood] that he was determined to capture the supreme power even by arms." And, as portrayed by Price-Mars, Vilbrun was the sort of man who "felt that he was capable of forcing the will of the gods."[14]

Naturally, Price-Mars was apprehensive, realizing that his own "Dream" depended on Vilbrun and he really did not know how the latter would react. But he was buoyed by the support of his grandmother's spirit: "Wearing a helmet and as agile in her peplos as an ancient Amazon, she showed me in the lordly beauty of an imperative gesture the ascending road of Hope." On the other hand, he knew how dear he had been to Vilbrun since childhood and perhaps more so after he began to serve as his secretary and political confidant.

One evening, returning from his long horse-back ride, Price-Mars falls back into hallucination. The ghost he sees this time is none other than that of Dessalines, "at the top of the hills [of Cormiers] whose fascinating beauty has been immortalized by the divine bard"—namely Oswald Durand, author of a celebrated poem "L'Epopée des Aieux" (The Epic of the Ancestors), two lines of which tell precisely what Price-Mars would like Vilbrun to do:

> Dessalines, with one leap, is in the West, Revolt
> vainly raises its head; he crushes it . . .

So Price-Mars went to Paroy in an unsuccessful attempt to talk Vilbrun into his dream. From historical hindsight, obviously Vulcan smiled at the idea of involving the gentle scholar in such an undertaking, for he would need him when the time came. After all, a war is not fought with the pens and pencils one uses to take notes or to write one's articles or lectures.

Thus, the interview brought the would-be avenger of history no closer to his goal. Still unappeased were the shades of Dessalines, Leconte and the three hundred guards. Still unrealized were the "foolish dreams" of his grandmother. Unable to start the Northern cavalcade on the road of Glory and Triumph, he could only return to his desk at the Department of Public Instruction. For relief he went off to France.

By the month of March when the poem appeared in *L'Essor,* President Auguste was moribund in his bed at the National Palace and Price-Mars' all-consuming desire to see him gone from the Capital filled him with deep melancholy. Price-Mars' poem, no matter how full of "verbomanie" was a call to Vilbrun to take up arms—a final attempt to stir him to action.

Seven

Triumph and Disaster

Price-Mars could very well have published his poem in the *Revue littéraire et scientifique* which had carried his article on the reorganization of primary schools. Instead, he chose the review *L'Essor,* probably to call Vilbrun's attention to a dimension larger than personal ambition. This magazine was created in 1912 and had gathered around its Director-Founder Hénoc Dorsinville the torchbearers of a new generation of writers who adopted the title of the review as their password. Literally *l'essor* means an upward flight; figuratively it denotes "development and progress." These young men had adopted Leconte's dream of the "reconstruction of the country." Taking their inspiration from this lofty ideal, they had enthusiastically undertaken to rouse Haiti's élite to their responsibilities as the brain of the nation in that "Reconstruction."

Before Vilbrun Guillaume became a soldier, he had taught primary school. Price-Mars knew that despite Vilbrun's frustration in being unable to achieve "intellectual conquests," he had remained keenly sensitive to things of the mind. Furthermore, as a military man, Vilbrun had helped Leconte to storm the National Palace. So, in telling Vilbrun of his own personal frustration from the latter's inaction at this critical moment of national emergency, Price-Mars also meant to inform the ambitious soldier that he was failing the militants of *L'Essor* and all the other intellectuals who had responded to Leconte's appeal for national reconstruction.

As one of the founders of *L'Essor,* Price-Mars was the most forceful challenger of the élite, particularly in the domain of public education. Still critical of French sociologist-anthropologist Gustave Le Bon, he made himself the new Defender of the Black Race, appealing for an all-out effort to educate the Haitian masses. In his article of July 5, 1912, he observed:

> They have often said that our race is inferior. Following in the footsteps of illustrious predecessors, I have rebelled against the pseudo-scientific arguments which have been advanced to support that ferocious doctrine. But it seems to me that no defense can be more peremptory and more decisive than the elimination of ignorance and superstition from the masses of our people. For if the proof has been given of the perfectibility of the Black brain, it

seems to me that such a demonstration has been confined to the élite. As a result, our apathy and bad faith have imposed on the underprivileged the double slavery of stupidity and poverty.[1]

President Auguste passed away on May 2, 1913, a month or so after the publication of Price-Mars' poem. Although this death was expected, the Northern military chieftains, usually so prompt in taking up arms, had made no move "to unfurl" their peasant-troops on the capital to storm the National Palace. However, on May 4, when the National Assembly met after the burial of the deceased President to elect a new Chief of State, the military commander of Port-au-Prince attempted to disperse the Assembly in a personal bid for the presidency, in the traditional fashion of his predecessors. The Chief of the Presidential Guard thwarted his effort, thereby allowing the Assembly to proceed with its important business.

Electing Senator Michel Oreste to the high office, the Assembly gave the Republic its first civilian President. Born in Jacmel, the new Chief Executive claimed to be a "self-made man." In addition to being a brilliant orator, "sans peur et sans reproche," as his partisans liked to describe him, he had taught Constitutional and Administrative Law at the National School of Law, to the delight and edification of his students. As a Senator, he had taken a firm stand for law and order. As President, he informed the Nation that his administration would devote special attention to the financial problem and the problem of public education. About the latter, he was somewhat romantic, being of humble origin: "We wish to see light penetrate everywhere," he said, "inundating with its rays our rural areas which have been left abandoned for so long."

He retained Tertulien Guilbaud as Minister of Public Instruction. Three months later Guilbaud resigned because the President was determined to entrust public instruction in the rural regions to the Roman Catholic clergy exclusively. On August 4, the Government signed a contract with Archbishop J. Conan of Port-au-Prince for the establishment of Catholic primary schools throughout the rural districts. Guilbaud had wanted a system of primary schools under the direct supervision of his Department that would prepare the sons and daughters of peasants for vocational schools. He planned to create five such schools, one in each province. As the President saw it, the Catholic schools were to train rural children primarily in agricultural methods.

The Michel Oreste plan was in all respects the program Price-Mars[2] had proposed in his article of July 5, 1912, in which he commented:

> Public school enrollment in the towns and cities is recruited among the people, since the well-to-do are in a position to pay for private

schools. The situation being such, what should be the aim of urban primary education?

First, it must be short, simple, substantial. It must not be a partial introduction to more extended studies which the poor have no time to undertake, nor a mass of fragmented knowledge; it must be a complete whole, an organized program sufficient to those whose difficult situation in life does not permit them to go further. I would wish it to be basically vocational, as I would like the rural school to be basically agricultural. This is the concept that a serious reform of primary instruction should tend to implement. The schools should put youngsters of fifteen into the struggle for life with enough knowledge for them to want to learn more, after acquiring a mind flexible enough and hands skilled enough for them to become social elements of considerable importance . . . [3]

In regard to Catholic schools, Price-Mars spoke about an experiment that was being conducted at the Catholic school for boys at Grande Rivière du Nord: "a practical experiment under private initiative," he called it. The principal of that school had instituted normal courses to prepare teachers for the rural schools of the North. "For fifteen years, the Catholic school for boys at Grande Rivière du Nord has been providing primary school teachers for the region. They have been admirably trained and they are true pioneers of progress." And he added:

In the present state of our public instruction, I can hardly see anything other than the good Catholic schools to achieve this double aim; and if I may express my deepest thought, I would gladly entrust to the Brothers of the Congregation of Christian Instruction the whole of our primary education in the rural areas as well as in the towns and cities. I want it to be well understood that I am not wedded to any religious cult. But judging from the results already obtained in some of our cities, we can only gain by entrusting the task of enlightening the uncultivated minds of young people in the rural areas to the Catholic Brothers.[4]

In his second article, that of September 5, 1912, Price-Mars returned to the same idea, suggesting that the Haitian Government enter into a contract with the Catholic authorities in Haiti to establish such a project:

I wish to add that I expect from it beneficial action in our fight against superstition. I caution myself against believing that this action will suffice to cure the disease overnight. Haitian superstition has deep roots, historical and psychological. With great insight, Dr. Dorsainvil is presently analysing its cause in the scholarly study he is publishing in *Haiti médicale*. And it is not the least service he has rendered us in showing that the mere acquisition of the notions of grammar and arithmetic is not sufficient to uproot ancestral beliefs. Something else is needed: the teaching of a higher moral sentiment, the purifying of the religious concept. It is a fact that some of us have materialized divinity to the extent of confusing the Christian faith with African idolatry.

No doubt the action of the clergy has not been vigorous enough in its fight against Voodoo. The Church too often has been content with a summary examination of global conversions that equated the salvation of souls with mere statistics. It has also let itself be deceived by the mechanical responses of neophytes to the questions of the catechism, without concerning itself with finding out whether adhesion involved an intimate profession of sentiments.

In the long run, it will be from the combined action of Church and school that good sense will overcome superstition.

Therefore, I would ask the Catholic schools to form both the character and the will; and since substantial nourishment is necessary for the spiritual needs of the masses, I would also ask the school to teach the spirit of love and abnegation that the humble Galilean preached. These are the reasons for which I prefer the Catholic schools.[5]

The same month Price-Mars published his follow-up article he published another one in *L'Essor* after Guilbaud had sent in July his plan for the creation of vocational schools to the parliament. In the article published by *L'Essor,* Price-Mars recalled what he had seen in the American southland:

The method of preparing the nation for a new life incontestably resides in the organization of technical education in the Anglo-Saxon manner. Hampton Institute and Tuskegee Normal Institute show what can be obtained from backward races when one knows how to direct them on the right path. It is that kind of education which is needed by the masses . . . [6]

Price-Mars was not content merely to indicate the way. He went farther to suggest the structure of the organization he envisioned for Haiti:

It is necessary to establish in each of our Provinces an important college on about a hundred acres of land, where from twenty to thirty trades should be taught by Anglo-Saxon educators, and where from 500 to 600 students would come to strengthen their muscles and develop their brains while at the same time elementary and agricultural instruction is being given in Catholic schools which should be created throughout the rural areas. These are, I believe, the practical means to be used to change the habits of routine and to combat the scandalous ignorance of our rural masses.[7]

These were deep convictions with Price-Mars; he did not write them to get on the Michel Oreste bandwagon. He had even expressed them to Minister Guilbaud before being appointed General Inspector of Schools. One might have expected President Oreste to call Price-Mars to head the Department of Public Instruction after Guilbaud resigned, but he chose instead Etienne Mathon, a prominent lawyer in the capital.

Price-Mars, however, had good friends in the Government.

Dantès Bellegarde was the President's Chief of Cabinet, and in that capacity directed the Administrative Office of the Chief of State; another friend was Seymour Pradel, who headed the Ministry of the Interior, in charge of Communal Administration and Internal Security. Both these men were friends Price-Mars had made in the group of *La Ronde,* and both were educators.

Perhaps Vilbrun Guillaume's shadow behind Price-Mars had made the latter *persona non grata* and unsuitable for appointment as Minister of Public Instruction in the Government of Michel Oreste. At any rate, he was retained at his post as General Inspector of Schools. At one time Vilbrun was arrested by the Michel Oreste Government and then released, if only to let him know that he was being watched. Perhaps the kind of technical organization proposed by Price-Mars with the participation of Anglo-Saxon (i.e. Negro American) educators displeased the citizens of the "Cultural province of France" to which Bellegarde, Pradel and lesser members of the Administration belonged. Moreover, Price-Mars himself made it difficult for his friends to help for he then sounded the death-knell of the "Cultural Province of France" with such passages as the following in his follow-up article:

> It is a rhetorical sin to speak seriously of our Latin mentality. Refined education, polite manners, well-groomed appearance, all that refers to the élite. But how strong is an élite consisting of only a handful of people—50,000 at the most—as compared with an amorphous mass of about two million primitive people? And does it not seem a scandal that these poor people are paying for the luxury of our education and elegance while we, of the élite, feel no obligation to compensate them in any way? Does it not seem a danger to foster the achievements of a civilization of the well-behaved vis-à-vis barbarian forces which a mere accidental impulse may unleash upon the city?[8]

On the other hand, the technical organization proposed by Price-Mars would obviously require some time to be established—to say nothing of the money that would be needed. President Michel Oreste seemed to have a nagging doubt about the length of time he would remain in power. While his election was being celebrated by some intellectuals as "a victory of the civil over the military," he doubted that anything of the sort had really happened. Surely to overcome the military it would take more than the Constitutional Law and Administrative Principles he used to teach. After peering into his own crystal ball, he had his Cabinet approve a decree allowing the State Treasury to pay him in a lump sum the total amount of money he was to receive during the seven years of his Constitutional term. This would cover the rental for his private residence where he had officially set up the National Palace.

The President did not have long to wait to see his doubt become reality. To some extent, he himself brought about the downfall of his government. In December he called for general elections, promising the Nation most emphatically that he would not intervene in the popular consultation. Evidently some "realist" advisors, who shared his doubts about the solidity of the unprecedented regime, succeeded in persuading him to brush aside his principles of law and order. Michel Oreste readily took the traditional road of militarily conducting elections. He was immediately accused of bad faith and, on January 1, 1914, a revolt broke out at Vallière in the Northern Province. When another erupted at Thomazeau, a commune near Port-au-Prince, Michel Oreste hurried to take a boat and left the country on January 27.

Before the end of the year Haiti had two Presidents, Oreste Zamor and Davilmar Theodore, both from the North, the latter a Senator, and the former Military Commander of the Province of Artibonite. They fought for the grand prize of the Republic until February 1915, when General Vilbrun Guillaume, feeling that his time had arrived, stood up at Cap-Haitien and announced, on the strength of his personal troops, the dismissal of Davilmar Theodore from the Presidency. He started out at once on the road to the capital and was met at St. Marc by government troops which offered him a determined challenge. But Guillaume had the advantage of numbers. In the early days of March, Vilbrun entered the capital at the head of an army of three thousand *cacos,* who proclaimed him President of the Republic. His second in command was none other than the poet Probus Blot.

Price-Mars, who had remained in the capital, met Vilbrun soon after his arrival. They met at the Dessalines barracks which Leconte had built during his presidency and where Vilbrun took up residence. According to Price-Mars' book on Vilbrun, when he and the victorious general were alone, Vilbrun told him, "I did my thing by myself, you see. Now I need your help and counsel."[9]

That night, while the exhausted poet Probus Blot slept in an adjoining room, Price-Mars prepared the "Proclamation" Vilbrun was to read to the Nation the following day. He also informed Vilbrun of the gravity of the situation in regard to the United States, and presented him with a list of names for the Cabinet, among them that of Ulrick Duvivier for the post of Foreign Minister. As for the next most important Ministry, that of the Interior, Vilbrun had his own man, General Joseph Misaël Codio, who had come along with the revolution. Vilbrun explained the reason for his choice as follows: "Codio has betrayed Davilmar Theodore on my behalf. I feel he is about to betray me at any moment on behalf of someone else. I must have him constantly in my sight to watch his slightest gesture. Unfortunately, he is not the only one in that situation."[10] And Price-Mars tells us: "The interview ended in complete agreement on the formation of the Cabinet." He left the barracks at 2. a.m. to get word to Ulrick Duvivier that he had been chosen as Foreign Minister and later returned to the barracks.

On March 7, 1915, the National Assembly convened and gave Vilbrun the legal seal of the Presidency. He took the oath of office on the ninth, under the name of Vilbrun Guillaume until his conviction as a "Consolidar," when he added the family name "Sam," vowing to restore its former glory. The very day Vilbrun took the oath of office, his military commander of Port-au-Prince, General Charles Oscar, rounded up some two hundred people and filled the government's prison with them as a revolt began in the North under the leadership of Dr. Rosalvo Bobo. Probus Blot was dispatched to the North and apparently succeeded in re-establishing order in that Province.

France and Germany, then in the midst of World War I, recognized the Vilbrun Government immediately. Thus the United States did not take the lead in recognizing the new regime; it even refrained from doing so after the two European Powers had extended recognition. Washington held back, wanting first to obtain from the Haitian Government control of Haitian custom-houses, as well as a guarantee that the Môle St. Nicolas would not be leased to any foreign power. If the Haitian Government was willing to enter into such agreement, then the United States would not only use its armed forces to protect Haiti from foreign aggression, but would also help to stamp out internal troubles in Haiti.

Similar proposals had been made to the last two governments of Oreste Zamor and Davilmar Theodore and had been rejected by both. For having said in the House of Representatives where he had been called to report on the U. S. proposals that he was "studying them with sympathy," Zamor's Foreign Minister, Joseph Janvier, was almost torn to pieces as he tried to escape from the angry lawmakers and the audience who cried shame on him for wanting "to sell the country to the United States."

Price-Mars advised the President not to reject the United States proposals, but to try to arrive at some compromise with Washington. The Haitian Minister to Washington at that time was Solon Ménos, who leaned toward the concept of a Pan-American "good neighbor" policy, a view he had expressed in his book, *L'Affaire Lüders*, published in 1898:

> I am inclined to think, as far as we are concerned, that the friendship of a great nation is a moral force, that is to say, one of those forces we sorely need and would be childish to neglect. Now, the power which is interested enough in our development to lend itself to this close relationship, to this kind of international intimacy, is not France which has become disdainful of our

traditional bonds of friendship and culture. The United States, on the other hand, usually wants to maintain with us relations practically of *good neighborliness*. We must take advantage of this tendency and seek, through a cordial entente between the two countries, a new guarantee to our external security . . . I advocate neither annexation nor protectorate, nor territorial concessions. It is and could only be a question of a *modus vivendi* guaranteeing to some extent our peace of mind through the maintenance and consolidation of harmony among the American States, thus fortifying our own moral and material position.[11]

But Washington was not thinking of dealing with Haiti through Pan-American involvement and channels. It feared Germany's ascendant economic position in Haiti, and this apprehension was intensified by the war then being waged in Europe. In May the United States sent Mr. Paul Fuller as a "Special Envoy" to Haiti. He told the Haitian Foreign Minister that as soon as the Haitian Government would sign the agreement with the United States, "it would be a great honor and pleasure for him to present to His Excellency the President of the Republic a special letter of recognition he had brought with him."[12]

While the pourparlers were in progress, Former President Oreste Zamor, who had probably taken refuge in the Dominican Republic, reappeared at Hinche in the Central Province. He was immediately arrested, brought to Port-au-Prince, and sent to join the other suspects in the government's prison. About that time, the judge who was conducting an investigation of the political prisoners rendered a decision of "No-cause," having found nothing against the accused persons. It so happened that President Vilbrun learned that Rosalvo Bobo had again taken up arms in the North. Convinced that the prisoners were in a conspiracy against him, the President demanded further inquiry into the case so he could keep them in jail. Tertulien Guilbaud, Minister of Justice, resigned in disagreement with the President over the order for additional investigation of the prisoners. Naturally, this created great tension in the capital.

Although the Vilbrun Government had agreed in principle that the United States would be authorized to intervene in case of foreign aggression against Haiti and that its assistance in Haiti's internal affairs would be welcome only after a formal request by the Haitian Government, Mr. Fuller abruptly left the country without even notifying the Foreign Minister of his departure. This happened in June, and by that time Cap-Haitien was practically in the hands of the rebel forces.

In the early hours of July 27, 1915, relatives and friends of the prisoners attacked the National Palace.[13] Hearing gunfire, the Military Commander of the capital rushed to the prison and gave the order to execute the prisoners. Some one hundred and seventy-six of them were slaughtered in their cells, including ex-President Oreste Zamor. Almost the entire population of the city spent the rest of the day either transporting victims to their family homes or watching the removal of bodies from the prison. To quote Dr. Bobo: "an immense drapery of mourning" fell over the capital.

The next evening, after the dead were buried, with practically the city's entire population again in attendance, on leaving the cemetery one could easily see the harbor less than a mile away, where an American battleship was on her way to the port. Thinking that the Government had asked Washington for help, the populace, infuriated, called for immediate revenge. They became even more enraged on learning that the President had taken refuge at the French Legation, and General Charles Oscar at the Dominican Legation. A mixture of personal hatred and patriotic indignation moved the crowd from the cemetery to the Champ-de-Mars. They broke into both legations, removed the President and the Military Commander from them, and killed them in the streets. A bloody revel followed the execution of the two men as their bodies were cut to bits; their heads were carried on sticks through the streets of Port-au-Prince.

That same evening of July 28, 1915, the U.S.S. Washington, landed her Marines who proceeded at once to restore order. History has recorded the names of only two Haitian privates who chose to be killed by the Marines rather than leave the posts where they were on duty: Germain and Pierre Sully.

Once again Price-Mars had been fortunate. He had left Port-au-Prince only a few days before the infernal turmoil. Earlier that same month, the Haitian Minister to France had died. Price-Mars got himself appointed to that diplomatic post and hurried to Paris. In his volume on Vilbrun he claimed to have rushed to Paris because there were pressing matters that demanded immediate attention. Strangely enough, the historian did not even bother to specify the nature of those matters.

One feels rather that, as a keen observer, Price-Mars no doubt realized that the days of Vilbrun's presidency were numbered, especially after the abrupt departure of U. S. Minister Paul Fuller and the Rosalvo Bobo revolt. He was perfectly aware that no help could be forthcoming from France that could enable him to redress the situation in Haiti. At the moment, France had her hands full with matters closer to home. As it turned out, he did not even get started, for the Vilbrun Government was overthrown before Price-Mars could present his credential to the French Government. He remained in paris.

Here he was again in 1915 as he had been in Grande Rivière du Nord five years earlier after the passing of his grandmother, "sad and alone" and feeling "useless to others." He previously told us that his grandmother wanted him to "become a model of virtue ... different from the men she knew." Vilbrun was one of the men she knew, and perhaps she did not want her grandson to resemble him. By the same token, one wonders whether Price-Mars was not thinking also of Vilbrun when he described as follows the "Haitian man" in the course of his recollection about Vilbrun:

> ... a bio-psychological left-over, a nefarious product of dehumanization from the three centuries of slavery in Saint-Domingue still weighs heavily on the Haitian society whose ethnic composition made up of elements originally disparate has not reached a state of perfect fusion, stabilization and coordination. As a result the man who in our community belongs to a superior social category by having received and assimilated a culture on the level of highly qualified Americans or Europeans goes through all his life with a split personality. He is drawn towards the summits by the high ideals of the Judeo-Christian morality to which he is related through Western civilization while some ancillary instincts insidiously pull him back towards "the bottoms" in the sense that "the intestinal functions belong to the bottoms" following the brutal expression of Keyserling.
>
> And often that man, subject to a sexuality he finds difficult to control, haunted by some childish beliefs of which he is as much ashamed as he is afraid, moves in a labyrinth of contradictions which baffle the keenest observer.[14]

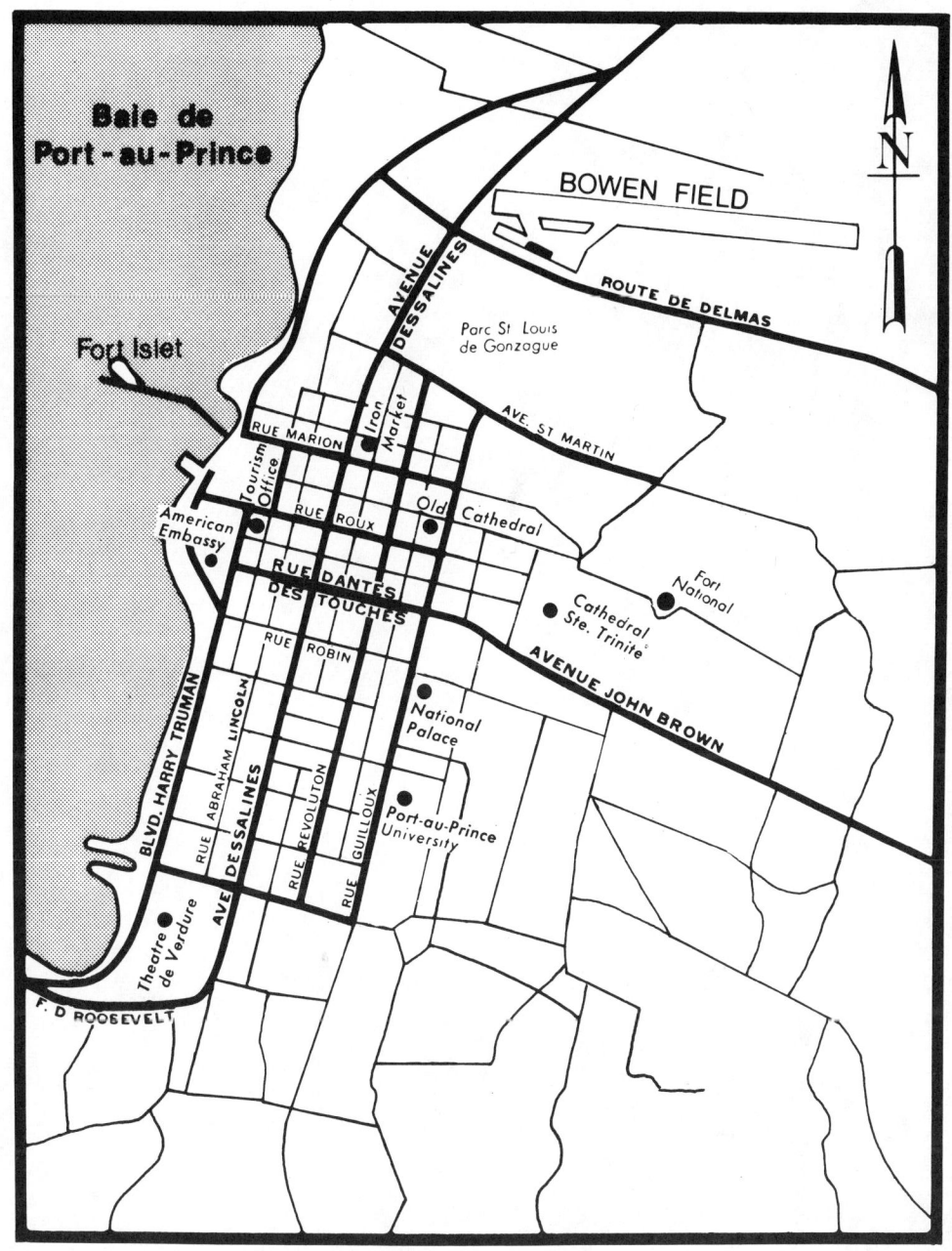

Port-au-Prince

Eight

Race, People or Fatherland

Admiral William B. Caperton disembarked from the U.S.S. Washington to set the stage on Haiti's political scene for Dr. Rosalvo Bobo's eventual arrival in the capital. A revolutionary committee of Bobo's partisans urged the National Assembly to elect him, but the great majority of the Assembly wanted Tertulien Guilbaud who, they felt, would be a neutral President. Admiral Caperton stepped in to delay things until he could ascertain Washington's intentions in the matter. On August 12, 1915, the National Assembly was permitted to reconvene, but only to elect Sudre Dartiguenave, then President of the Senate, to the Presidency of the Republic. Guilbaud had shied away from the high post. Admiral Caperton then offered it to Bobo, who indignantly rejected the offer as an insult coming from a usurper.[1] Dartiguenave accepted after Admiral Caperton had made this solemn declaration to him prior to his election:

> The only object of the United States is to insure, establish and help to maintain Haitian independence and the establishment of a stable and firm government by the Haitian people. American forces will be kept in Haiti only as long as will be necessary for this purpose.[2]

In 1912, the United States had landed Marines in Nicaragua and had removed them the same year. But in the case of Haiti, with the war on in Europe and the German threat, the so-called "humanitarian" move of President Wilson was likely to be superseded by the U. S. national interest, as concern about the Panama Canal increased.

The Haitian élite, though smarting from the injury to their national pride, were so distressed by the Vilbrun holocaust that many of them probably prayed secretly for the occupation to last at least a decade or perhaps a score of years. In his last presidential message to the Haitian Council of State (1929), President Louis Borno expressed their feeling: "Haiti's dignity and sovereignty could not mean the right to present to the civilized world, in the middle of the twentieth century, the endless spectacle of a scandalous slavery hidden under the false appearances of popular elections and legislative chambers." Thus, those of the élite who felt that way were ready, even eager, to collaborate fully with the Americans.

Price-Mars did not return home until 1916. While in Paris, he had decided to have a personal confrontation with the French sociologist-anthropologist Gustave Le Bon, remembering perhaps Frederick Douglass' interview with his former master. To be sure, Price-Mars did not just want Le Bon to look at him, to hear how well he could speak French, and to realize how much knowledge he had accumulated. For Le Bon had not denied that an individual Negro could reach a high level of education. One rather senses that Price-Mars sought the interview in order to prepare his return to Haiti and to appear there not as the actual or presumed power behind ex-President Vilbrun, but rather as the man who effectively crossed swords with the French racist scientist on behalf of the Black race. No doubt he hoped that Le Bon would retract his "insolent," "erroneous" views about the Haitians and other Blacks under the weight of his arguments.

Thanks to Sorbonne Professor Guignebert, Price-Mars obtained the interview. The two men had a most courteous discussion on the theories Le Bon had affirmed in his *Psychological Laws of the Evolution of Peoples.* The author adamantly maintained his views, while Price-Mars, with no less ardor, contended that "the offspring of European adventurers and African slaves had been able in less than a century and in the worst of conditions, to produce Haitians capable of measuring up to the accomplished offspring of the white race."

"Le Bon conceded," Price-Mars told Emile Paultre, "that he had expressed his ideas 'in a somewhat categorical form.' Suddenly feeling a vague sympathy for the Haitian people, he could not help asking his interlocutor: 'But why, Monsieur, don't you write a book about your country?' "³

Back in Haiti, Price-Mars resumed his articles on education for *L'Essor.* In April 1914, he had written an article about the education of retarded school-age children. In a follow-up article (July 1916), he probed more deeply into the situation of those children, declaring that their miseducation "constituted an enormous waste to the great despair of both teachers and parents, because they are victims of a pedagogical error that applies to them the same curriculum as to normal youngsters the same age." Fearing that some of his readers might willfully misconstrue his remarks, he hastened to qualify his thought:

> Oh no, I beg you not to twist my words. I do not intend to imply or affirm that our people are affected by any physiological degeneracy. But it is no less painful to observe that, masters of our

own fate for more than one hundred years, we are still, the great majority of us, in a state of intellectual backwardness caused by a lack of development of our mental faculties.

As Price-Mars saw it, this human "waste" as well as the presence of the foreign invader resulted from a failure of leadership on the part of the Nation's élite. On his return to Haiti he had been dumbfounded to learn that some of the "haute société," mostly mulattoes, had found it possible even to go dancing at Haitian social clubs with American Marine officers, including Admiral Caperton, only a short while after the Occupation started. In reaction to this, Price-Mars became even prouder of his blackness, so closely allied to Haiti's past glory. The black peasant had taken up arms against the invader, while the intellectual élite had sunk to the depths of despair. On all sides he heard them lament: "Il n'y a plus rien à faire" (There is no longer anything that can be done).[4]

In a fearless and determined attempt to transfuse some of the black blood boiling in his veins, Price-Mars undertook a series of lectures in Port-au-Prince and other cities of the Republic. He began in the capital at the Parisiana Theatre in April 1917, speaking on "The Postulate of a Social Education." The self-appointed Doctor to the moribund Fatherland gave the following diagnosis:

> ... we have inherited from colonial society certain tendencies that today are alarming anachronisms. For example, this sort of moral Pilateism which prompts us to detach ourselves from all solidarity with those at the bottom, seemingly in order to avoid getting mixed up with bad company, whereas we are eager to make a thousand advances to the white man, wherever he may come from, without even asking for his birth certificate or his police record.[5]

This "danger of dissociation from the elements that insure the existence of the City—this danger of destruction of the City itself," perhaps upset Price-Mars all the more because the Vilbrun boat had capsized before he even had a chance to launch it on the high seas of human and material progress. Continuing his analysis, Price-Mars said:

> It is a fact established that when a people does not instinctively feel the need to create a national soul by the close solidarity of its diverse elements with common aspirations toward high ideals— even if chimerical—when the governing class loses interest in the masses, and the masses are almost completely unaware of the existence of the governing class because they share only economic relations—this people is faced with imminent disintegration. It then suffices that an external danger threaten their national existence for each part to revert to its own interest, thus making it impossible ... for them to unite in resistance, even of a moral nature, against the invasion of their soil, in whatever form it may take.[6]

Price-Mars gave notice of his self-appointed mission as the

Fatherland's physician by declaring: "It is because I have detected this danger in the present crisis that I have thought of trying to find the means to stop it." He believed in self-help, in private initiative, and for that reason, he wished that his words could be heard beyond the confines of the Parisiana Theatre, by "all, who, in this country, are endowed with intellectual power or manual talents and who have attained a high social echelon." Thus they may join hands with him in combatting ignorance and disease, not just as a "charitable act of their blasé elegance," but as the manifestation of their collective consciousness of their moral, patriotic duty toward the country. "Get it straight," he warned, "the only criterion by which an élite can be judged is its social usefulness."

Six months or so later Price-Mars was back at the Parisiana with another lecture on "Economic and Political Domination of the Elite." By that time many painful events had occurred: since the vote of the Haitian-American Convention of September 16, 1915, an American protectorate had actually been established over Haiti. The following April President Dartiguenave had dissolved the Senate by a decree that turned the House of Representatives into a Constituent Assembly. This Assembly was presented several constitutional amendments to which the Senate had objected, thus bringing about its dissolution. The House likewise refused to pass the amendments and was also disbanded. The main design of the change demanded by Washington was to eliminate the refusal of the right to land ownership to foreigners—a stipulation found in every Haitian Constitution since that of 1805, under Dessalines.

Dartiguenave called the people to the polls to elect new legislative chambers on January 15, 1917. Price-Mars presented his candidacy to be Grande Rivière's Deputy, but was defeated. In June of the same year, both Senate and House were again dissolved by Presidential Executive Order, as the new legislators also opposed the amendments. Finally the President abolished both Senate and House by a decree which established in their place a Council of State whose members he himself appointed.

Recalling his electoral defeat, Price-Mars told his audience: "tears involuntarily streamed from my eyes, a sob went up to my throat. For, resounding on the ancestral soil were the rhythmic steps of the American officers who had come to ensure an honest election." He had not, of course, the slightest chance of being elected, considering his participation in the Vilbrun Government. At that time the American Occupation forces were engages in a bitter war with the *cacos.* The latter had taken up arms in protest against forced labor to which the Americans had subjected the peasants in order to build a road from Port-au-Prince to Cap-Haitien. This revived an old law requiring the *corvée,* which President Boyer had instituted. The peasants resented it so intensely that they fought with only their machetes against the machine-guns of the Marines; their resistance was so tenacious that the Marines finally resorted to bombing to quell the revolt.

Such was the background against which Price-Mars delivered his lecture, illustrating what Rosalvo Bobo had called "the enslavement of the Negro by the Negro," with economic and political measures taken against the rural areas. He underscored the fact that the "Haitians' immense pride" in being citizens of a free and independent Black nation until 1915, had derived from the deeds of the Black masses whose labor had given the nation its economic basis. The peasants, he said, have paid twice for Haiti's independence. "The first time by their heavy contribution in blood during twelve years of an atrocious, savage war; the second time, by their enormous contribution in labor for the Liberation Indemnity."[7] That indemnity was paid, as Price-Mars put it, "by the sole class that produces: the peasants . . . and they continue to pay all the debts the governments of Haiti have so criminally contracted abroad without the nation ever receiving any tangible benefit from them."

He proceeded to point out that the rural people, who comprised four-fifths of the voters in national elections, were illiterate and inarticulate. Consequently, the democratic principles in Haitian Constitutions and laws were empty words only used to cover up the exploitation of the masses by the élite of the so-called Republic: "Liberty? A grimace! Equality? A lie! Fraternity? Dupery!"

In his first talk at the Alliance Française, Price-Mars had lauded Toussaint-Louverture for having engineered and eventually achieved the liberation of his slave-brothers. In this second lecture, as he looked at "The First of the Blacks" in the light of his economic policies which were an essential part of the Haitian heritage, Price-Mars became an unholy iconoclast. What benefits, he asked, had the former Black slaves received in compensation for their heroism and their blind allegiance to Toussaint?

> Alas! the answer to that question is the eternal shame and the eternal iniquity we have inherited from our forefathers, the indelible stigma of which we are still carrying with an indifference bordering on both insanity and cowardice . . . Immediately after the victory of our arms, we proclaimed emphatically that slavery was forever abolished on the soil of Haiti; it was, however, Toussaint-Louverture, our immortal statesman who, with the tacit or effective authority in the colony during and after the bloody struggle, inaugurated a policy of conciliation with the former masters whose main objective was the disguised reconstruction of the system that had just been abolished thanks to the untiring devotion of the docile masses.
>
> Historical evidence establishes the fact that, as the General-in-Chief drove the enemy from the colony, he hastened to organize the recovered plantations under severe statutes aimed at re-

establishing the work-shops as well as handing back to the former owner the land from which he had been dislodged by the war.⁶

Price-Mars then remarked that it would be interesting to travel back along the road of history to examine social legislation since 1803 so as to determine how these laws had fostered the evolution of Haitian customs and especially how they have satisfied the élite's sense of justice and their leadership responsibilities. But he could not possibly do that in only one hour. So he was going to jump over a whole century to examine the Rural Code. He said:

> Thus, there exists on our territory a category of persons whose social and economic role deserved definition by special laws, the better to show that they have nothing in common with us, and that we can dispose of their property, of their freedom, and even of their lives as we see fit. This seems a bit paradoxical to you, doesn't it? I am really sorry not to be able to comment on certain articles of the rural code, as I should like to do if time permitted, but there are two or three articles I wish simply to read.
>
> Chapter VIII
>
> Article 19. The working days are Monday, Tuesday, Wednesday, Thursday and Friday of each week. The working hours are: in the morning from six to eleven and in the evening from two to six.
>
> Article 11. No worker, employee or day laborer is permitted to leave his work to take part in feasts on working days. Dances and feasts shall end at midnight. Those who break these regulations will be sent to jail.
>
> Article 12. No agricultural worker on a rural estate shall be permitted to leave the district for more than 24 hours without the permission of the chief of the district.
>
> And the rest is the same. But the quotations I have selected suffice, no doubt, to show the arbitrary nature and the abomination of the legal system to which we have subjected our peasants. Those quotations suffice to make you realize what inhuman, ugly treatment, what moral suffering can ensue when that system is implemented under the Haitian-American Treaty by the kind of gendarmes we have.⁹

Although Price-Mars knew that the Haitians were no longer master of their immediate future, he did not believe that the Americans wanted to eliminate the whole Haitian people. To him such thought was ridiculous. The facts which created that fear in the minds of many Haitians were officially brought to light subsequently by a United States Investigating Committee, the McCormick Committee, that was sent to Haiti in the 1920's following vehement protests by the late James Weldon Johnson, Executive Secretary of the National Association for the Advancement of Colored People. The McCormick Committee presented a voluminous report producing evidence of atrocities committed by the Marines in their attempt to "pacify" the Haitian peasants: they were stoned, burned to death, beaten, tortured, and, in at least one instance, a woman was burned alive in broad daylight in one of the Gendarmerie's courtyards. In addition, their cattle were killed and their crops destroyed by fire.

Although the records kept by the Marines show that only 3,250 Haitians and twelve U. S. Marines were killed during the five and a half years of the war, the *Union Patriotique,* a Haitian association created to oppose the Occupation by peaceful means, claimed that more than twice that number of Haitian deaths had occurred in the Marines' concentration camps, where Haitian prisoners died either from starvation or unattended illness, not to mention the "practically indiscriminate killing of natives," to quote Major-General Barnett, Marine Corps Commandant, who was horrified by what he had heard his Marines were doing in Haiti.

However, Price-Mars was confident that the nation would not perish from the face of the earth. He felt that the élite should give serious thought to the role they themselves must play in the developments taking place in their country without their consent. And he returned to the idea of National Reconstruction voiced by President Leconte in December 1911. The phrase became Price-Mars' motto. "I do not know if I am in error," he said in closing his lecture, "but it seems to me that, though one may not be aware of it, by precipitating catastrophes the World War has served to make us recognize the necessity for the complete reconstruction of the City."

* * *

Price-Mars again emerged unscathed from the debacle of the Vilbrun Guillaume Sam Government, as he did from the damage done to the good name of President Tirésias Simon Sam by the Consolidation Trial. The tragedy that befell Haiti with the American Occupation offered no time or opportunity for witch-hunting. Although he had played an important, conspicuous role in the Vilbrun Government, even his enemies probably gave him credit for sensing the impending troubles and seizing the providential opportunity to escape abroad, as Haitian Minister to Paris. Realizing that he could no longer be useful to the Government and that he could not change Vilbrun's impulsiveness or excessive drinking, he had merely been clever enough to abandon the sinking ship. Now, with American Marines trampling on the Fatherland, the main concern was to keep Haiti from losing her sovereignty completely. All Haitians, of whatever past political affiliation or social and economic standing, were expected to stand together.

The fact remains that it took a great deal of self-assurance, determination and courage on the part of Price-Mars not to let misgivings about himself force him into a prudent silence after he returned from France in 1916. His personal commitment to the whole Haitian people was deep and obsessive. Even more profoundly conscious of his blackness than at any time in his life, he became belligerent toward the élite. But he would never give up that name *Price-Mars* which he had taken at St. Louis, Missouri on August 19, 1904 to symbolize Haiti's greatest need: Fraternity.

In his last talk, after crying out, "Fraternity? Dupery!" he gave the following definition of a true solidarity, the rock on which he fervently hoped to reconstruct the City:

> Social fraternity is above all else a reaction of Reason against brutal injustice of Nature or Society; it is above all else an inclination of the heart toward more kindness and mansuetude for the humble. If you have not first found it inside of you, if you have not been nourished by this milk of human kindness of which the poet speaks, you need not look for it in the empty formula of a text. It is inscribed in the shadow of our conscience because it is a command of the moral law . . . [10]

As he saw it, though the élite no longer had a hand in the making of national policy, they had at least an immense field of social work open to individual and group initiative. This they had neglected through the years and that neglect had been stressed by foreign civilian observers as it has been exploited by foreign military expansionists. In his follow-up article of September 1912, he had said: "But they are right to claim—it is a truism to repeat it—that nowhere else is there greater separation between the masses and the élite. They know only too well the extent to which our masses are engulfed in ignorance and superstition. So much so that a noted observer, Sir Harry Johnston, in his celebrated book, *The Negro in the New World,* has written that the Haitian peasant of today, except for language and dress, does not present any difference whatsoever from his African ancestor."[11]

President Leconte and his Minister of Public Instruction, Tertulien Guilbaud, were particularly fearful of the dichotomy between the Haitian élite and the masses. "They hoped to remove the danger that was smoldering between an enlightened minority and an illiterate majority. They feared our future absorption by a more advanced neighbor, and often the Minister reminded the President of these words by an American philosopher: 'When two peoples are facing one another, one highly organized and the other with an inferior or rudimentary organization, the outcome is not doubtful. The first one ousts the second. The right of prior occupancy vanishes before the superior right of the exploiter.'"[12] The President and the

Minister were so disturbed by this thought that they had it published in the official bulletin, *Le Moniteur.*

Obviously, if the Vilbrun Government had lasted, Price-Mars had intended to devote his most serious attention to Foreign Affairs and Public Instruction which caused him great concern as they had Leconte and Guilbaud, and for the same reasons. He grouped those two ministries under Ulrick Duvivier. On the one hand, considering the gravity of the American threat, Duvivier would naturally be under Price-Mars' direct supervision for the latter served as Vilbrun's eyes and ears. On the other hand, considering Price-Mars' personal interest in education, Duvivier was more or less compelled to follow his suggestions. Price-Mars also took two seasoned educators into the Vilbrun Cabinet: his former chief, Tertulien Guilbaud, and Auguste Bonamy[13], but he sent the latter to the Ministry of Finance and Commerce, and assigned the former to the Ministry of Justice. He probably felt that Duvivier would be more amenable to his views on education than the other two men.

Engrossed in his self-appointed mission of moral evangelization to the Haitian élite, Price-Mars hardly took time to catch his breath. After his talk in November, he was back in the lecture hall the following month to discuss "The Vocation of the Elite." He repeated the lecture later that month at St. Marc in the Province of Artibonite and at Cap-Haitien in the North, the two regions most involved in the war between the U. S. Marines and the Haitian *cacos.*

Most of the Haitian intellectuals felt completely demoralized, overwhelmed, put to shame by the foreign occupation. They were also humiliated by the thought that the peasants, whom they had always scorned, were the only ones sacrificing their lives in defense of the Fatherland. Price-Mars himself was no less ashamed of the part Haitian leaders in his own family had played in the loss of Haiti's sovereignty. Nonetheless, he vigorously took the leadership of the panic-stricken intelligentsia. By his severe judgment of Toussaint-Louverture, he won the confidence of most mulatto intellectuals, whose minds were still welded in blind affection to the memory of President Pétion, just as most Black intellectuals worshipped at the shrine of Toussaint. They might deplore Price-Mars' criticism of their idol but they knew he had spoken with the honesty of a scholar, and that the facts were such as he had described them.

Price-Mars took advantage of the circumstances to level two broadsides at the élite in general, charging them with lack of vision and lack of sensitivity in their failure to promote the welfare of their compatriots and defaulting on their mission to foster the rehabilitation of the Black race.

Returning to what he had called in his first lecture "the dissociation of the elements that ensure the existence of the City,"

Price-Mars now undertook to analyze the economic and psychological forces that had caused "this harmful gap between the élite and the masses to such an extent that at present they constitute two nations withint the Nation, each with its own interests, tendencies, and outlook."

He affirmed that the abolition of slave labor, which had been obtained at so great a cost in blood, had merely brought superficial changes. "In fact," he declared, "legal slavery has given way to a hybrid form of bondage with a mere change of persons and responsibilities. For, despite the expulsion of the French masters, despite the new laws and the goodwill of well-meaning individuals, the new society insidiously and tacitly retained the class system of the former colony. The unassailable proof of this, he claimed, was the fact that the people of the lower strata continued to be engaged in the same type of work as before, with only a few changes which consisted in allowing them part of the crop they had cultivated, but not one day's salary. He argued that such a system was not adequate and could not have fostered progress among the masses. To bring progress, the post-colonial system should have been viewed less as an end than as a means: "a means would be a progression from slave labor to paid labor commensurate with the specific value of the work and technical skill of the worker . . . "

In his 1906 lecture on "The Prejudice of Races," Price-Mars had said that, according to statistics in the U. S. census, there were nine million Negro Americans and sixty-one million whites. Out of one hundred landowners, seventy-five were white and twenty-five Negro. He further told his audience that the Negroes "own 130,000 farms valued at 2 billion francs; some public buildings (churches, etc.) estimated at 109 million francs, and some 150,000 other real estate properties worth 2 billion francs."

By contrast, in Haiti, the system of sharecropping, known as "half-and-half," had been the only form of compensation the land owners have ever accorded the masses. This has fostered a sense of routine that has retarded progress and improvement in agricultural methods, to say nothing of other ills that the system has created. The State, he explained, in taking possession of most of the land by right of conquest, distributed it either in large lots or small parcels or into rentals for farming. Thus it created a new privileged class:

> If these privileged people had had a clear vision of their responsibilities, they would have been agents of progress in setting an example by personally working their land . . . But alas! they had neither the energy nor the wisdom, and probably no capital with which to rebuild the plantations they had received from the State's generosity. They chose, while maintaining nominal control over the land they had acquired in that manner, to live elsewhere, in the cities, enjoying easier and more immediate profits from politics,

leaving the administration of their plantations to the ignorance and routine of the sharecroppers. This was the first great mistake of the élite: the desertion of the land.[14]

Price-Mars then explained how, imitating colonial methods, Haiti's rural regions were divided after independence into two groups of plantations: those on the plains and those in the mountains. The privileged beneficiaries are to be found in the plains, where large plantations still exist, while the peasants are located on the mountains where their land has been subdivided time and again. "The problem of existence was not complicated for them by any luxury of attire, of jewelry or even of mere comfort. They contented themselves with tilling the soil which generously yielded enough to sustain a primitive way of life without aspirations, without curiosity, without concern." The peasants continue to live that way even now. They are spread out on the mountain tops, on the mountain slopes or in the gorges, in total isolation . . . Many of them, by far the greatest number, were in the past and still are "half-and-half" farmers like those in the plains. But the latter have roads at their disposal and many work for industrial enterprises which pay more or less adequately. Moreover, they are in contact with the urban middle class. Some have taken advantage of these circumstances to better themselves to some extent.

> The others, who comprise two-thirds of the total population, abandoned to themselves, resigned beforehand to their fate—the tragedy of which they do not even sense—rhythmically alternating the thud of the hoe and the click of the machete, repeat the same ancestral gesture that welds them to the land and makes them a group of people different and distinct from the rest of the nation in terms of language, dress and way of life.[15]

Price-Mars remarked that some members of the élite have attained the heights of knowledge, while the peasants still remain in deepest ignorance. But as he saw it, the élite's knowledge has been limited to "specialization in literature." He felt that the élite must come from all segments of the population and must present commercial, industrial and agricultural skills as well. Both segments should be able to engage in the various fields, all of them aiming at improving the well-being of the entire nation. He was, of course, proud of his compatriots' accomplishments in literature as well as in music, sculpture and other arts. But he could not reconcile himself to the fact that the élite had evolved through the years "like an external appendage to the rest of the nation." For this has caused the division of the Haitian people into two hostile groups, the one having no faith in the other.

In his lecture on the "Economic Domination of the Elite," he had tried to rouse them to constructive action by a series of questions and answers:

"Do you really wish to retain the historical prestige and moral authority of leadership?

"Be a true élite by your proven intellectual and moral worth that should continue to develop.

"Do you want to prevent the foreign menace from some day exploiting the ignorance of the masses against your privileges?

"Be a truly social élite by bridging the abyss between the poverty of the lowly and your apparent wealth. Create works of social action and rehabilitation."

At the conclusion of his lecture on "The Vocation of the Elite," he again tried to rouse them by delivering the *coup de grâce* to their pride:

> ... we are also below our congeners in the United States. Yes, every time I receive newspapers from there, joy fills my heart as I applaud what they are accomplishing, while shame bows my head because in our inferiority we are unable to follow them. Would you like some examples? Here is what I learned from the *Crisis,* a Negro magazine published in New York:
>
> 1. "The fourth meeting of the Masons in Alabama has presented a report on funds collected this year for the activities of their Temple: $118, 855."
>
> 2. "The 23rd meeting of the Lott Cary Baptist Foreign Mission (Va.) has collected $11,000 for expansion of their religious work."
>
> 3. "At a convention held in Tyler, Texas, Bishop Carter of the African Episcopal Church has collected on the spot $14,000 for educational activities."
>
> 4. "The Negroes of Texas have given $10,000 to the Freedman's Aid Society for their schools."[16]

Price-Mars then noted that the single State of Texas, whose Blacks contributed $24,000 in one year, had only 690,049 Negro inhabitants, three times fewer Black people than Haiti with her two and a half million citizens. And he asked his listeners if they did not feel "humiliated" in being unable "to offer anything that could resemble such initiatives and such movements of social solidarity."

> Ah! yes, we are ready to spend thousands of gourdes[17] to set up clubs for play and pastime, to go to the theatre, but we are unable to support a good literary magazine, to create clinics, night schools, or to establish a good college where ... we might offer a better education to our élite of tomorrow ...
>
> Each day I hear it said there is no longer anything that can be done because political power is no longer in our hands. Well, this is only the resignation of slaves and the treachery of eunuchs ...

All social forces—Church, school, corporate association—must have but one doctrine, one goal: to save the moral patrimony from the disaster that has engulfed the political patrimony. And that can be done only through private initiative providing for a better education.[18]

As an antidote to despair over rights seized by the American invader, he reminded his listeners that "the right to make an effort had not lapsed." By his own attitude he had indeed proved his courage as he tried to overcome the odds against him in the realm of politics. Perhaps he was already once again under the spell of "Pan's foolish dreams." Perhaps he had boosted his own morale by prescribing a remedy for the national malaise. In any event, he would surely find satisfaction in the rural Haitian expression: *m'buté mais m'pas tombé!* (I stumbled, but I kept my balance!)

Nine

Ministering to Youth

The impact of the American Occupation on Price-Mars was doubly painful for he could not help viewing it through the assertions of French anthropologist Gustave Le Bon. In light of the general philosophy underlying imperialism, particularly the United States brand of Manifest Destiny, the presence of U. S. Marines in Haiti implied the superiority of the white race, if only in Caucasian minds, while the past one hundred years of Haitian sovereignty seemed to corroborate Le Bon's views and thus justify the pretext that foreign intervention was necessary to help "civilize" Haiti.

Colonel Littleton W. T. Waller, one of the invading American Marines in 1915, was convinced of the Haitians' racial inferiority. He described the élite in a letter to his superior, General J. A. Lejeune: "They are real niggers and no mistake. There are some very fine looking, well-educated, polished men here but they are real nigs beneath the surface."[1]

Price-Mars knew very well that the collapse of Haitian sovereignty had little to do with skin color. From his own anthropological studies he was absolutely certain that the Black man is a full *homo sapiens* with the same human potential as any other man. However, as he faced the American Occupation, a torturing question plagued his mind: "Why have the élite found themselves powerless to prevent or control the series of crises which have furnished the pretext to justify this intervention in our own eyes and in the eyes of the whole world . . . ? And why have the élite proved themselves imcompetent to cope with the tragic realities?"[2]

Price-Mars had long since detected the roots of the problem that had produced the national catastrophe: the Nation had foundered because its sociological base was weakened by a psychological ailment among its élite, who were divided as to their real identity. Thus their very concept of nationality suffered from the lack of a cohesive element that would have ensured the development of a national character. The self-appointed physician to the Fatherland turned the scalpel deep in the wound to remove the cancer. In a sense, he was also operating on himself, because he felt profoundly guilty, both as an individual and as a citizen, of having shared the élite mentality. Now he was ready to prescribe the unpalatable remedy: Black consciousness and Black pride are the *sine qua non* if Haiti is to become a truly healthy nation.

In a lecture on "The Woman of Tomorrow" in 1917, he declared: "We cannot disengage from our filiation with the past, not only the past of our national history, but also the remote past of our ethnic origins."[3] He went on to stress that Africa was still part and parcel of Haiti. After some three or four centuries, the human transplant from Africa to the Caribbean obviously has not greatly changed. From their African ancestors, Haitians have inherited and retained "some ways of thinking and believing, a whole concept of life that persists because it rests on the foundation of instinct and volition."

Price-Mars realistically described the abject condition of the peasant women, whose men use them as mere instruments of their prosperity and pleasure. But the lecturer was thinking less about the rural women, though he sympathized with them, than about the élite women. After all, he felt that the difference between the life of the peasant woman and that of her élite sister is only one of degree.

Price-Mars had alluded to the problem in his first literary attempt, and if the circumstances related in that short story are true, he personally must have suffered at the hands of a woman of the élite. In "Son Idéal," Pierre Dufailly (alias Price-Mars) had fallen head over heels in love with a Haitian girl, a *griffon* named Marguerite Rouvier. She was studying in Paris while he was attending medical school there. Eventually Pierre Dufailly lost her to a Monsieur Philippe de Chateaunoir, natural son of a certain Count Jacques Léopold de Chateaunoir. The father had made a fortune through dubious if not scandalous means as a banker in Haiti. After his death the son had inherited the fortune that enabled him to win Marguerite's family and then the girl's hand. Pierre's frustration would be mildly consoled by the fact that he later became the lover of the married Marguerite.

Frédéric Marcelin's first novel is much more explicit on the problem now obsessing Price-Mars' mind. As we have already seen, his main character is Thémistocle Epaminondas Labasterre, an educated young Haitian who had followed in his father's footsteps as a businessman. He fixed his choice upon the daughter of one of the more powerful businessmen in the country. but when he tried to court her at a social affair, her girlfriends were scandalized: "What a nerve!" They could not conceive of the possibility that anyone among them might someday be called Madame Epaminondas. Like their mothers before them, these young women dreamed only about having foreign white husbands. And in 1901, when Marcelin's novel was published, most of the Haitian female dreams centered on Germans, for German men were then more numerous and more prosperous than Frenchmen.

If such an attitude had only mildly upset Price-Mars in 1900, now in 1917, in the midst of the national ordeal, he was highly incensed as he watched these ladies gaily eating, drinking and dancing with U. S. Marine officers at the Bellevue Club. He had come to believe that this was an intrinsic part of the political problem that had brought about the nation's collapse. He felt that Haiti's sociological pattern derived in large measure from the psychological conditioning of the élite through their women.

In the rural areas, he charged, the peasant woman had been turned into a mere "instrument of work" in the fields, with no possibility to help in the physical and mental evolution of the Haitian people. Subjected to this kind of "slavery," she is physically disfigured:

> One need not be a technician to discover that among the female peasants the skeleton appears to show a clear curvature toward the loins; their musculature presents more vigorous protrusions in certain parts of the body; these increase neither their grace nor their charm. The epithelial tissue hardens into a corneous layer under the foot and in the palm of the hand. The arch of the heel deviates and spreads in noticeable disproportion so as to maintain a balance between the person's growth and the inevitable conditions of her milieu; thus the individual becomes more readily adapted to the necessity of her work. The function creates the organ. We are hardly surprised that these hard, rough creatures bear almost no physical resemblance to the fashionable women we encounter in the city streets and drawing-rooms.[4]

On the other hand, the élite woman is made an "object of luxury and pleasure," and exerts considerable influence on her man. He is as much flattered as she by the compliments she receives.

Happy to be an object of luxury and pleasure, living in a society where the display of costly dresses, costly carriages and costly houses, the bourgeois woman is not only the barometer of social values but of all human values. She has narrowed her horizon to the extent that her own ideal of happiness boils down merely "to cut a figure . . . "

We never even suspected that she, too, was insidiously leading us to the political and administrative 'bankruptcy' that they (the Americans) have so gleefully pointed out.[5]

Although Price-Mars had suffered from the ostracism of the mundane élite, he is not thinking of personal revenge, for he sees more than one side of the issues, more than one dimension to his own responsibilities, more than one meaning in the words "Black" and "National." At forty-one, still relatively young, he set out in 1917 on his crusade to revamp Haiti's national soul with constructive values in order to protect the sacred Fatherland from complete absorption by the United States. In reminding the élite, men and women, of their responsibilities, he continually referred to the importance of education:

> If someday the Haitians regain control of their nation's destiny, one should not hesitate to impose another program of action that will finally completely revise our public education so as to develop intensively the moral preparation of the élite up to the level of its intellectual preparation.[6]

The verb "to impose" clearly show how intensely he felt on the subject, for he was a gentle scholar and seldom tried to coerce. But in the "Reconstruction of the City" which, in his mind, is tantamount to a rebirth of the nation, he wanted the women of Haiti—all of them—to be among the workers who will build the "City" anew for "more justice, more kindness and more human compassion in our land."

> Finally, the Woman of Tomorrow will bring into the life of the City the beneficial breath of her heroic virtues. She will no longer be ashamed to accept herself, to present herself, and to act fully as a Haitian. Becoming aware of the country's past, she will learn that at the birth of the immortal epic, her female ancestor stood as the fierce, fervent inspiration of the unique exploit that made this corner of the earth the independent fatherland of the Black man.[7]

* * *

The educated Haitians who had overtly supported the Treaty with the United States in 1915 had done so in the sincere hope that conditions in the country could improve. By the time the Marines landed, Haiti's reputation as a "civilized" country had been completely destroyed by bloody upheavals within the Republic, though these upheavals had often been sparked by greed from without.

Although many of the educated Haitians found it possible to amass considerable wealth under the century-long military regime, they were the first to be horrified by the amount of bloodshed caused by the Generals. I need not mention their shame on being obliged to play the role of jesters at the Generals' court to save their own skin. Even those like Price-Mars, who had strong family connections with the military, were impatient to move into a new era. Frédéric Marcelin, who had served in the Cabinets of three Generals, would say: "The good ministers will be of no use to them whenever they (the Generals) feel that their personal interests require them to tighten their grip. Name even one Minister of Justice who has prevented an illegal act, the imprisonment of citizens or placing them before the firing squad. Usually he only learns of the act after it has been perpetrated."[8]

Consequently, those who had supported the Treaty hoped that they had moved toward the reign of Law and Order in a climate of

Freedom. They were encouraged by President Woodrow Wilson's declaration that the sending of the Marines stemmed from a genuine humanitarian motive.

Yet, from the inception of the Occupation, the United States clearly showed its determination to reduce the Black Republic to the status of a colony. In 1917, while Price-Mars was lecturing, he avoided overt mention of the great issue of the amendments to Haiti's Constitution, which Washington demanded. After the Haitian Legislative Chambers had bitterly resisted those proposals, they were eventually approved on June 12, 1918, through a plebiscite, with U. S. Marines managing the affair. They provided entertainment and refreshments to enliven the proceedings and they counted the ballots on behalf of the Haitian Government. Under the pretext that the great majority of the Haitians could not read and write, the Occupation authorities prepared two sets of blank ballots: a white one meaning "yes" and a pink one meaning "no." But few pink ones were distributed, just enough to create the illusion of an honest popular suffrage. The amendments were accepted by a vote of 98,225 to 769. However, the *cacos* were still fighting over a large part of the country. They would continue their guerilla warfare against the Occupation until the death of Charlemagne Péralte, on November 1, 1919, when the revolt lost its impetus and rapidly dsintegrated.

The new Constitution, the "Constitution of 1918," set up a dictatorship apparently vested in the hands of the President of the Republic. The real situation was described as follows by a former American Treaty official, Arthur C. Millspaugh:

> Nominally, the treaty officials are responsible to the President of Haiti or to their respective Ministers; in practice, they are directed by the High Commissioner who is at once an appointee of the President of the United States, the diplomatic representative of the United States Government, and the Commander of the Marines in Haiti. He not only vetoes but also drafts Haitian legislation. He negotiates contracts with American companies, determines the administrative attitude to be assumed toward them by the American treaty officers, and interests himself in the details of claims, the collection of revenue, road construction, and in agricultural, educational, and sanitary matters. American treaty officers have little official contact with the Haitian executive and their relations with the Ministers have necessarily become perfunctory or formal.
>
> On its face the arrangement is characterized by division and confusion both of authority and responsibility; in practice it leads to a relationship between the President of Haiti and the representative of the Government of the United States which emphasizes the authority and responsibility of the United States in the domestic affairs of Haiti.[9]

While Haiti was going through the second stage of her trauma, Price-Mars was himself engaged in a daily struggle for his own survival. Whatever money he had made between 1905 and 1915 was completely gone. He found himself obliged to sell his books to pay his daily expenses. The need was compelling because he had to take care of a twelve-year old son he had had out of wedlock by a Northern woman while a member of the House of Representatives. The boy, who had received the Christian name of Louis, was at the time in Cap-Haitien attending the Catholic Brothers' school. Nevertheless, Price-Mars remained active in politics, if only to the extent of meeting with friends to discuss current events. He lived in Pétionville, not far from the most prominent politician after President Dartiguenave—Louis Borno, Minister of Foreign Affairs. Borno was then attracting many admirers, including Price-Mars, by his proud, firm stand in dealing with officials of the Occupation.

Soon after the new Constitution was voted, the Americans began to show both President Dartiguenave and Minister Borno who the real masters of Haiti were. When the President refused to rubber-stamp the Financial Adviser's views on the budget, the latter, Addison T. Ruan, simply stopped paying the Chief Executive and Ministers their salaries. Ruan's action was also prompted by the fact that Washington wanted a new Cabinet in Haiti, primarily to get rid of Borno. Before long Ruan got his wish.

The new government contained two staunch friends of Price-Mars: Pauléus Sannon and Dantès Bellegarde, respectively Minister of Foreign Affairs and Minister of Public Instruction. Another friend of Price-Mars, Auguste Bonamy, was also appointed by Dartiguenave as Chief Justice of the Haitian Supreme Court. Thanks to these friends in high places, Price-Mars' financial difficulties soon found relief, for Dantès Bellegarde offered him a teaching position at the Lycée Pétion.

Price-Mars asked to teach Haitian history and geography and civics. His wishes were immediately granted by Bellegarde. The previous year during his lecture tour, Price-Mars had had some contact with lycée students. His audience on June 4, 1917 at the Parisiana Theatre consisted mainly of young people. In December he addressed another group of young people in Saint-Marc. One of these, Justin J. Kenol,[10] still remembered twenty years later the profound impression made on the "enthusiastic audience" by the closing words of that speech on "The Art of Reading as a Discipline of General Education":

> Do read, young people who are listening to me; and do not shy away because the advice comes from us. I know well that we of this generation growing in years, already out of breath and tired, are transmitting to you a degraded, tattered and mutilated national heritage. I know we are continuing to offer you the spectacle of our

miserable hatreds and pitiful rivalries.

Yes, I know all that, and therefore I do not have too great a right to stand up either as a critic or as an advisor. But, comrades, are we not brothers in shame and misfortune? Well, without going further in examining our right to speak to you, first look and consider the gift we bring. If you judge it worthy, take it and enjoy it without asking whether it was prompted by a fraternal intention.

Now the good news I bring this evening is that the reading of great works is one way to liberate yourselves, even temporarily, from the state of turpitude in which the ignorance of some and the cowardice of others have submerged us. Read to develop your mind, read to learn how to become better than we are, and momentarily to escape from the evil realities of our life. For, to read a serious book is often to admire and to pray, and that prayer is within reach of everyone.[11]

The appointment of Price-Mars to the Lycée may appear as simply the deed of a Good Samaritan, but it was more than that. It was the decision of a lucid mind. Although Bellegarde and Price-Mars did not always see eye-to-eye, they had remained warm friends through the years. In fact, when Price-Mars came to the capital in 1911, following Cincinnatus Leconte, it was on the advice of Bellegarde's mother that he went to live in Pétionville. There, in the temperate climate at the foot of the Kenscof Mountain, he was able to convalesce. Dantès Bellegarde, himself a great patriot, devoted like Price-Mars to the progress and dignity of the whole Haitian People, knew the importance and quality of the service that his friend would render to the youth of the Lycée Pétion.

Minister Bellegarde had appointed Price-Mars in an effort to save the century-old institution. The preceding year the lycée's students had exhibited the inferiority of their preparation in the State's examination for the baccalaureate degree. Bellegarde feared for the Lycée because of the Occupation's attitude toward the Haitian schools. In his own words, "Returning in July 1918 to the Department of Public Instruction, this time as Minister, I had at once to fight against the evident determination of officials of the American Occupation to destroy our educational system. Our secondary education was particularly threatened."[12]

In addition to Price-Mars, Bellegarde brought a number of respected Haitian educators to the Lycée, among them Seymour Pradel, a former Minister of the Interior and one of the most prominent lawyers in the capital. Like Price-Mars, Pradel was an alumnus of the Lycée. He returned to his Alma Mater to teach without pay. True enough, Price-Mars badly needed his salary, but he was motivated above all else by the thought that "he could undertake in a more direct manner the great struggle for the restoration of the national soul."[13]

The above-reproduced conclusion of his speech to the young people forecast the direction his teaching would take in the classroom, as it sketches the intellectual, moral, emotional and spiritual personality of the instructor he would be. Two of his students rose to the Presidency of the Republic under his intellectual and inspirational banner. In his lecture on "The Vocation of the Elite" he had voiced the thought that he would hammer into the minds of his *lycéens:*

> Our duty at the present hour is to contribute to the creation of a national thought to express our feelings, our qualities and our shortcomings. We can do it if we endeavor to find inspiration in great works that are the pride and the common heritage of the human race. It is only for that purpose that meditation on and assimilation of intellectual works are indispensable for the improvement of our own culture.[14]
>
> If you consider for one moment the detrimental results to which I have called your attention in regard to our educational system; if you choose to think about the insufficient and precarious intellectual preparation of our élite that has resulted from it; if finally you wish to consider the various reasons which divide our epople into two hostile groups, full of misgivings and antagonism toward one another, you will admit with me that all these causes put together make our social milieu presents an overwhelming reaction of moral depression against any attempt at continuous progress. You will finally admit that a combination of those causes had made us all accomplices in the state of affairs which permitted the Americans to plant their flag on the moral ruin of our fatherland.[15]

Revealing once again his integrity as a scholar, when Price-Mars mentioned the name of Le Bon in his speech on "The Art of Reading . . . ," he chose a quotation that seemed to merit praise rather than condemnation. Referring to the French anthropologist's book, *Psychology of Education,* he said:

> Here is a volume based on psychological considerations and full of facts, taken primarily from official documents on the reform of education in France, and published in 1893. The author, thought-provoking as usual, attracts one's attention from the first pages by his ardent criticism of the methods used in the University; then in the constructive part of the work, he sums up his doctrine in this formula: the object of *all education consists in the art of transferring the conscious into the unconscious.*[16]

After discussing what he called Le Bon's aphorism, he made the following comment which indicates how his own intellectual personality had been influenced by his adversary: "Is the conclusion that we have briskly drawn from Gustave Le Bon's aphorism well-founded? Perhaps so. What is certain is that it has made us reflect, and what is no less certain is that from the effort of our own intelligence, we have derived the undeniable benefit of meditating on one of the most serious problems of human life."[17]

But Price-Mars never forgot Le Bon's contention that no education could ever give the Black man "the forms of thought, the logic and, above all, the *character* of Western man," because these things are created by heredity alone. On the contrary, Price-Mars expected education to do precisely that: "to develop or help to develop, along with the intrinsic qualities of the intelligence, those no less important and no less precious qualities of character which give worth to the dignity of life and imprint the sense of responsibility in the heart of man."[18]

He felt that this, more than anything else, was what his compatriots needed. "The Haitian," he said, "whatever his social class, has acquired the habit of tortuous words, of roundabout periphrases, of ingenious circumlocutions to hide his thought to avoid displeasing the masters of the moment, for fear of becoming involved by simply expressing his opinion."[19] In this context, he quoted his old idol, Jean Jaurès, on courage:

> Courage means to rise above your own faults, to regret them but not allow yourself to be overwhelmed by them . . . Courage means seeking and speaking the truth; it does not mean yielding to the triumphant lie of the moment, nor does it mean concurring, with soul, lips and hands, in stupid applause or fanatical derision.[20]

After teaching history, geography and civics for a year, Price-Mars gathered his various talks and published them in book form under the title, *The Vocation of the Elite*. Again, as he had done in one of his talks, he underscored in the preface, the widespread despair, the hopelessness that still permeated all factions of the élite.

As a matter of fact, in September of that same year (1919), Léon Laleau, one of the most talented younger authors, began to write *Le Choc* (The Impact)[21], a novel about the Occupation. He described the despair of his generation in the presence of the invaders. The principal character of the novel felt, at one time, an impulse to take up arms to resist the Occupation. But he gave up the idea, discouraged by the low morale of his élite friends. Heeding the advice of a Catholic priest, also his friend, he voluntarily sought exile in France.

Regardless of the dejection of Laleau's main protagonist, the role played by the French priest in the latter's decision could not but infuriate Price-Mars. For in one of his lectures, he referred to the Catholic Church which had remained aloof from the Haitian ordeal: "If the Church has a role to play in the current crisis, it must be a national one that makes the Haitian cause and the Haitian's suffering its own."[22] But the armed phase of the national cause would soon come to an end: on November 1 of that year, Charlemagne Péralte fell into a trap and was put to death by the American Occupation forces.

In *A Marine Tells It To You,* Colonel Frederic May Wise had this to say about Charlemagne: "Under the corvée system of building the road from Port-au-Prince to Cap-Haitien, the peasants had been drafted and forced to work far beyond legal requirements, they claimed. All they needed was a leader. In Charlemagne they found a damned good one . . . Charlemagne's various bands raided town after town. Those raids looked like bravado to me. A few Haitians known to be sympathizers with America were killed now and then. But there was no looting to speak of."[23]

Charlemagne, whose life was cut down at the age of thirty-three, was an educated Haitian. He had been arrested by the Marines for *corvée* service but had escaped and joined the peasants' guerilla. The rebel was dear to Price-Mars personally for he and his older brother, Saül, had participated in the conspiracy that brought Vilbrun Guillaume to power. And Charlemagne had started his revolt against the U. S. Marines, who had himself been arrested in 1918 for *corvée* service[24] but released, drew the following conclusions from the uprising. They serve at least to illustrate his own spirit at the time as a teacher of civics at the Lycée, though, for obvious reasons, his words did not appear in print until a decade or so later:

> Charlemagne Péralte, declared a bandit because he refused to submit to the *corvée*, despite the American Occupation's bombs, dynamite, and the machine guns of its combat airplanes, led his fanatical, ragged bands, armed with only their courage, to the heart of a Port-au-Prince that was surprised, fearful and dismayed.
>
> When, in the history of a century and a half of independence, one finds such sporadic feats of heroism and sacrifice, it is not possible to believe that the race has degenerated; that the sense of honor is lost; that the value of human dignity has depreciated. Let the cowards grovel before money and the pleasures it provides. Let the snobs consider themselves above the crowd because their wealth frees them from material needs. What constitutes the beauty of life is the only imperishable wealth that makes life worth living: the nobility of the heart, moral solidarity and human brotherhood. If there are still Haitians for whom these things exist, a great future for this country is still possible . . . [25]

At the Lycée Pétion, Price-Mars soon won the admiration and affection of his students for his exceptional talents as a scholar and lecturer and for his inherent kindness as a man. From that moment on he would prove to be "the greatest friend of Haitian youth." Attaining his objective as a teacher, he refurbished the "National Soul" among his students, and for that matter, among the whole younger generation in Haiti, kindling their minds and keeping their hearts aflame with the intellectual convictions and the passionate faith he had in the Haitian fatherland and the Black Race. One of his students, who later became a professor of law and president of the Bar Association of Jacmel, recalls that the "intense patriotism" exhibited by Price-Mars in his classroom at the Lycée was "however, devoid of xenophobia, sectarism or intolerance."[26]

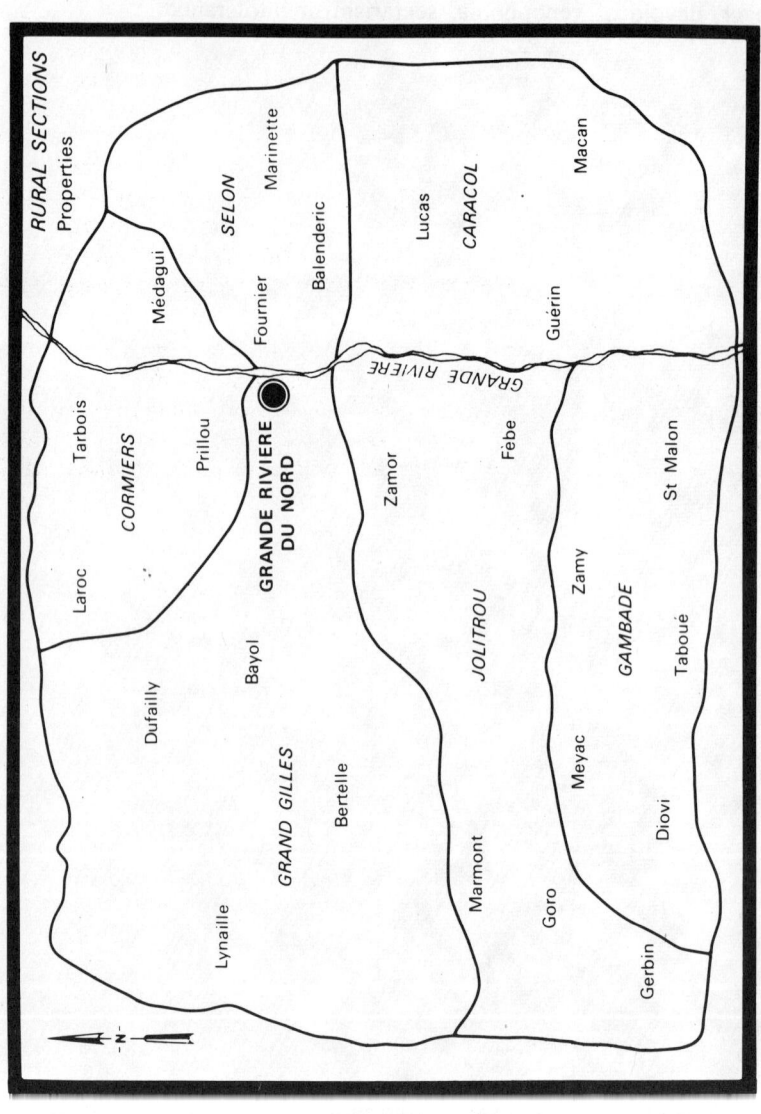

GRANDE RIVIERE DU NORD: Urban Center

Names in italics: Rural Sections
Names in regular type: Private properties, farms, etc.

Ten

The Country Doctor's Elixir

The year 1920 marked a turning point in Price-Mars' life both politically and intellectually. That year opened with great excitement in Haiti as well as in the United States. The Navy Department in Washington communicated to the American press in December of 1919 a letter from Major-General Barnett, Marine Corps Commandant, to Colonel John H. Russell, Commandant of the U. S. Occupation Forces in Haiti, in which the General reported having heard that "practically indiscriminate killing" of Haitians "had been going on for some time."[1] Obviously the information was given to the press by mistake for the General's letter was marked "Personal and Confidential." The publication of this statement in the newspapers was followed immediately by violent protests in the United States. And in March the prominent Negro writer James Weldon Johnson and Mr. Herbert Seligmann, a white American, arrived in Port-au-Prince as the Representatives of the National Association for the Advancement of Colored People to investigate conditions in Haiti in the light of the Haitian-American Treaty. Johnson spent only six weeks in Haiti, but his visit had a tremendous impact both in Haiti and the United States.

During his short stay in Haiti Johnson managed to have talks with practically all prominent Haitians, including President Dartiguenave. Back in the United States, Johnson sounded the alarm that roused Negroes throughout the United States in defense of Haiti. Writing in the *Crisis*, he declared:

> The United States has failed in Haiti. It should get out as well and as quickly as it can and restore to the Haitian people their independence and sovereignty. The colored people of the United States should be interested in seeing that this is done, for Haiti is the one chance the Negro has in the world to prove that he is capable of the highest self-government. If Haiti should ultimately lose her independence, that one best chance will be lost.[2]

While in Haiti Johnson had insisted in his talks with the Haitians that they ought to create an organization on the pattern of the NAACP without distinction of political tendencies among its members and with agencies in the most important cities of the Republic, to undertake the defense of Haiti at home and abroad. Under the name *Union Patriotique,* that association was created on November 17 on the initiative of Georges Sylvain and with the blessing of President Dartiguenave. It had, said the *Crisis,* "as its prime object the working, in accord with the defenders of the Haitian cause in the United States, for the abolishment of all restrictions placed upon the full exercise of sovereignty and independence on the part of the Haitian Government."[3]

Naturally Price-Mars was among those who enthusiastically welcomed the American Negro writer whose poetry and songs he had mentioned in his first talk about his visit in the United States in 1904. In the company of his good friend Pauléus Sannon he had several conversations with Johnson who underscored that fact in his book *Along This Way:* "I saw a great deal of Mr. Sannon, who had resigned as Secretary of Foreign Affairs rather than sign the Haitian-American Convention by which Haiti was forced to abdicate it sovereignty. A huge man, pure black, and with exceptional intellectual powers. I saw as much of Mr. Price-Mars, formerly Secretary of the Haitian Legation in Washington, a gentle scholar, as slight in bulk as Sannon was huge, and also pure black."[4] About Georges Sylvain, he said, "With him, the cause of Haiti seemed to dominate every other interest."[5]

Upon his return to the United States Johnson had immediately denounced the atrocities committed by the Marines in the New York review *The Nation* and in a booklet entitled *Self-Government.* This had much to do with the sending to Haiti of the Mayo Commission, named after its chairman, Admiral Henry T. Mayo, Chief of U. S. Naval Operations in the Atlantic. The Commission came to investigate the facts about the "indiscriminate killing" of Haitians by the Marines. After a fortnight or so the Commission departed, leaving the inquiry in the sole hands of one of its members, Admiral Knapp, who simply white-washed the Marines. The Mayo Commission's report to the Navy Department declared that "General Barnett's accusations had no serious basis." It further stated that the accusations constituted "a regrettable outrage" to the Marines who had accomplished a difficult, dangerous and delicate work in Haiti for which they deserved instead "the highest praise."

The *Union Patriotique* played a significant role in presenting witnesses before the Commission. Although it had failed in its first endeavor, Haiti now had a potent voice which, coupled with the hue and cry of the *Crisis, The Nation* and the *Chicago Defender,* succeeded in causing the U. S. Senate to send the McCormick Commission the following year, and prompted Senator Warren Harding to make Haiti an issue in his presidential campaign against President Wilson. Again the McCormick Commission produced no satisfactory results on behalf of Haiti. Senator Harding, elected President of the United States, chose to maintain the *status quo* in Haiti. But the Occupation's shameful dossier had been thrown open for all the world to see.

In "The Vocation of the Elite," Price-Mars had advocated the creation of an organization such as the Union Patriotique which "would bring before public opinion in Haiti and abroad the rightfulness of our cause so as to exert moral pressure on the decisions of the Authority."[6] He used the word "Authority" to mean the American Occupation for he voiced that opinion in connection with rumors that the Occupation wanted to do away with the principle of free admission to Haitian secondary and graduate schools. Price-Mars felt that in a country as poor as Haiti which had emerged from slavery, free admission to those schools was a legitimate means for the Black nation to produce the physicians, professors, scientists and men of letters it needed both to promote the welfare and to foster the intellectual and moral development of the Haitian people.

In 1920, when Dantès Bellegarde left the Department of Public Instruction to become Haitian Minister to France, the American Occupation wanted nothing less than to take over the entire Haitian public school system. A proposal to that effect was officially made to the Haitian Government during that year although the Treaty did not provide for such a thing. The proposal was unanimously rejected by the Haitian Cabinet. Arthur C. Millspaugh, who served as United States Financial Adviser to Haiti under the Treaty in 1928, described the method the Occupation used to reach its end: "All financial means were refused for Haitian schools until they were absorbed."[7]

Under such circumstances and considering the new blood James Weldon Johnson had injected into the intellectuals of the *Union Patriotique,* one is not surprised to see Price-Mars move from his restrained position as school teacher to the militant ground where his good friend Pauléus Sannon then stood. The following year as the latter was sent by the *Union* to the United States along with two other members, Sténio Vincent and Perceval Thoby,[8] to present the plea of the Haitian people for the restoration of Haiti's sovereignty to the Congress of the United States, Price-Mars began to make speeches at the meetings of the *Union.* He was separated from his teaching position at the Lycée Pétion without receiving any reason for his dismissal in 1922.

This was a presidential election year in Haiti. The *Union Patriotique* wanted President Dartiguenave to call first for general elections to replace the American-made "Council of State" by Haiti's traditional two legislative chambers, and as the President showed he was not so disposed, the *Union* became violently opposed to the Government, accusing the President of being a willing tool in the hands of the Occupation for his own personal financial gain. As journalists were arrested, the political tension in the capital rose to fever pitch and rumors spread at times that President Dartiguenave would be assassinated.

Price-Mars decided to return to the Haitian Medical School to complete the medical education he had begun in Paris. He was still living in Pétionville. When he did not have to go to Medical School he spent a large of the morning in the company of such friends as Pauléus Sannon, Eugène Roy, Alexandre and Drossaint Lilavois who also lived in Pétionville, on the main square of the town.[9] They certainly spoke a great deal about politics and the forthcoming presidential election. The President of the Council of State, Stephen Archer, the principal contender for Dartiguenave's seat, had a magnificent summer villa bordering the park where he usually spent the night. At first the President had wanted another term in office but under the pressure of the Opposition he had deferred to Archer. The small country town became even more animated with the coming and going of politicians because another prominent public man, Louis Borno, lived a short distance from Archer at the end of the only street going up from the park. Another candidate much admired by Price-Mars, was Auguste Bonamy.

Mr. Borno, in Creole parlance, was a candidate *en bas feuilles* (under leaves), that is, feigning disinterest in the contest. His presumed presidential ambitions were being dismissed in the newspapers by his adversaries who declared that he was not born a Haitian citizen nor from a Haitian father as Article 73 of the Constitution of 1918 required for election to the Presidency. He had been born a French citizen like his father, in 1865, and had become a Haitian citizen nine years later by naturalization in 1874.

Ironically, although Borno had been an intransigent Foreign Minister in dealing with the American Treaty officials, he was the candidate of those who wanted closer cooperation between the Haitian Government and the Treaty officials for rapid implementation of the Treaty. James Weldon Johnson gives a good picture of Borno in *Along This Way:* "Mr. Borno, a lawyer, was former Secretary of State for Foreign Affairs. He was one of the most accomplished men I have met; tall, slender, bronze-colored, with the face and hands of an artist; a linguist, a fine poet, and a very astute statesman."[10]

President Dartiguenave had rejected a loan of forty million dollars from the National City Bank of New York which had been offered under the auspices of the U. S. Government. The President feared that the loan would lead to the complete engulfment of Haiti's sovereignty. Borno, on the contrary, through his many friends among the élite who had social contact with the American officials, let it be known that, if elected to the Presidency, he would accept such a loan, promising in addition "a frank and loyal collaboration with the Americans."

One of the projects being contemplated for immediate realization with the loan money could not but make Price-Mars an ardent partisan of Borno if only in the secret of his heart—the establishment of a Technical Service of Agriculture as he had advocated in 1912 in *L'Essor*. Although Price-Mars had lost his position at the Lycée, he was nevertheless a man of considerable importance both on account of his influential friends and the publication of his book which had established him as a leading intellectual.

At that time to cover the eight miles between Pétionville and the capital, people of Price-Mars' social status needed a horse. Thus Price-Mars had acquired this means of transportation when he went to live in Pétionville during the Cincinnatus Leconte government. Now, on afternoons when he did not have to to go to Port-au-Prince either to attend Medical School or Union Patriotique meetings or take care of some other business, Price-Mars would get on his horse and roam about the countryside in the immediate vicinity of Pétionville or climb Kenscoff Mountain to investigate the peasants' way of life, collecting information directly from them as to their religious beliefs and old legends in the locality. He had been doing this research in the vicinity and elsewhere for over a year. According to Courtilien Charles he met the peasants during those trips as if they were old friends of his, giving them advice on occasion and sometimes offering little gifts to the women who had readily answered his questions. In learning at close range the thinking of his "good people of Haiti," Price-Mars entered the field of ethnography and ethnology with no less enthusiasm than he had previously shown in the fields of anthropology and sociology. And it was from the new field of his interest that he brought back the ingredients to make the elixir that will in no time revitalize the moribund "Fatherland."

In April, Mr. Borno was elected President through a burlesque maneuver of the Council of State by the Head of the American Occupation. The same month Price-Mars was warmly welcomed by the worldly young women of the exclusive Primavera Club of the capital as a lecturer. He told the aristocratic, Houbigant-scented young females and their mothers, "I would readily bet that you have felt some discomfort, even some serious apprehension when you learned I would discuss the family of the peasant."

He presented what he called "the results of my investigation on the folklore" in the vicinity of Pétionville and Kenscoff, remarking that he had noticed there that the peasants had retained some obvious physical similarities with the Congolese type which belong to the largest African human importation to Haiti. Then joyfully he described rural customs in other parts of the country, recalling some he had enjoyed in his childhood in Grande Rivière du Nord. With a wealth of details he described courtship, betrothal and marriage among the peasants, pointing out what both Voodoo and the Catholic Church have contributed through the years to customs in rural Haiti.

"Do you want to see, for comparison, the establishment of a family somewhere in the Congo, Sudan or Dahomey?" Price-Mars asked his listeners. Then he exclaimed:

> Ah! I know the sort of repulsion I am knocking against in daring to speak to you about Africa and African things. The topic seems inelegant to you and totally devoid of interest, is it not so?
> Beware, my friends, that such a feeling does not have as its source a scandalous ignorance. We are living on rancid ideas from the appalling stupidity of an ill-arranged education, and as a result our childish vanity is only satisfied when we repeat like asses the words written for others to glorify 'The Gauls, our ancestors.'[11]

Price-Mars repeated a sentence from his talk "The Vocation of the Elite" which was to inspire two young Black students at the Sorbonne, who later became two of the most prominent protagonists of "Négritude," Léopold Sédar Senghor of Senegal and Aimé Césaire of Martinique, who himself coined the word "Négritude." The sentence Price-Mars repeated was: "We have no chance of becoming ourselves unless we do not repudiate any part of our ancestral heritage." He added, "Well, that heritage constitutes for eight-tenths among us a gift from Africa," and he went on to say:

> Our ancestors? They are first the dead whose centuries long sufferings, courage, intelligence and sensitivity have mixed together in Saint-Domingue so as to make us what we are: Free people ... It is because our ancestors were men who suffered, who loved and hoped that we, too, can aspire to the full dignity of being men despite the brutal insolence of imperialism of all kinds.[12]

At the end of his talk Price-Mars told his audience that those who study the ethnic and historical background of the Haitian people "are fascinated by a luminous intuition that their past constitutes a guaranty of their future." This talk stands as the landmark of Black consciousness and Black pride in Haitian literature. Until then the Haitian intellectuals had taken great pride in their Black ancestors viewing them as heroic and sublime *va-nu-pieds,* just as the French had viewed their 1789 revolutionists as heroic and sublime *sans-culottes.* But the doubt about the human potential of the black man as expressed by Chanlatte during the very year of Haiti's independence was still in the hearts of the Haitians. A case in point is Massillon Coicou's famous *Complaintes d'esclaves,* a poem whose last stanza reads as follows:

> But why am I a Negro? Oh! why am I black?
> When God threw me into the bosom of my mother
> Why did not jealous Death so prompt in her duty

> Rush to remove me from the earth?
> Ah! if you hear me well you must also see me.
> If I am blaspheming, alas! you surely see I am weeping?
> You know, you who know everything, that I'm suffering
> At every hour because I am black?
> Well, I've suffered for too long in silence
> Lord, forgive me if I am learning to curse.

Coicou had written those verses with a mind obsessed by the repeated failure of the Haitian élite to raise themselves from their selfishness and division up to their high Destiny so as to lift in turn the Haitian masses from their abject condition and the country from its economic stagnation. It was this frustration that led him to his violent death.

On the contrary, Price-Mars' mental courage before the predicament of the Haitian masses and the shortcomings of the Haitian élite has its source, not in despair but in the unswerving faith he had in his race—the Black Race. He ended his talk at the Primavera Club with those words:

> I beg you, my friends, let us no longer despise our ancestral heritage. Let us rather repeat the words that the old poet put on the lips of one of the inhabitants of Olympus: 'There is nothing ugly in the house of my father.'[13]

In December of that year (1922), Price-Mars, along with Pauléus Sannon and some other intellectuals, created the *Society of Haitian History and Geography,* with Sannon as its first president. The following year, President Borno reinstated Price-Mars to his teaching position at the Lycée Pétion. Again he was assigned to teach history, geography and civics but in the higher level classes. He found among his students the same veneration his past students had shown him. There were in the Lycée at that time a Dumarsais Estimé and François Duvalier[14] as well as Price-Mars' son Louis, who had come from Cap-Haitien to pursue his education at the capital.

Price-Mars completed his own medical education during 1923, and joined a group of physicians of Port-au-Prince at the Coicou Clinic, named after its senior partner; he also practiced at the Péan Clinic which his other good friend, Dr. Léon Audain, had established in 1903. The latter had died in 1914, while serving as Haitian Minister in Paris. But Price-Mars did not abandon his rural activities in and about Pétionville. Now he could dispense medical care to his humble and abandoned friends in the valley or on the mountain with all the authority his medical diploma conferred on him. The Haitian writer Thomas Lechaud gives the following amusing sketch of the physician:

> Dressed in khaki as one who had become converted to the color of the uniform of the U.S.M.C.'s boys, the calves of his leg covered

with leather boots like an officer of those boys, a sun-helmet on his head—a brown one, over his black face, the effect is most charming: Price-Mars on horseback, followed by his dog, roaming about Pétionville as a traditional country doctor.[15]

The sight offered by Price-Mars was doubly unusual at that time. Not only did the great majority of the physicians practice their art exclusively in the cities, the wealthier ones going on calls in their buggies; practically all of them wore woolen clothes which was also the vestimentary tradition in the halls of government as well as in the drawing rooms of the élite, in spite of the ardent tropical sun all the year around. However, Price-Mars never lost a mild preoccupation for a well-groomed appearance at social affairs, a habit acquired in his youth during his student days in Paris.

In view of some revelations that came to light during the Mayo Commission inquiry, one is not surprised that Price-Mars' next intellectual effort in providing his elixir of Black Pride to his fellow-countrymen, particularly to the Mulatto élite in the cities, was to undertake to rid them of their fear of Voodoo as he tried to destroy their shame about their African blood. This he undertook against odds that would freeze to inaction most other Haitians of the élite. For at the National Palace stood Louis Borno, one of the most polished images of Western Civilization, a product of the Law School of Paris and a "Catholic Musketeer" as Georges Sylvain had nicknamed him.

Ever since the *Pellé Affaire,* the élite mother, more often than not, associated blackness of the skin with cannibalism. Whenever an old black man or an old black woman would come to their door either to offer his ware as a merchant or to ask for charity, the élite mothers would send their children into the house if they were on the outside when these "characters" presented themselves to view. The children were instructed never to look straight into the eyes of these black people for fear that the latter would "steal away their souls" by hypnotic power.

The American Occupation used this fear among the Haitian élite to maintain their hold on them more securely: "When we arrived in 1915," wrote Colonel May Wise, "the Haitians of the better classes, the Church and the foreign colony had received us with open arms."[16] One of the victims of the Marines, we are told by the Colonel, was an "old Haitian" who had been arrested by an American officer, Lt. Brokaw, at Croix des Bouquets some fifteen miles from Port-au-Prince. One night after some heavy drinking with three other Marines at the military post there, Lt. Brokaw, claiming that the "old man" was a "Papaloi"—a Voodoo priest, executed him. Colonel May Wise says that being a "papaloi" was supposed to be against the law. He described the execution of the "old man" as follows: "They took him out with another native who was in jail, led them to the outskirts of Croix des Bouquets, made them dig their own graves, stood them up on the edge of the graves, and shot them. Just for excitement."[17]

Colonel May Wise reported another story which he said "sprang up in the interior and swept the island." Another Marine officer, Captain B. F. Hickey, from whom the story originated, spoke of a Voodoo priest, who presumably after having been turned down by a girl, had announced that he would cause the girl to die and then bring her back to life. Effectively as the story goes, the girl became ill. The old French Catholic priest at the village was summoned to her. He told this story to Captain Hickey: I administered the last rites of the Church to the dying girl . . . I saw her die. I officiated at her funeral. Now, months later, I have seen walking in the streets of this town the same girl I saw die and saw buried."[18]

Colonel May Wise arrived in Haiti in 1915 with the invading Marines. After the United States entered the European conflict he was sent to France and returned to Haiti in 1919 when he was given the command of the Haitian Gendarmerie. After underscoring the warm welcome the Marines had received in 1915, he remarked: "But by one blunder after another, we had succeeded in four years in getting everyone down on us."[19]

He knew Haiti well, as he himself said:

> Haiti, as I know thoroughly, is composed of two classes, the gentry and the peasants. The peasants, forming the vast majority, are simple and kindly, good-natured and responsible. The gentry are a proud, formal race. Some of the best blood of France is in their veins. They are descended from generations of rich plantation owners. Their sons got their degrees from European universities. Their daughters were educated in the convents of France and England. They were at home in the drawing-rooms of any capital in the world. They looked upon France as their mother country, and when money was plentiful visited it yearly. These were the people among whom one of those American Treaty officials arrived with a book entitled "The Development of the Negro Mind", from which he quoted on all occasions.[20]

Admiral Knapp, of the Mayo Commission, levelled a most devastating charge against the Haitian society which naturally infuriated the Haitian élite, but helped to increase their antagonism to Voodoo. It became known in March 1921 that Admiral Knapp, in addition to the Mayo Commission's report, had presented a personal one in which he affirmed that cannibalism was being practices in all strata of Haitian society.[21]

This was the prevailing mental climate among the Haitian élite, the French clergy and the American occupants when Price-Mars spoke in 1926 at the Society of Haitian History and Geography on the subject "The religious sentiment and phenomenon among the

Blacks of Saint-Domingue." Not only did he not let that climate deter him from defending the Voodoo cult, he attacked the problem without even the fear of alienating his old friend Pauléus Sannon. Price-Mars undertook in his talk to project the light of African ethnography on general history, as he said, "to establish the map of religious faith of the Negro according to the map of the slave trade."

The talk contains a wealth of information which evidences Price-Mars' long and patient research on the various peoples of Africa. In regard to Saint-Domingue he quoted Moreau de Saint-Méry to the effect that all the Africans who had been taken from the various points over some 300 leagues on the African coast from the mouth of the Senegal River in Sierra Leone "are Moslem." The famous author of *Description of the Island of Saint-Domingue* further indicated that among the Africans many, particularly the Congolese, had ideas of Christianity they had received from the Portuguese. The latter generally branded the Africans as fetichists having noticed that the Africans seemed to show reverence to certain material objects.

The Portuguese word "fetichism," Price-Mars affirmed, had only covered part of the phenomenon it pretended to qualify and explain. "Fetishism," he went on to say, "is not a religion":

> The Blacks of Africa do not pay hommage to material objects. They venerate the spirits they believe are embodied in certain forms of matter and particularly in cosmic forces: Sea, Earth, Rivers, Forests, etc. This is what modern science, after painstaking research, has called Animism. And it is Animism which is the universal religion of Africa. Even after having yielded to some fanatical currents which have implanted in their land the banner of the Prophet or the Cross of Christ, the Blacks very often remain animist.[22]

Price-Mars not only affirmed that Animism constitutes a "true religion" with a "body of cosmologic doctrine," he pointed out that it requires in certain regions a sacerdotal hierarchy to perpetuate the cult, as in the regions of South-East Sudan where the religious chiefs bear the name of "Bougho" or "Hogon," meaning fire or the heat of fire. He reminded his audience that this title is still borne by the religious chiefs among Haiti's rural populations of the North and South-West. These chiefs, he said, go through initiation ceremonies. They are compelled to live an austere life which gives them the great moral authority they enjoy. Then he asked: "This animism which divinizes the forces of the Cosmos, pays tribute to spiritual generations which these forces embody; this animism which renders to the dead ancestors a cult of veneration and requests their blessings and protection, is it a religion that is in opposition to the religion of the Universal God, sovereign and supreme master of the Universe?" He answered, "No, certainly not."

The African man, Price-Mars declared, is under rigid moral code, the more binding because he believes as does the whole community in which he lives, that the gods themselves demand the observance of the moral code which prescribes:

> A ban on killing, except for an enemy of the tribe; a ban against stealing, or casting a bad spell over someone. Interdiction of sexual relations between a couple when a mother is nursing a child or with a woman who is having her period. A ban against women in the latter case participating in religious services. Punishment of the adulteress. Respect due to old people, to the Spirits and the interpreters of their wills as well as to their places of cult and everything consecrated to them. Obedience to those who are the holders of public powers and had been consecrated as such by the will of the Spirits.[23]

All these prohibitions, Price-Mars said, constitute the structure of all religious frameworks, of the simplest ones and the most complex as well. The African dogma appears to him as "a twin sister of the famous precepts Yahweh dictated to Moses on Mount Sinai: Thou shalt not kill (probably the man of the tribe). Thou shalt not steal. Thous shalt not commit adultery. Thou shalt have no other gods before me, etc. . . . " And Price-Mars remarked, "After all, Negro ethics, Jewish ethics, double face of a same coin. This appears to me to indicate a universal phenomenon, inherent to the very nature of man."[23]

From his analysis Price-Mars reached the conclusion that the great mass of Negroes taken from various regions of Africa and brought to Saint-Domingue were pious people, devoted to Islam, to the Dahomeyan cult (Voodoo), and to some extent to the Catholic faith, "although the latter was forced on the Blacks more often than not hypocritically and in an unskilled manner which hid badly the design of maintaining the Blacks in their slave status." But why, asked Price-Mars, have the Haitian historians from the first ones, the Brothers Ardouin, Madiou, "up to our distinguished colleague Monsieur Sannon," so mercilessly crushed the Blacks with the reputation of being fetishists. "Is it misinterpretation of facts, a deliberate attitude or self-consciousness?" He answered as follows:

> I believe one can detect a little of all that with various nuances in the severe judgment of our analysts. They have been obsessed and very much so by the false opinion that Europeans generally express or have expressed about African religions. For all authors of General History and Geography as well as for travellers, and the first analysts of religious history, Africa is the classical land of fetishism. It is not surprising that on this side we, Black Haitians, who take pride in our Christian faith, we repeat: 'The Negroes of Africa are fetishists,' and then, as a consequence, the Blacks of Saint-Domingue also were fetishists. Et voilà![25]

Price-Mars did not gloss over the fact that magic and

superstition have entered the African cult. They have also, he pointed out, entered at times the Christian religion to the great scandal of some of its pontiffs. In any case, the Voodoo religion, as it presents itself with its air of mystery which one finds at the origin of all religions, is nothing else than a syncretism of beliefs. Price-Mars became quite heated as he asked this other question: "Were the Blacks of Saint-Domingue really the crude superstitious people our historians speak about?":

> No, I shall answer from a saner analysis of the religious sentiment and a better interpretation of the facts. There are no superstitions capable of engendering the magnificent élan of spirituality that lifted the souls of our forefathers and made possible the miracle of 1804.
>
> Superstition? The faith that drove the black bands of Hyacinth in 1791, in the Plain of Cul-de-Sac, to rush without arms against the artillery of the French soldiers of Artois to plunge their hands into the cannons to remove the bullets?
>
> Superstition? The faith that engendered such sublime acts along with the thought that the souls of the martyrs would be born again in a black fatherland where justice may find a better soil to grow than in the inferno of Saint-Domingue?[26]

At the end of his talk Price-Mars expressed a great apprehension on his mind coupled with a great sorrow in his heart as he spoke of the "awakening of the peoples of Africa (following the First World War) from North to South, from East to West, under the double banner of race and religion—nationalism of the young Senegalese, of the young Dahomeyans, of the *young Turks* in general."

From what he will say just a while later, one is almost certain that he was deeply distressed as he thought about the young Haitians. During the same year he delivered this lecture, Léon Laleau published a book of verses *La Flèche au Coeur* (Arrow in the Heart) whose theme was love with some of the poems taking their inspiration from classical Greek poetry, to say nothing of M. Etzer Vilaire, a poet of the generation of the centennial of Haiti's independence. Vilaire had found it possible in 1919 when Charlemagne Péralte was actually crucified by the Marines to escape to a French literary period dating back one hundred years. He wrote poems about peaceful sunsets with the Romantic's sense of detachment.

At the time Price-Mars delivered his talk "The Vocation of the Elite," some of the younger writers of Laleau's age had created *The League of Haitian Youth* which published a "Bulletin." The publication did not last long and Price-Mars lamented the fact. Perhaps he was thinking about them when he advised his audience not to let failure cripple them, to try again, saying, "The right to effort has not lapsed."

As he had espoused Cincinnatus Leconte's plan for the "Reconstruction of the City" he was naturally most interested in finding out what the younger men were thinking about, and he consulted the *League's* bulletins. He was glad to acknowledge that some of the younger writers showed promise of real literary talent. But he said he had found it impossible to detect the "true trend of thoughts of our young élite," either from his personal investigation about them or from the reading of their writings. In the League's bulletins appeared some suggestions regarding the "Reconstruction of the City." Although these suggestions depicted preoccupations perhaps of a high order, he said, "strangely they seemed to me only mere echoes, slightly attenuated, of things from overseas." On the one hand, their preoccupations were concerned with the implementation of the ideas of the French Revolution, which prompted this remark from Price-Mars:

> Unless I am mistaken in viewing the thoughts of two or three writers as the preoccupations of a whole group, it seems to me that from among the ideas which dominate the minds of our youth one may detect a certain apprehension regarding the legal structure of the City and moreover a restrained fear, even a certain bewilderment that the City might be too democratic.[27]

On the other hand, their preoccupations had to do with the role of the Catholic Church in the National undertaking. About that, Price-Mars commented that "the gods of Africa have not completely yielded to Jesus of Nazareth ("among the immense majority of the Haitian people"), and even (you hear me) among many of us of the élite ... the cooperation and juxtaposition of the two creeds works as a sort of mutual counter-insurance against the mysteries of the life-beyond."[23]

Obviously Price-Mars was painfully shocked by the fact that the minds of the younger generation were not running at all in the same direction with his in the search of an elixir that would revive the moribund Fatherland. Some other realities perhaps affected him still more painfully. On November 22, 1922, the Council of State had passed a law establishing a "Service Technique d'Agriculture," Price-Mars' great dream. Whether or not he had had anything to do with that, President Borno immediately invited Dr. Robert R. Moton, President of Tuskegee Institute, to come to Haiti to discuss with the Haitian government the possibilities and conditions for establishing Vocational schools in Haiti on the Tuskegee pattern. Unable at that time to make the trip, Dr. Moton sent his assistant Mr. W. T. B. Williams. But this move fell through as a result of criticism by the citizens of the "Cultural Province of France" who showed the greatest hostility to such a project. They feared that the racist Americans would only make "hewers of wood and fetchers of water" of Haitian youth.

It was perhaps about this incident and many other indications of the same psychological reaction on the part of the Haitian élite that Price-Mars was thinking when at the end of his talk he attempted to speak as a prophet:

> I do not know what will become of Haiti around the year 2050, because the confused data I have are obscuring my anticipations. I see an élite thirsty for lively pleasures, without zeal or faith whatsoever. And what is even more serious, it has lost the sense of solidarity both social and ethnic. For, you see, no greater offense can be done to a man of our élite than to tell him he is a Negro—whatever may be the color of his skin, black as the night or fair as the day.
>
> Ah! one may be a refined Black—please admire the euphemism—marabou, griffe, chabine, mulatto, white.[29] But to be Negro, collectively and conventionally speaking, no one deigns or wants to be so. However, it is the fact that we are Negroes that gives us some originality.
>
> I do not know what will become of this country in a not too distant future when I look at the mass of the people bound by the fetters of ignorance under a superficial sprinkling of formal Catholicism, while the élite camouflage their shortcomings under an attitude of elegant detachment. Anarchy at the base and cowardice and hypocrisy at the top. I do not know what will become of this country—maybe a mere geographical expression in the American Mediterranean, inhabited by industrial pariahs.[30]

But Price-Mars' soul rebounded from the combined action of his natural confidence and enthusiasm as he thought about his black brothers on the American Continent and the Dark Continent:

> But on the contrary, I perceive an immense future of glory and progress for the black communities of the United States as a revenge of immortal justice. I foresee a glorious triumph over the forces of oppression: physical forces, economic forces, social forces, in behalf of the black communities of Africa. And all these things will come to pass as a result of the spiritual élan which is carrying these people under the double banner of Race and Faith.[31]

Happily indeed Price-Mars' words proved to be true in regard to the Blacks in the United States and those of Africa. But he was wrong in his morose prophesy about Haiti's youth. Long before his predictions will be fulfilled in the United States and Africa, the youth of Haiti—in their early twenties and some of them still youngsters—"will come marching on," proudly keeping step with him under the double banner of Race and Faith, only a few months later.

Eleven

Thus Spoke The Uncle . . .

In 1926, "the Occupation was expanding in all its beauty," with an iron fist. And President Borno warned the Haitian People that the American Forces would not leave the country until after they have finished helping his Government "to concretize" its plans for a more prosperous and dignified Haiti. He defended his policy of "frank and loyal collaboration with the Americans" during the past four years as he approached the elections for the Presidency of the Republic, the lone candidate.

Ever since Borno's inauguration to the High Office in May 1922, the country had been under a strongly welded two-headed dictatorship, made up of the President and General John H. Russell, who had returned to Haiti in March 22 as the first civilian head of the Occupation with the title of U. S. High Commissioner and the rank of Ambassador. The Opposition had found itself powerless before the bicephalous government which made the subservient Council of State pass laws in 1922, 1923 and 1924, restricting constitutional liberties. Georges Sylvain died on August 2 of that year and was buried amid national consternation, baring his soul in one of his last poems:

> Haiti, arise! the monster which is dragging you
> To the abyss, to shame and grief will be frightened
> If it sees the conscience of Mankind rise!
> Make the world shiver by your cries of pain!

> Show the wound of your soul where your dream is dying
> So that in the far away nights of time your fate shall not
> Have to suffer this funeral offense. They failed to defend
>   themselves.
> It's sinful for Right when violated not to protest!

> Even if the whole world should remain deaf to your cries
> Make your voice louder and increase your lament
> So their ardent and superhuman tone may arouse
> The ancestors sleeping in the peace of their graves.

> O Land of epics, of fierce warrior,
> Knowing your History I have faith in your destiny
> Despite your neglect, your doubts, your poverty.
> I love you and wish you to be free: Haiti, arise!¹

Price-Mars continued his teaching undisturbed at the Lycée and his work in the field of ethnography. He worked the more diligently because he felt that under the prevailing political circumstances in Haiti the United States might eventually "erase her from the map of the world."² However, he was deeply confident that the herbs he had gathered in the field of Haitian folklore, which he first presented to view at the Primavera Club in 1922, could prevent the death of the "Fatherland."

His confidence and hope received a great stimulus in 1925, when at long last two young writers began to scent the very aroma that had intoxicated Price-Mars, that of their own land. In the July issue of *La Nouvelle Ronde,* of that year, Antonio Vieux, a Black, and Philippe Thoby-Marcelin, a Mulatto, both 21, undertook jointly in an article to question the authenticity of Haitian literature:

> For a Haitian literature to have existed it would have been necessary for the works to reflect more of the aspirations, the temperament, the very soul of the country . . . Our elders have produced some works of worth. However, they have not produced works that were profoundly ours. The Haitian soul must be uncovered and analyzed in its bareness. Only by doing that can we get the originality that has been sought after with such obsession, which has been sought after so far away, except where it was possible to find it.³

Nevertheless, these young poets presented at that time in their works nothing which was vividly Haitian. Obviously, Philippe had got his inspiration for the above statement from his great-uncle Frédéric Marcelin, without giving too much thought to what the author of *Autour de deux romans* had in mind. Curiously enough, it was from a profound reflexion on Frédéric Marcelin's thought that Price-Mars had come to think about the elixir to save the "Fatherland" and invigorate him for new triumphs, to be sure, not on the field of battle, but in the field of the arts and literature. For he believed with Frédéric Marcelin that "To a great extent, it is literature which makes the soul of a people. It is . . . the most educational, the most precious testimony of its genius and originality. We must direct our effort to this task and toward this most desirable end."⁴

And the moment to do so—more urgent than at any time before—was now, when the "Fatherland" was on the verge of perishing for the simple reason that it had been living on a borrowed soul—an artificial one which had kept it weaker and weaker since

Independence until its pitiful fall under foreign white control. And this was the thought which had crystallized in Price-Mars' mind and became so painful that he had not cared about hurting his old and proven friend Pauléus Sannon in his last talk.

For lack of financial means *La Nouvelle Ronde* soon disappeared. Another review, *La Trouée* (The Break-Through) also created by young writers in their 20's appeared on July 1, 1927 and took up the fight against "pastiche" in Haitian letters, affirming that "Literature . . . is the cry of the people who want to say what is boiling inside of them."[5] But for the same reason, like *La Nouvelle Ronde* it published only one issue. The same month of July one of its editors, Jacques Roumain, joined another group of young writers to create *La Revue Indigène* under the editorship of Normil Sylvain,[6] the son of Georges Sylvain of l'Union Patriotique.

The founders of *La Revue Indigène* were seven in number. They were the brothers and friends of the young ladies of the Primavera Club. Only two of them had never left Haiti. All the others had lived in France where one of them had published his only book, *Poèmes d'Haiti et de France* (Poems of Haiti and France).[7] Nevertheless they took up the ax to proceed on the demolition of the Temple of French Imitation. They created quite a stir in the Haitian Parnassus less perhaps by their works than by their attacks on their elders and sometimes by the violence and disorder of their lives. They were determined to nail Lamartine to his "Crucifix"* or to drown him in his "Lac,"* as they would say around the tables in the cafés they frequented.

They came closer to Price-Mars. In the second issue of the review, its editor wrote: "Our folklore is full of . . . songs. It is the sound of tam-tams . . . the call of the conch-shell . . . the agitated and sensual rhythm of the meringue with its lascivious melancholy which must condition our poetry."[8] However, they wrote in French not in Creole, and in ultra-modern French. "They imitated in that respect French writers like Toulet, Eluard, Carcot and Drieux la Rochelle, just as their predecessors had imitated Hugo, Lamartine, Coppée, Rostand, Verlaine, Mallarmé, de Lisle or Baudelaire. But, though cutting their cloth according to French patterns, they added to the design of the garment their local or racial inspiration, an art both personal and new."[9]

However, they had come closer to Price-Mars only to a certain degree. Their movement was primarily literary, except perhaps for Jacques Roumain and Carl Brouard who breathed also an air of social revolution. In December of that year, Price-Mars had completed work on his second book which, he said, was written from "a long ambition to restore to the eyes of the Haitian people the

---

*Titles of two famous poems of Lamartine.

worth of their folklore."[10] Philippe Thoby-Marcelin had said in 1925, "The Haitian soul must be uncovered and analyzed in its bareness." In 1928, Price-Mars did just that with his second book *Ainsi Parla l'Oncle* (Thus Spoke The Uncle) which shook Haiti to her foundations.

Haiti, said Price-Mars in that book, from her independence and through the years that followed, had tried to achieve what she thought to be her superior destiny: to fashion her thoughts and sentiments after those of her former mother country, to look like and to identify herself with France. As a result of this long and patient endeavor the Haitians have fallen into a "collective bovarism," that is, seeing themselves other than they really are. But as a result also of an "implacable logic" as the Haitians strove to pretend to be French and wished to establish themselves as such among the peoples of the world, they were undoing themselves as Haitians—people born in a certain historical framework who have amassed in their souls, as does any other human group, a psychological complex which gives the Haitian community its specific physiognomy. As a consequence, all that is truly indigenous became suspicious and of bad taste in the eyes of the country's élites in their nostalgia for the lost "fatherland." Thus the work "African" has always been and is still the most humiliating adjective that could be applied to the Haitians. "The most distinguished man of this country," affirmed Price-Mars, "would prefer to be told that he resembles an Eskimo, a Samoyed or a Toungouzeen rather than to be reminded of his Guinean or Sudanese ancestry."[11] Then Price-Mars asked the following crucial questions:

> Does Haitian society have a background of oral traditions, legends, tales, songs, riddles, customs, observances, ceremonies, and beliefs which are characteristic of it or that it has assimilated so as to give them its personal imprint? And if this folklore exists, what is its value from the literary and scientific point of view?[12]

No other country, Price-Mars felt, has a richer stock of stories and legends than Haiti. And if one studies them it will not be unusual for him to find among them some subjects which combine the various literary genders: epic, drama, comedy and satire. The comic and the satiric, he pointed out, are brought forth more often not through the narration of the story, which is always simple and naive, but from "the realism and picturesque appearance of its characters."[13] Obviously he was thinking here of Frédéric Marcelin, for later on in the work he will say: "Who before Marcelin had ever thought of gathering these sheaves of popular beliefs so as to bring forth the realistic and picturesque effects he has imparted to some of his books."

Ainsi Parla l'Oncle is illustrated by the picture of an old, ragged peasant, called "Uncle Bouqui" who with "Ti-Malice" is the most popular character of Haitian stories and legends. For Price-Mars, Bouqui represents a certain force made up of patience, of resignation and of wit "as it is possible to detect their expression among the masses of our peasants in the mountain regions." Whereas Bouqui's inseparable companion, Ti-Malice, is worldly and crafty. It is obvious that now Price-Mars identifies himself with "Uncle Bouqui."

The author takes great pleasure in telling some of the stories that have charmed the imagination of all Haitian children, regardless of their social condition, and in which everything generally enters: heaven and earth, men, animals, plants and trees. But he warned:

> ... as interesting as the oral traditions are ... as suggestive as they may appear, they constitute only a very small part of the entangled mass of our folklore. The beliefs are its most apparent and the most suggestive expression.[14]

Then Price-Mars undertook to ascertain the origin of those beliefs while trying to bring forth their symbolism. He did that through five chapters of the book under the following titles: 1. Popular beliefs; 2. Africa, her races and civilization; 3. African societies and the outside world; 4. African animism, and 5. Religious sentiment among Haitian masses.

In the course of his long journey across Africa, Price-Mars indicated the source of the various Haitian beliefs and explained how eventually they amalgamated into a special form of religion in Saint-Domingue, the colonial Voodoo, which from then on evolved under the influence of Catholicism into a close association with the latter.

Besides, knowing that in the eyes of Haitian intellectuals, from the haphazard information they had gathered from authors usually unsympathetic to the Black man, Africa was the land of barbarism where only the crudest forms of superstition were to be found, Price-Mars undertook in those chapters to destroy that traditional stereotype of the "Dark Continent." He recalled the memory of the theocratic state of Fouta-Djallon in French Guinea where Peuhls and Mandingos "constantly showed a taste for the study of belles-lettres up to our days." The people of Bénin and of Yoruba have made themselves known by their works in bronze as well as in clay, "revealing a remarkable sense of beauty." Then he recalled the memory of the political and social organization of the Kingdom of Dahomey whose civil administration, army and sense of discipline were of the highest order. Thanks to the Kingdom's cohesion it remained independent under the same dynasty from the sixteenth century until the French conquest in 1894.

Price-Mars alluded to the U. S. Marine office Hickey's and the French priest's story about the girl who had been killed by a hougan and then revived by the hougan. He blamed such stories, on the one hand, on the "almost general Haitian belief in supranatural illness." More often than not, death is considered as the result of malefic and mysterious power vested in Voodoo believers. On the other hand, referring to the French priest of the story, he said:

> ... these legends are not new. A long long time ago, had not a Father Labas brazenly declared that a slave girl by mysterious means had stolen the lives of five officers of the ship that was transporting her and that she had even given the spectacle of sucking from a distance the pulp of a melon? The good Father's imagination raises no questions.

Price-Mars recalled the *Pellé Affaire* of 1863 to reject the thought that such practice of human sacrifice is currently happening in voodoo, though in a remote past it may have been part of the African religion as it was for the Jews to show their gratitude to Yahweh for his protection over Israel. Even in the twentieth century in Catholic Spain superstition had engendered the barbaric killing of a boy in the witchcraft drama, known as the *Léona Affaire*. This took place in the village of Gador in 1910, in the Province of Almeira. There, too, the culprits were brought before the criminal court and sentenced to death. Price-Mars believed that the juxtaposition of the two creeds since colonial time has brought about a confusion of their principles:

> Don't the Catholic, and the Voodoo worshipper believe in the existence of a supreme God? Don't they both believe in His unceasing intervention in the course of human life as well as in the realm of universal phenomena? Don't they believe Him sensitive to offense, terrible in vengeance and yet merciful, responsive to prayer and to the offerings of his poor creatures lost in misery and sin? Don't they both believe in supernatural beings—saints, angels, and demons—who stand between man and his creator and are ever disposed to concern themselves with the affairs of this world? Don't they trust in the power of saints as intercessors before the Supreme Divinity on behalf of a pitiful humanity? Isn't it true that both of them maintain that reason is important to explain the most essential things of life, which are its origins and end? Isn't it a fact that both have found almost the same term-mystery–to envelop their ignorance of any phenomena that seem unexplainable to them? Moreover, are they not both obsessed by the fear of Satan? But despite these elements of similarity it is the differences that stand out when one compares one belief with the other. These differences manifest themselves especially in the cults through which Catholics and Voodoo followers express their religious sentiments. These differences increase in proportion as the Catholic faith acquires intellectual bases and justifies its existence by a body of dogmas whose purity and integrity are placed under the custody of a spiritual authority *realus* of preserving their tradition and character. Whereas the Voodoo ceremony displays the emotional bareness of its symbols,

unintelligible even to those who use them, the faithful Catholic can establish the relationship between the smallest detail of the Catholic ritual and . . . a revelation received directly from heaven. The origin of this faith confers upon its considerable prestige and authority over most religious manifestations, and so it exerts a great attraction on unorganized cults whose secret ambition is to assimilate some of the elements which assure the prestige of the Church. Hence the clumsy imitation by Voodoo worshippers of all that constitutes the outward aspects of Catholicism: the pomp and magnificence of the Catholic ritual, the mystery of signs, the sumptuousness of sacred vestments.[15]

In going over the subject once more, what Price-Mars was aiming at primarily was to contradict the Haitian historians, among them Pauléus Sannon, who view the independence of Haiti as the brain-child of the freemen of Saint-Domingue and who moreover "take pride in being good Christians." On the contrary Price-Mars gave most of the credit to the ignorant Blacks of the former colony, putting the emphasis on the inspiration they had received from their African gods in the historic and heroic struggle:

The savage struggles that marked the beginning of the fight for the rights of man in Saint-Domingue found expression during the outbreak of 1791 in a completely Voodoo-like ceremony—the oath of blood. During thirteen years of violence, privation, and bitter suffering the Blacks found in their faith in the African gods the heroic strength that permitted them to face death and accomplish the miracle of 1804: the creation of a Black nation in the West Indies.[16]

Price-Mars, who confessed in his youth to a burning desire for literary triumph, shows in both his first works the effects of that obsession which lead him to be pedantical at times while often involving him in an array of long sentences for oratorical effect. But one finds really good prose in *Ainsi Parla l'Oncle* such as the description of Ville-Bonheur,[17] the picturesque hamlet in the Artibonite Province where on July 16, a multitude of faithful of both the Church and Voodoo meet for syncretic religious devotion in daytime as well as for demoniac orgy at night.

The fact remains that Price-Mars seems to be monotonous in the larger part of his first two books for he is dealing all the time with one question: the Black Man. While the young writers of the *Revue Indigène* staged a revolt in the Haitian Parnassus, he, Price-Mars, was thinking of a Cultural Revolution that would shake the nation to its foundations so as to rouse the people from their lethargy and project them on the road of progress. One of the Haitian legends he recalled in *Ainsi Parla l'Oncle* tells us of his continuous concern, apparent in all its writings:

Is it the question to explain the diversity of man on the planet and how, we Haitians, are still bringing up the rear in the race toward progress? A legend will tell you that on a certain day God having finished the work of the Creation called before His throne the White, the Mulatto and the Black and told them this: 'I wish to endow each one of you with special aptitudes. Tell me your wishes, I shall fulfill them at once. The White immediately asked for world domination through wisdom, wealth, the arts and science. The Mulatto wanted to resemble the White—which meant that he would follow the latter—but when the time came for the Black to speak, the story reached the height of burlesque. 'And you, my friend, said the good Lord, what do you want? The Black became intimidated, chattered some unintelligible words, and as the good Lord insisted, the Black turned about and finally said, *'M'pas besoin angnin. Cè ac ces Messiè là m'vini'* (I don't need anything, I just came along with these gentlemen).[18]

As Price-Mars saw it, only through creative activity in the arts and literature based on their folklore, will the Haitians get rid of their inferiority complex through discarding their borrowed French soul and becoming wholly Haitian. He is terribly singleminded about that, and for that reason he seems to produce the impression of monotony in his two books. Actually, though he is dealing with one question: the Black Man, he is dealing with two different things now for two different ends which intermingle, however, in his mind. On the one hand, from his first talk in 1906, he has been viewing the Black man through Haiti both as a historian and a sociologist. Like Firmin and Hannibal Price he saw only the Haitian. The historian was proud of the glorious deed of the forefathers while the sociologist was ashamed of the kind of society in which the Haitian people had lived since Independence.

But beginning in 1922, when he lectured at the Primavera Club, still speaking of the Black man, as a Haitian, Price-Mars viewed him no longer through Haiti but through Africa. Thus he no longer sees only the Haitian; he only sees the Black man whose native country is Africa. The black man of the United States and the black natives of Africa are no longer his brothers. They have become his very self. And in shaping his own personality, beginning in 1922, he is no longer so much concerned with becoming a great Haitian writer as was Delorme and Firmin. He is endeavoring to make of himself an authentic Black Man, adorned with all human potential, but evolving within his special black cultural climate. His works, however, must go into the mainstream of civilization for the benefit of the Black Race and the general progress of mankind as a whole.

The Occupation of Haiti and the World War which are coincidental in terms of time, constitute the line of demarcation between the two Price-Mars, the Haitian and the African. The first believed with Hannibal Price that Haiti was "the Mecca, the Judea of the Black Race . . . to which every man with black blood in his veins should go in pilgrimage at least once in his lifetime, because it is there that the Negro had made himself a man." The second Price-Mars is no longer looking toward the past. In light of developments brought about in Black Africa at the end of the World War by the "young Turks" marching "under the double banner of Black Pride and faith in the Black race," the pilgrimage for men with black blood must now be toward Africa. The Negroes of the United States have already started on the journey—spiritually with their so-called "Harlem Renaissance." The Haitians, too, must get on the way. And they are the more compelled to rush on the spiritual trip because the American Occupation has placed a "tragic uncertainty" over the destiny of their moribund "Fatherland."

In a booklet he published the following year under the title *On the "Negro Renaissance" in the United States*, which he said he wrote in an attempt to bring to the attention of the Haitian public this movement of "Black values" so as to shake some Haitian intellectuals from their lethargy and others from their stupidity, Price-Mars deplored the fact that the white world had denied the black man any intellectual capacity in order to turn him into an agricultural instrument for creating wealth for the sole benefit of the white world.

Considering the surge of black talent of the "Harlem Renaissance," he asked this question: "Should not one call this movement 'The Negro revenge?'"[19] And he went on to quote the following passage from President Lincoln's Second Inaugural Address:

> Fondly do we hope—fervently do we pray—that this mighty scourge of war may speedily pass away. Yet, if God wills that it continue until all the wealth piled by the bondman's two hundred and fifty years of unrequited toil shall be sunk, and until every drop of blood drawn with the lash shall be paid by another drawn with the sword, as was said three thousand years ago, so still it must be said, "The judgments of the Lord are true and righteous altogether."[20]

Price-Mars then depicted the "formation of the élite" of the Black community in the United States, extolling their solidarity "based on common suffering and common aspiration" which constitutes the strength of the American black community. He added, "that this solidarity reveals itself by the development of an unequivocal black consciousness and black pride, this is what makes its originality."[21] He quoted W. E. Burghardt DuBois: "In my veins flows a little of Dutch blood, a little of French blood, some drops of Anglo-Saxon blood happily submerged by a large wave of black blood, Thank God."

The conclusion Price-Mars drew from his study of the "Harlem Renaissance" was presented in the form of a question, which is his usual manner of emphasizing this thought:

> Does it not appear that we (Haitians) ought to make an effort of introspection so as finally to take consciousness of ourselves, of our qualities and shortcomings in order to draw from them some subjects of literature and art as well as of applied psychology and even of experimental pedagogy?
>
> Does it not appear that it is time for us to stop leaning on the window to listen to the notes of flutes others are playing while applying them to ourselves as if they express either the joy or the sadness of our souls?[22]

This was the import of *Ainsi Parla l'Oncle*. In returning to the same subject with the express purpose indicated in his booklet on the Harlem Renaissance, Price-Mars obviously was aroused by the criticism made of his work. While a Dr. Dorsainvil declared that *Ainsi* was a remarkable work, presenting a better analysis of theories than Firmin's *De l'Egalité des races humaines*,[23] an anonymous writer published in the newspaper *La Presse* a series of humoristic jabs at the author under the title "Thus Spoke the Nephew." The second oldest newspaper of the Haitian capital, *Le Matin*, published a criticism of *Ainsi Parla l'Oncle* which was about the length of the book, from the month of November 1928 to January 1929, chiding the author either about his bookish knowledge of Africa that he had never visited or about his pretention of wanting to restrain the writers' freedom of inspiration and choice of subject matter. Such a reaction, of course, was that of the citizens of the "Cultural Province of France."

Indeed Price-Mars was very hard on the later. Even Demesvar Delorme, whom he called in his book "our greatest man of letters of the past century," was furiously lashed by Price-Mars for his lack of sensitivity in regard to Haitian things and for having situated the plots of his novels outside of Haiti:

> In our opinion Mr. Delorme has sacrificed to one of the most stupid among the shallowest prejudices that restrain Haitian productivity, namely that our society, in the past as in the present existence, offers no interest to the art of the novelist. Thus he has ignored a thousand and one moving dramas, troubling incidents of the tragi-comedy of which Haitian life is woven; he has ignored this perplexing human group where collective and individual vanity, social hypocrisy and solemn stupidity attack most fiercely the simplicity of the heart, serene devotion, the proper development of the mind as well as the moral sense. He was not even aware of the fact that these things exist.[24]

Price-Mars remarked that while Delorme, thanks to his prodigious literary talents, could have easily been a great French writer, he was not known in French literature, and as far as Haitian literature is concerned he "almost does not exist." Price-Mars is far from thinking about restraining the writer's freedom: "We are not thinking, and I want to repeat it, we are not thinking about restraining the writer's freedom." He agreed that some Haitian writers have given to their works an "indigenous character" thanks to their talents and the use of Creole. And in that connection he criticized Georges Sylvain, the author of *Cric-Crac*, for translating La Fontaine's fables into Creole in that book:

> By the languages he makes his characters speak, people and animals, even when they are not of our land, he succeeds very often in giving them the intonation and the appearance of people of our land. One asks but why did he feel the need of modeling his thought on that of the outstanding fabulist?
>
> Do you see the magnificent original creation Georges Sylvain would have made if he had forgotten La Fontaine and had got his subject entirely from the legends and popular stories of Haiti? Is it not unfortunate that we lost this great opportunity of having a literary masterpiece of Haitian folklore?[25]

In writing about *Cric-Crac* Price-Mars certainly remembered his joy on listening to similar stories of his father based on Haitian folklore as a child at Grande Rivière du Nord and his subsequent amazement on discovering the work of the French fabulist at the Grégoire College in Cap-Haitian. But in 1928, discussing Haitian literature and art in *Ainsi Parla l'Oncle* these brought him no merriment. More importantly, he was not discussing for literature's and art's sake. Literary talents like those of Georges Sylvain and the use of Creole by Haitian writers may have produced books presenting an "indigenous character" but for him now that was not enough:

> ... besides that there must be something else that is larger, truer in terms of human and Haitian life. It is necessary that the material for our works be drawn sometimes from this immense reservoir of our folklore, where for centuries the motives of our will have been condensed, where the elements of our sensitivity have been built, and where the fibers of our identity and our national soul have been woven.[26]

Price-Mars remarked that in the sole novel dealing with Voodoo, *Mimola*,[27] by Antoine Innocent, the story "is swaddled with apologetical worry." He wanted Haitian writers and Haitian artists to free themselves from such mental straight-jackets in order to produce works in literature, art and music that "make obvious the aptitude of the race for a personal art, generator of thought and emotion." And it is precisely Voodoo that he saw as the source of Haitian creative works "of a new and original vein" in those fields, viewing primarily such works as the elixir made of black consciousness and black pride that was needed to revive the moribund "Fatherland."

The reaction to *Ainsi Parla l'Oncle* among Haitian youth was no less immediate than that of their elders. But it was an exultant approval of its author's pronouncement, which the young took much less as a literary and artistic guide than as a spiritual and patriotic credo—exactly what Price-Mars intended it to be. At that moment when the Bicephalous Government indicated its firm resolve to carry on indefinitely,[28] the young taking at once a strong dose of Price-Mars' elixir of black consciousness and black pride, were ready to challenge both the "racist Uncle Sam" and his Haitian "lackey" at the National Palace. Some of the more radical among them went so far as to advocate making Voodoo the National religion, perhaps more in defiance of the "Catholic Musketeer," who had a chapel set up at the National Palace where every morning he attended mass said by a French priest; and obviously the French Catholic hierarchy had washed their hands of the Haitian national ordeal.

Thus the phrase "Return to Africa!" in a fervent exclamation became the password of nationalist proselytes throughout the capital. The elders of those belonging to the mundane élite—fathers, mothers, uncles and aunts—repeated in the form of a question "Return to Africa?", the males with a smirk on their angry faces and the females whispering a "Jésus-Marie-Joseph" while lifting their hands to the sky.

Price-Mars' first book, *La Vocation de l'Elite*, had established him as a crusader for social justice among the young people at the Haitian capital and in other Haitian cities. *Ainsi Parla l'Oncle* concretized the very dream he had nursed ever since he was a boy at the Grégoire College, establishing his name this time as a scholar and a scientist among Haitian intellectuals. It also brought him a much larger fame than either Delorme or Firmin had ever enjoyed beyond Haiti's frontiers—that of becoming the Patron Saint of a world-wide cultural revolution: *négritude*. In that respect Senghor had this to say:

> There are names that sound like manifestoes. Price-Mars' name was revealed to me as such when I heard it for the first time. As a student at the Sorbonne I had begun to ponder on the problem of a cultural Renaissance in Black Africa, and I was looking for—we were looking for—a sponsor who could insure the success of that undertaking.
>
> At the end of my search I was to find Alain Locke and Jean Price-Mars. And I read *Ainsi Parla l'Oncle* at a breath as one drinks water from a cistern, in the evening, returning from a long trip in the desert. I was gratified to the full. The Uncle was supporting the reason for my search, approving what I had felt. For, as he showed me the wealth of Négritude he had discovered on and in Haitian soil, he taught me how to discover the same value, but virgin and stronger, on and in African soil.
>
> ... all black ethnologists and writers of French expression owe a great deal to Jean Price-Mars: essentially this truth that "we have a chance to be ourselves only if we do not reject any part of the ancestral heritage." Particularly the writers. First the Haitians—

Roumain, Dépestre and others—but also the Caribbeans and the Africans: a Damas, a Césaire, a Niger, a Birago Diop, and especially myself.[29]

Georges Sylvain

Twelve

The Inveterate "Foolish Dreams"

Apparently Price-Mars had no quarrel with President Borno about the way the latter was administering the Republic, for there is no record of his writing or speaking about the renewed political tension. By the Plebiscite of February 1929, the Bicephalous Government had amended the Constitution to bring under its thumb all the magistrates of the Republic, including the Justices of the Supreme Court, heretofore independent and irremovable. The President had formed the National Progressive Party which practically bound together all public functionaries under his leadership. While many of its members were dithyrambic boosters of the Government's achievements, a public servant was not compelled to join the Party and could remain in his position if he kept quiet. Obviously Price-Mars remembered how he had been dismissed from his teaching post in 1922. In 1929, as in the past, his salary as a teacher was about all he had to keep body and soul together.

As a matter of fact, Price-Mars seemed to enjoy the Government's favor for he was invited to speak on October 9, 1929 at the Central School of Agriculture. Such an invitation could not have been issued without prior approval of the National Palace at a time when some of the students had started to voice dissatisfaction with the policies of the school's American administrators.

Price-Mars accepted the invitation, fully aware of the political importance he had acquired among Haitian youth with his recently published *Ainsi Parla l'Oncle*. Speaking on the subject, "What the country may expect from the Technical Service of Agriculture," he began tactfully:

> Of the Technical Service I only know what I read in your publications. Should I know more about it my method of work would prevent me from expressing a valid opinion unless I were in a position to exercise a strict control over what I read, what I see and what I hear . . . However, I came, responding to the cordial invitation . . . And why? Have I succumbed to some taste for parade or to a secret inclination for the tinsel of vain words?
>
> I came to you because in fact I am in communion of thought with you. I came to you because I am in sympathy at least with the

principle of your institution. Many years ago I called for such a realization with all my heart.¹

He then read part of the article he had published on the matter in *L'Essor* in 1912. With the flair of a politician he declared: "The creation of the Central School of Agriculture is in conformity with one of my most formally expressed and reaffirmed plans for social transformation." And he went on to say:

> If human geography is understood as the facts of transformation of a part of the world by the will of man, is it not true that all the transformations of the Haitian land have been accomplished by the black man ... If the principal factor of these transformations is the black man it seems correct to say that he is the greatest wealth of this country.²

Calling attention to the fact that Haiti had never had an agricultural school from 1804 to the present day though she is primarily an agricultural country, and viewing that fact as "a tendency toward contradiction which is at the basis of our collective personality," he explained:

> All Haitian education has had but one objective, a latent rather than a formal objective, dimly felt rather than clearly expressed; an objective which consists in producing highly educated men so that by their very existence and great culture, they can refute the thesis upheld by others that the black man is inferior.³

Paying no attention to the political hue and cry against the Americans, Price-Mars told the people at the School of Agriculture that they were applying "fruitful pedagogical method, the American method *par excellence:* Learning by doing," and that what was expected from them was the transformation of the peasants through the renovation of their agricultural methods so as to enhance in their own eyes the use of their lands. He ended his talk with this warning:

> Without deep sympathy the human material you are manipulating will rebel and will be recalcitrant in your hands. But I have faith in the remote future of your work because its success depends on time. This is why I came simply to tell you what people expect of you for a higher standard of living.⁴

A fortnight later some of the students of the Central School of Agriculture went on strike, protesting against a measure taken by the American head of the School, a Dr. Freeman, who had diverted scholarship money from students to hire more American experts for the institution. As the striking students were expelled on November 4, the politicians at the capital began to stir, and on December 6, when the tragic event of Marchaterre took place⁵, Port-au-Prince erupted in anger and the Opposition openly joined the young demonstrators of the Central School of Agriculture in a general strike which in no time spread throughout the country.*

*At that point the Occupation imposed Martial Law in Haiti.

It was about that time that Price-Mars published his third book, *A Stage of Haitian Evolution*. The main purpose of the book was to refute Gustave Le Bon's contention that the mixed-blood are inferior to their progenitors. Price-Mars tried to show that the offspring of African slaves and French settlers of Saint-Domingue had reached such a high degree of intellectual development that this fact by itself conclusively demolished the contention of the French anthropologist who would have us believe that his fantasy was supported by some law of heredity:

> So many conditions are necessary to produce a man that it is futile to simplify the role of the various influences which form his character, his temperament, his psychological constitution. All these elements mixed together fashion his personality, explain his conduct, and finally create a man. Therefore it is absurd to believe that all these complex components can be reduced to the simplicity of the law of quarters.[6] True and verifiable in the elementary life of plants, the doctrine is inadequate for human life. Because the human organism is complicated to the extreme. For thousands of years man has been a product of cross-breeding, living according to his whims. The idea of a pure race is a myth in anthropology. On the contrary cross-breeding is a biological fact as certain and undeniable as the connection between our organism and some humbler form of the animal series. The only thing which is still debatable is the quality of the cross-breeding in a given group, the stablilization more or less achieved in the various mixtures, which gives a more or less accentuated homogeneity to the products and which molds the physiognomy of the various human species according to the circumstances of time, climate and history. One does not pretend to deny that a greater homogeneity, a perfect stablization of the diverse elements entering in the make-up of a human race . . . nation or people being led to progress by the development of their minds, the spirituality of their beliefs and the exaltation of the character among them would not offer a magnificent example of collective organization where all that makes the pride and glory of our species we call civilization would find its highest expression.[7]

Price-Mars went on to say that most human communities are trying to reach that ideal with untiring endeavor and countless vicissitudes as well. But none of them can pride themselves on having fully realized that ideal. So he felt that in the present stage of socio-psychology it is somewhat foolhardy to crystallize idle affirmations into the term of "laws." Moreover, it will be necessary to attach oneself exclusively to man's biological nature in order to determine his capacity for progress. Price-Mars thought that the work of determining the mentality of a human group was a delicate and complex matter which in any case could not depend on the static morphology of its components. But he conceded that the Mendelian theory may help to understand certain atavistic oddities,

Price-Mars quoted from a book published anonymously in 1799: "There have been for two centuries more than 200,000 freemen and not one of them has left a name which the friends of science and letters remember." To this he retorted that, although most of the mixed-blood freemen who distinguished themselves in Saint-Domingue had studied in France, one could fairly say that none of them had reached a high degree of culture, and except for Moreau de Saint Méry, one could make the same observation about the white creole who represented the élite in Saint-Domingue and were the heirs of fifteen centuries of Christian civilization.

He ascribed the reason for such penury to the Saint-Domingue society itself:

> There was a degrading apathy in this milieu. Slavery produced not only the humiliating depravation of the victim, it also engendered the perversion of the master whose moral sense became dull and his will weak and who often drowned his idleness in debauchery of alcohol, gambling and women.[8]

But as the French Revolution broke out in Europe the revolutionaries undertook daily to realize the dreams of the philosophers, destroying the old concepts on which French society rested. However, the shortsightedness of the men in Saint-Domingue prompted them to try to take advantage of the principle of liberty and equality proclaimed by the Revolution for the sole benefit of their respective classes. This selfishness of the social classes brought about the violent convulsions from which Toussaint-Louverture emerged:

> On the theatre where he exercised his activities he was the greatest among all the men around—blacks, whites and mulattoes, whom he used to reach power. He was stronger than the events which he overcame and directed so as to realize his thought of domination and grandeur . . . He was neither a freeman nor a mixed-blood. Coming out from the herd of slaves he used the slaves as the potter does the clay to form a new human material from which Haitian nationality will emerge. Wendell Phillips indeed is right in saying that this prodigious black man has no match in human history, and it was with the intuition of a visionary that Lamartine would say of him, "This man was a nation."[9]

Price-Mars remarked that Toussaint's human potential remained latent until he reached the age of fifty when, usually in the Tropics and under better conditions than those Toussaint knew, most men begin to decline. Using Toussaint as a case in point he said: "It was the magnificent adventure of the French Revolution that brought about the atmosphere, the circumstances and the most favorable conditions for the emergence of this phenomenal genius." And he added:

> At the same time the same events created a group of remarkably talented men as the brilliant stars of a radiant constellation. A

Rigaud, a Dessalines, a Christophe, a Pétion, a Beauvais willingly or unwillingly went along with Toussaint until they got the opportunity one way or another to fashion by their own talents and heroism and even by their faults the dream of the genial promoter.[10]

Then Price-Mars proceeded to show both the difficult social conditions of the new black nation in 1804 and the sustained endeavor of each successive generation to produce the intellectual leaders the nation needed. With the writer's art, coupled with the erudition of a solid historian the author paints vivid frescoes of the various eras of Haitian life from independence to the time of Delorme and Boyer-Bazelais. Up to the time of the Nationals and Liberals the intellectual productions in the field of science and letters were rather scarce. The educated men of the past were primarily men of action. He remarked that as a result of the historical formation of the Haitian people it has always been in public life that the educated elements have revealed their talents. At this point Price-Mars shifted to the task of determining whether or not Haiti was going through "a crisis of men" for having failed to produce in the nineteenth century men of the stature of Delorme, Bazelais, Firmin, Edmond Paul:

> Already as it presents itself to our examination our era is one of the evolutionary stages which, by taking advantage of past achievements, shows our aptitude to increasing knowledge as well as to more efficient application of the intelligence. It predominates over the previous epochs . . . In that respect it only confirms one of the essential conditions of progress. If our era had failed in its task of producing men better educated and in greater number than those of previous generations, our society would have furnished the most conclusive evidence of the inferiority of our race. I am also confident that our children will surpass us and will give new luster to the Haitian concept of life. For it seems to me that in the evolution of peoples, in the elaboration of human thought and the progress of mankind we, too, have a role to play, and this role seems to be the result of the psychological complex that gives a specific mark to our collective personality.[11]

What he gave in support of his view is in the main an uncritical list of the outstanding intellectuals of his own period, writing this time in a somewhat rhapsodic style bordering on grandiloquence. Ernst Trouillot*, writing about *Uncle* with the greatest sympathy and veneration, warns us about Price-Mars' evocation of Haitian writers in *A Stage of Haitian Evolution:* "One must not see, Trouillot writes, "in those pages any very deep analysis of the various aspects and many tendencies of the writers. Nor must one view Dr. Mars as a literary critic in the proper meaning of the term, but rather as a

---

*Brother of Henock Trouillot, Price-Mars' close ideological friend and his long associate at the Société haitienne d'histoire, de géographie et de géologie.

scholar who wishes to justify his thesis: the aptitude of the Negro mind for the most varied intellectual productions." And he added: "Dr. Mars looks at the writers more on the surface than in depth."[12]

Ernst Trouillot's opinion naturally calls to mind the original concept of the book which *A Stage of Haitian Evolution* hardly fulfills. The subject of the book had been on Price-Mars' mind for many years. In his 1906 speech, "The Prejudice of Races," he had stated: " . . . what characterizes our evolution is the harmonious development of our mental faculties, the rapid conquest we have made in the intellectual domain . . . " And later, in his talk on "The Vocation of the Elite," delivered in 1917, Price-Mars told his audience:

> I had planned—and to offer it to you as a tribute—to examine the whole of our intellectual achievement, not only in establishing the number of works that have been produced in our country for about a century but also in giving my opinion as to their real worth so as to better measure the importance of the progress we have made.[13]

Price-Mars then confessed that he had failed in the attempt because "The ambition was too grandiose." He hoped that "others will take up the idea and carry it out better than I did."[14] This was indeed the subject matter of a monumental book of "sociopsychology," to use Price-Mars' own terms in describing the nature of the studies he was presenting in *A Stage of Haitian Evolution*. One is therefore suprised to see that after all that time and on a subject so close to his heart, both as a Haitian and a Black, Price-Mars finally decided in 1929 to produce only 208 pages. Only half of those pages deal directly with the subject matter indicated by the title of the book. The author himself found it necessary to defend the arrangement of his work, saying in his preface: "One would be quite wrong to think that the various materials included in the book are not closely related to the subject matter that gives the book its title."

A Stage of Haitian Evolution is divided into three parts. Part one contains some fifty pages which deal directly with the subject matter indicated by the book's titles; the rest of Part one is devoted to the discussion of the question of whether Haiti is going through a "crisis of man." The material that makes up Part two is a talk delivered in 1926 under the title, "The religious sentiment and phenomenon among the Blacks of Saint-Domingue," a critical analysis of Seabrook's *Magic Island*[15] and a short story, "Christmas of the Humble." Part three contains an exchange of letters between Price-Mars and Mrs. Blair Niles about her book *Black Haiti*. Like W. B. Seabrook, she was an American white.

A Stage of Haitian Evolution was published within a year of *Ainsi Parla l'Oncle*. Its haphazard arrangement reflected Price-Mars' obvious desire to ride the wave of consciousness caused by the appearance of *Oncle*, as well to keep himself in the limelight for another reason. For just as the publication of his poem "The Mutilated Victories" in 1912-1913 had been Price-Mars way of responding to the urgent political, social and intellectual challenges of that period, the author of *A Stage of Haitian Evolution* was feeling the same internal pressure to respond to the challenges of the Haitian situation in 1928-1929. Underlying his compulsion to remain at the center of the Haitian intellectual arena—even at the expense perhaps of his "scholarship"—was Price-Mars' urge to realize Pan's "foolish dreams" of leading the Haitian Republic..

* * *

Price-Mars quotes Taine on the title page of his book:"There is a Phidias in each one of us. Every man is a sculptor who has the duty to correct his marble or his clay until he succeeds in bringing out from the mass of his crude instincts an intelligent and free person." This had been Price-Mars' goal through the years. It is also what he likes about Toussaint-Louverture whom he depicted in *A Stage of Haitian Evolution* as "a potter who fashioned the clay"—himself and the other black slaves—"to bring out from it the new human material from which Haitian nationality will be born." This achievement had been Price-Mars' dream ever since his student days in Paris. He was satisfied that he had finished the work of the "potter" or "sculptor" of which Taine speaks.

Ainsi Parla l'Oncle had established Price-Mars as a scientist and a scholar. But this was only half of the "foolish dreams" his grandmother had infused in him. The other half must be accomplished through action in public life, and that is what his address to the Central School of Agriculture had been about: "The creation of the Central School (of Agriculture) is in conformity with *one of my most formally expressed and reaffirmed plans for social transformation.*"*

Though he had reached a position of power in 1915 through Vilbrun Guillaume Sam and his *cacos,* he had not had the opportunity to fulfill his dream of bringing about the transformation of his beloved people, particularly the Blacks whom he views as "the greatest wealth of Haiti." But the present political situation in the country is pregnant with change, he feels, for he seems to have a flair for smelling the winds which carry such change.

At the time Price-Mars began to prepare *A Stage of Haitian Evolution,* the idea of a possible change in Haiti's political situation was, by no means, a far-fetched thought. In 1925, President Borno had refused to call for general elections to re-establish the Senate and House of Representatives, claiming that the Haitian people were not

---

*Emphasis added.

yet fully prepared for that. Thus the Council of State remained as the Legislative body and re-elected him. Regarding the Presidential election of 1930, Borno had indicated to General Russell, as early as April 1928, that he would not be a candidate for a third term. However, Borno was determined not to call for general elections to re-establish the Senate and the House to elect his successor which meant that he intended to handpick the man to replace him.*

In the meantime, Herbert Hoover, elected to the U. S. Presidency in 1928, decided before taking office to make a goodwill tour to some of the larger countries in South America. He wished to learn firsthand the growing feeling of fear and mistrust among Latin Americans toward the United States as a result of the occupation of Haiti and Nicaragua by U. S. Marines. In December of the same year, Professor Philips Marshall Brown of Princeton University, speaking at a meeting of the Foreign Policy Association and referring to a Pan-American Conference on Arbitration which was to take place in Washington that month, observed:

> Mr. Hoover without doubt will understand that it has become imperative to launch a completely new policy toward the countries of Central America and the Caribbean and South America. The general hostility and mistrust which has been caused by United States' aims and methods there must disappear. Protestations of unselfish intentions and assurances of friendship are not enough. There must be concrete evidence of a new policy.[16]

The thought of a change in Haiti's political leadership did not obviously leave Price-Mars indifferent. He was indeed prepared as the publication of his *A Stage of Haitian Evolution* demonstrated. Price-Mars introduced his discussion of the "crisis of men" in the early pages of his work against the background of Haiti at the end of the Dartiguenave Government, in large measure identical to that of the closing days of the Borno Government:

> ... Mr. Dartigenave, President of the Republic, at the end of his term, stubbornly tried to remain in power and, maneuvering to have the Council of State re-elect him, he refused to re-establish the Legislative Chambers.
>
> Anxiety ran high. Of what will tomorrow be made? People met one another only to exchange morose words on the general situation. Some felt that the men had been left behind by the events. And the anguish was so great that it was thought that there was a lack of qualified elements to take in their hands the affairs of the country.
>
> In the midst of these apprehensions and the confusion of the moment I was asked this question: Is there not a crisis of men? Is it

---

*Borno's own partisans suspected that the man was Léon Déjean, Haitian Minister to Washington at that time. Borno's daughter had married the brother of Déjean's wife.

possible to find now ten men of the *worth* of a Bazelais, an Edmond Paul, a Firmin, a Thoby?

On the Government's side as well as on the Opposition's side the Mulattoes occupied the prominent strategic positions in the political field and the social field as well. Price-Mars was aware of the unpleasant impact *Ainsi Parla l'Oncle* had on the Mulattoes. Its publication had made him the *bête noire* of the élite to such an extent that ten years after its publication Dantès Bellegarde thought it necessary to defend Price-Mars against the Mulatto reaction to the ideas discussed in that book. Bellegarde attempted to soften Price-Mars' words by stating:

> In a book of great scientific construction and of great psychological insight Dr. Price-Mars has established that Voodoo presents its substance the elements of a primitive religion . . . Of course, Mr. Price-Mars in writing his book wanted to act as a scientist and not as a proselyte: the thought of advocating Voodoo as a national religion could never come to a Haitian of his high intellectual level as some literary dilettantes who falsely claim him as their leader have dared to write on the pretext of nationalism. He recognizes that that religion constitutes "a stage" on the painful road humanity is following, but a stage less advanced than Christianity, "which has risen from the start," he himself wrote, "to a moral height it would be difficult at least to surpass.[17]

And Bellegarde added:

> Some Haitians, partisans of a "closed" society, find it little glorifying that Haiti may be considered as a French intellectual province, likewise they feel it is humiliating that the Catholic Church of Haiti is held as an ecclesiastical province of Rome. They do not want to hear one speak about French culture nor of Latin culture. What is good for Walloon Belgium, for French Switzerland or French Canada has no value for Haiti. Why? Because the Haitian people is of African origin. Therefore it must have as its ideal to create, in the center of the Americas, a Dahomeyan kingdom with a Bantu culture and a Congolese or Arada religion—for the entertainment of Yankee tourists to the joy of the Seabrooks and the Loederers[18] searching for sensational topics.[19]

In the light of these comments by Bellegarde and of the style Price-Mars used in presenting the Haitian writers—even the dead who were still an integral component of the Haitian political scene and practically all Mulattoes—one has the impression that Price-Mars published *A Stage of Haitian Evolution* as a conciliatory gesture to the Mulattoes whose opposition would decide any presidential election against him. Price-Mars even paid tribute to Dr. François Dalencour whom the black intellectuals, particularly those of the Northern Province regarded as an enemy for his sustained attacks against Toussaint-Louverture, Dessalines and

Christophe as well as his continuous praise of Rigaud, Pétion and Boyer.

In this study of socio-psychology by which he proposed to refute Le Bon's thesis, Price-Mars offers no analytical discussion of the works of the scions of Haitian intellectuality or spirituality. He does not even bother to mention the works of those writers. Price-Mars devoted about two pages to Sylvain:

> ... he possessed in a marvelous manner the qualities of the great writer: happy choice of expression, atticism of speech, magnificence of thought, and finally that indefinable something which prompts one to say on reading one of his pages: "He is a master of the language." And endowed with such gifts he presented himself before the French Letters as the Ambassador of Haitian spirituality. Never has a Haitian Plenipotentiary—except for Bellegarde—had the success he enjoyed in French political and literary circles.[20]

Then Price-Mars recalled the commemoration of the twenty-fifth anniversary of the founding of the Alliance Française in Paris in 1909 which he attended and to which Sylvain went as the Delegate from Haiti, having been named that year Haitian Minister to France. The ceremony took place at the Sorbonne under the chairmanship of French academician Paul Deschanel who was later to become President of France. Delegates from many parts of the world and local participants made up an audience of about a thousand people. "When the time came for the Haitian Delegate to speak," wrote Price-Mars, "Georges Sylvain made such a fine speech that the audience gave him an indescribable ovation. The fact is that Georges Sylvain made the best and the most eloquent speech for the occasion."

Price-Mars went on to praise the talent of Clément Magloire as a journalist and editor of *Le Matin* as well as his "rich sensibility" as a man. About his brother Auguste, to whom the long anonymous criticism of *Ainsi Parla l'Oncle* in that newspaper is generally attributed, he added to his praise a grain of irony:

> August Magloire, disciple of Le Play[21] to whose school he went to fetch the directives of his analytical method, has applied himself to the study of Haitian society. He has pointed out its errors of orientation in many monographs of great doctrinal severity. An abundant and stern writer, he enjoys meandering through ideas with the secret pleasure of a teacher who, sure of his method, takes the longest road to arrive at the demonstration of his theorem. And his studies are solid constructions fashioned with skill and ingenuity.[22]

Of President Borno Price-Mars had this to say:

> And what shall I say of Mr. Louis Borno at this present moment which may be considered as the expression of an objective truth?

> Mr. Borno occupies at the same time the highest office of the State and the leadership of a political party. His exceptional situation creates for him many partisans as intransigent enemies. Is it possible to remove the writer from these contingencies in order to examine him in the light of some cold critical doctrine? Such would have been our attitude and the only one capable of obtaining the agreement of his friends and that of his enemies as well, if we could find, condensed somewhere, Mr. Borno's thought. Alas! with him as I have said about so many others, we have found his ideas spread all over, in the newspaper articles, in speeches, etc. without having been gathered together in some work on which we could render our verdict. Besides, Mr. Borno is in the midst of action; it is perhaps more fair to postpone our judgment until history will be able to support the verdict in all serenity about the man and his work.[23]

Of Seymour Pradel, likely contender for the Presidency of the Republic with the widest support from the Capital's élite, Price-Mars commented:

> Seymour Pradel's curiosity for things of the mind and the richness of his gifts have developed in him the most solid qualities of lucid and clear-sighted criticism. He has proved this on many different occasions, especially in his study on "The two tendencies". With sagacity, versatility and prodigious competence he has demonstrated the mechanism of the movements that had engendered the generation of men of letters to which he belongs. Only a little amount of determination would suffice for him to complete that study which would reveal the extent of that talent which has excelled in all the literary styles he has attempted. Alas! Seymour Pradel, a sportsman smitten with sculptural beauty, a poet who has escaped from the voluptuousness of dreams, a hero who has fled from the adventurous life, is wasting around the clock the best part of himself.[24]

This criticism was the more potent because in the preface of *A Stage of Haitian Evolution* Price-Mars had made this comment:

> In truth, I cannot manage to understand how some men who believe they are truly men can content themselves with a vegetative life where earning money, eating, drinking, sleeping and the rest, can be the supreme aim of life. Could it be that going to the movies, visiting the sick, studying a dossier, reading a newspaper article, demolishing political adversaries constitute the utmost effort of an educated bourgeois of our time?
>
> If this were so, people would have to relinquish the task of fashioning an ideal of human worth for the feeding of the citizens of this nation, it would be necessary to declare them unworthy of all transcendental aspiration and let them offer their necks to the political and economical slavery which is the fate of all the pariahs who have ceased to try to ennoble their existence on this planet, even by caressing some utopian dream.[25]

In concluding the list of the writers he would honor Price-Mars lost all fear about his teaching position, for what was at stake now was so considerable in its dimensions—so much more important indeed than the meager check he was receiving for his service at the Lycée. He selected only two young writers to receive, along with Joseph Jolibois Jr. and Elie Guérin, his awards for their journalistic efforts:

> Has there ever existed in this country, except for the beautiful era of the Revolutionary Epic, a greater demonstration of pluck than that by a Jolibois Jr., an Elie Guérin, a Jacques Roumain, a Georges J. Petit?[26]

Including the names of these people constituted an act of revolt against the Borno-Russell regime. For Jolibois was the editor of the *Courrier Haitien* and had been arrested more than ten times under both Dartiguenave and Borno. With the passing of Georges Sylvain, he became chief of the Opposition.

Elie Guérin was an apiculturist in the Cul-de-Sac Plain when the American marines landed in Haiti in 1915. He abandoned this work at once to take up the pen as a journalist. By his caustic pamphlets against Haitian politicians and his passionate defense of Haiti's rights to live as a sovereign nation, he soon made himself the high priest of Haitian nationalism by preaching the gospel of resistance to the Occupation. He did this principally through his newspaper, *Haiti Integrale,* uncompromising always in spite of repeated imprisonment and his failing health. (Guérin died a few months after the publication of Price-Mars' *A Stage of Haitian Evolution.* Léon Laleau portrayed him in the novel *Le Choc* under the name of Emile Verin.)

After the disappearance of *La Revue Indigène,* Jacques Roumain had joined hands with Georges Petit, the editor of the weekly paper *Le Petit Impartial.* Whereas Roumain was the grandson of the late President Tancrède Auguste, Petit was from the common people.* Together they attacked the bicephalous regime no less fiercely than Jolibois and Elie Guérin did at the *Courrier* and *Haiti Integrale.*

These four gentlemen were not, however, the only ones to receive all Price-Mars' accolades for moral courage. Price-Mars extended his consideration in that respect to the entire Haitian élite retracting his own words about their pitiful shortcomings in his closing to the first part of the book:

> ... In an article published in the March 13, 1921 issue of *L'Essor,* which initiated the discussion on the "crisis in men," I had declared that in my view there was not an intellectual crisis but a moral crisis. And I qualified it as a collapse of Haitian character on

---

*His mother worked as a cook for the family of Léon Laleau's wife at one time.

Jacques Roumain

confronting the American Occupation. Thinking things over, it seems that I had exaggerated our moral deficiency a little.[27]

Price-Mars was a very subtle man. While he gives the impression of trying to please all sides in Haitian society in his work, he realized he did not want to give the impression that he was abandoning the blacks by his conciliatory overtures to the élite. Thus he included his 1926 talk "The Religious Sentiment and Phenomenon among the Blacks of Saint-Domingue." Moreover, while discussing *Magic Island* by the white American author Seabrook, Price-Mars seized the opportunity to offer himself as the prototype of the Black Man in universal indignation for his race.

The passage in the book that contains the one word that unleashed Price-Mars' rage—*sauvagerie*—must have been deeply gratifying to him. For it illustrated strikingly what constituted the core of his thought on Haitian evolution as well as Negro American evolution in the area of physical beauty, particularly that of the women. A skillful writer, Seabrook described a ball at the Bellevue Club in honor of the officers of a Swedish ship visiting Port-au-Prince:

> Here was assembled the native aristocracy of Haiti, its brains, wealth, and beauty, its inner circle; and recalling that these people had come up from plantation slavery in the brief cycle of a century, it was very interesting.
>
> . . . .
>
> Between these pure blacks and the dominant pale mulatto tone with its lighter shades of quadroon and octoroon, there was considerable element of brown like my friend Monsieur Baussan, who had appeared meanwhile and was escorting us to the terrace opening on the ballroom, where we found Madame Baussan with Seymour Pradel, the leading lawyer and bachelor beau of Port-au-Prince society . . .
>
> It required no poring over the historical pages of Moreau de Saint Méry to understand that the seventeenth-century slavers had been, to say the least, careless in selecting their supposed "human cattle" for West Indian export. Here flowed the blood of warriors and chiefs. Revolt, uprising, massacre, were bound to follow the enslavement of such types as these . . .
>
> While dancing with Madame Baussan, I noticed, gliding in the arms of the tall flaxen-haired Swedish admiral, a tall, pale-brown-skinned lithe creature of whom my hostess said proudly in answer to my query, "That is Thérèse, our daughter." She was slightly darker than mulatto. She was a tall, strong, slender hamadryad in pale bronze . . . Her figure was revealed candidly as the current world-wide fashion is. Her legs, her ankles, arched instep, and long, slender feet were Louis Quinze rather than sculptural. It was interesting because of the general Anglo-Saxon belief that persons of partial African descent invariably lack grace in this particular.
>
> As Mlle. Thérèse glided close beside us in the arms of the blond

Swedish admiral she said, "Tu t'amuses bien, Maman." Big, sultry brown eyes flashed, wide-set beneath a low forehead; there was a touch of cruelty, *sauvagerie,* I thought, in the wide, short chin, cobra-like cheek bones, the mouth like a slashed red fruit, a touch of negroid too in the chin and slightly retroussé nose, a touch also which suggested the face of Faustina on old Roman golden coins, Pola Negri as the wife of Pharaoh. Her hair, bobbed in an almost Egyptian style, was crinkly. She was too wise in her sure beauty to straighten it by pomades or tricks. She was African, yet not quite Africa, Africa of the poets rather than of the ethnologists and explorers . . .

Sitting opposite Mlle. Thérèse at midnight, with Monsieur Baussan at the head of a long table, glittering with long-stemmed champagne glasses . . . I reflected on the strange biological-hereditary processes that had culminated in his daughter. It occurred to me that in terms of cold science, if not by more conventional standards, she represented a fusing of the highest selective elements in both the white and negro races. I shall try to explain presently what I mean by "highest." Assuming that these highly selective elements were fused in her, I wondered whether she represented some ultimate future type, superior perhaps to anything that either race alone could breed, and which, a thousand years or ten thousand years hence, might become the dominant superior world-type. I wondered whether even now, an unprejudiced, detached ethnologist visiting the earth from another planet would not deem Mlle. Thérèse superior in physical beauty and strength, in richness of potentiality, perhaps also in pigmentation, to any purely white or purely negro type.[28]

Price-Mars contradicted in his gentlemanly manner many of the assertions presented in *Magic Island* about Voodoo which the author claimed to have gathered while watching Voodoo ceremonies in Haiti. Coming to the word *sauvagerie* in the text, Price-Mars recalled his trip to Italy during which he visited the Museum of the Vatican one morning. He left at noon, feeling hungry, and on his way to get something to eat, the thought came to him to look into the Basilica. The esthetic splendor of the church overwhelmed him. "I lost the notion of time and the sensation of hunger. Throughout the afternoon I roamed about Saint Peter's of Rome until closing time, when I was forced out."[29] Then, erupting into anger about the word *sauvagerie* in *Magic Island,* he wrote:

> In truth, I do not know if my low forehead, my woolly hair, my flat nose have stamped on me a special accent of sauvagerie. What I know very well is that if an artistic emotion has had the power to abolish the sensation of hunger, in me, the offspring of slaves from Africa, I can consider myself no inferior but equal to this brute with an aquiline nose, blue eyes, and an orthognathic jaw who, somewhere, having behind him twenty centuries of Christian civilization, hanged "niggers" by their thumbs, and low enough to

offer their sexual organs to the ferocious appetite of his trained dog.

I cannot consider myself on the level of these men who yearly burn at the stake scores of "niggers" *accused* of rape and who enjoy the odor of the burnt flesh of their victims and quarrel over the pieces of their charred skeleton to keep as relics.[30]

In the course of his discussion on *Magic Island,* Price-Mars peremptorily denied what he called "the stupid legend that I advocate a return to Africa."[31] To be sure, the peasants of his "Christmas of the Humble" are not thinking about that either. They have come down from the mountain of Kenscoff and from the surrounding countryside to attend Midnight Mass at Pétionville, joyfully, in their best dress, commemorating Christ's birth. And Price-Mars, making himself their spokesman, asks, "But when shall your reign come, O Christ?"

Testifying to his own deep Christian feeling with the candor of a child, the author went on to say:

And here on Noël night the humble of my village will commemorate the Message to Mary made two thousand years ago that somewhere in the world Thou shalt be born from a woman for the redemption of mankind . . .

Do come at last. Come here first . . . come to deflate the vanity of all the sadducees of vice and ostentation . . . Come to deliver us from those who are stealing our daily bread . . . Come to inspire them with pity for the weak and fraternity which links man to man whatever his race and wherever he may live . . .

Hurry up. The times are hard. The crop is ready . . . Come to us the children, as in the past between the mule, the donkey and the lamb. We shall open wide the doors of our peasant homes while whispering the hosanna of the saints . . . [32]

But honest to the hilt even while playing politics, Price-Mars, also wanting to make it clear where he stood and would always stand, published in Part II of the book a letter of Mrs. Blair Niles in which the American woman author echoed his own thought as follows:

. . . I felt that the great service that I could render to the Haitian was to try to show him that the ethnic genius that he possesses and which is African is one of the elements of his evolution of which he has the right to be proud as those of any other race from which he has also received in part his heredity. It is to the shame of our arrogant race, to us Caucasians, that the African has come to despise himself. And as long as he feels that way I am certain that in trying to rid himself of the African genius he is denying to the world qualities which the world needs as much as those from the Orient, from the Latins, from the Germans.[33]

If Price-Mars' intentions in publishing *A Stage of Haitian Evolution* at that time were truly to placate the mulatto bourgeois of

The "Foolish Dreams"

Haiti, his attempt would have found its immediate justification in the very mores of Haitian society. Besides, such artifice is part and parcel of political life in any country. Once Theodore Roosevelt told the boys at Groton while his young cousin Franklin Delano Roosevelt was attending school there: "In politics it is not enough for a man to be good; he has got to be shrewd too."

Price-Mars, too, was a very shrewd man. He had arrived once again at the crossroads to await his destiny. His goal was the National Palace and he hoped, with almost childlike faith, that he would realize his dream to become Chief Executive and be able to minister to his black brother of rural Haiti "to rouse him from his long slumber, from his rut, and from his dejected resignation."[32]

Léon Laleau

Thirteen

Again, Victory and Defeat

Whatever the author's reasons for rushing into print with *A Stage of Haitian Evolution,* the volume served no discernible useful purpose. No sooner had it appeared than it became obsolete or almost non-existent insofar as Price-Mars' presidential campaign was concerned. Events had moved faster than the printing presses. The tragedy at Marchaterre, escalating the student strike to national protest, shattered all plans and prognostications. What Price-Mars seemed to fear as the stumbling block to his presidential aspirations—his advocacy of Black Consciousness—proved to be the trump card in the exciting political developments of the moment. Somewhat paradoxically, it was a young mulatto, Jacques Roumain, who introduced that explosive formula which blew the bicameral Government to bits.

After the students' strike began, General John H. Russell, who had previously depicted the Haitian people as having the mentality of a seven year old child, invited Jacques Roumain to a dinner at the American Embassy along with other Haitians in an attempt to defuse the growing hostility in the Capital against the Americans. Jacques returned the invitation on which he had written: "The black Jacques Roumain does not dine with the white racist Russell." Published in the Opposition newspapers, Roumain's *RSVP* set the tone immediately among the young strikers. Roumain belonged to the new brand of poets who viewed poetry as an arm for combat in the political arena, as he said himself:

> First, we must do away with the myth of the freedom of the poet. Far from being as Valery pretends "a very ancient man", the poet is above all a contemporary man, the reflecting conscience of his time. If his thought is not action, the poet is not free. He is not so if he evades the imperious necessity of making a choice. He must choose between Garcia Lorca and Franco, between Hitler and Thaelman, between peace and war, between social democracy and fascism. His pretended freedom can be summed up in what one might call Pontius Pilate's complex which covers all the artifices of coward and renegade. The poet is at once witness and actor of the historic drama. He finds himself drafted with his full responsibility. And particularly in our time his art must be an arm on the first line of combat in the service of the people.[1]

One is therefore not surprised to see Roumain join the young strikers at the Central School of Agriculture with the heedlessness of youth and a fanatical social consciousness. He soon became a hero to Haitian youth throughout the country for his increasingly violent attacks on the Government and the Occupation and for the repeated brutal beatings he sustained by the police. Yet, in addition to being a poet, he was a scholar. A great admirer of the "Uncle," he had joined Price-Mars several times for ethnological investigations in the countryside.

Borno was also confronted by another young poet, Jean F. Brierre, the leader of the striking students, who had risen to mourn the death of Haiti's "liberties" at the hand of a President acting as the "lackey" of a foreign master. The furious young poet attacked him in passionate steel-like alexandrines in *In the Heart of the Citadel* and *Poem to the Marchaterre Cross.* In the presence of large crowds, Brierre recited the vibrant fragments of his epic before the monuments of the heroes of Haiti's Independence. Two years later he published *The Flag of Tomorrow,* a dramatic poem in two acts, which repeated what Price-Mars had been preaching in effective prose over a quarter of a century: that the Black man is not inferior, though he is oppressed in Africa and persecuted in America. The means of his liberation is within his power provided he realizes that his strength lies not in childish imitation of divisive prejudices. It lies in the exploitation of the resources of his own genius in racial unity and solidarity:

Forward! Forward! oppressed of the Race!
You can, be proud, climb in the light.

Eventually an exposé of the Haitian situation written by Dantès Bellegarde, Jacques Roumain, Constantin Mayard and Charles Moravia[2], was published by the New York *Herald Tribune* in its edition of February 16, 1930. As a result, the United States Congress was finally moved to approve the sending of an investigative Commission by Mr. Hoover to Haiti. The Commission arrived in Port-au-Prince on February 28. Not until then did the French hierarchy of the Catholic church in Haiti decide to side publicly with the Opposition. The Chairman of the American Congressional Commission was Cameron Forbes, former Governor of the Philippines. After about two months of consultations with both Government and Opposition, the Commission, with the approval of President Hoover, struck a bargain with both sides in Haiti. Mr. Eugène Roy, Price-Mars' Pétionville friend was elected President of the Republic on April 21 by the Council of State as a neutral, temporary President with the proviso that he call for general elections as soon as possible to re-establish the traditional Legislative Chambers which in turn would elect a Constitutional President.

Soon after Mr. Roy went to the National Palace as President, Price-Mars, then fifty-four, married a beautiful mulatto girl, Clara Perez, who also lived in Pétionville. She was the owner of a small general store in Pétionville. She was well-educated and possessed great charm and exquisite manners. When President Roy called for general elections on October 14, Price-Mars presented himself before the people of the Northern Province as a candidate for a seat in the Senate, campaigning also for the Presidency of the Republic as Seymour Pradel and Sténio Vincent were doing in the Western Province. On Election Day, by order of the Government, the military—officers and soldiers—were confined to their barracks while the Haitian people went freely to the polls and made their choice.

The racial factor, which had characterized the attacks on the Americans after the students' strike and Marchaterre, had given way to a purely nationalistic feeling among all sectors of the Haitian citizenry after the arrival in Haiti of the Forbes Commission. For that reason, Price-Mars, who had become the idol of the black intellectuals throughout the country, did not fare as well as he would have if the initial racial trend of the protests had continued. One of the most important members of the Commission, Henry P. Fletcher, of the State Department in Washington, described as follows the attitude of the Haitians after the arrival of the Commission in Haiti:

> Witness after witness publicly testified that the people of Haiti would not accept the choice of the Council of State as the next President of the Republic, and that if the Council of State attempted to elect anyone a revolution would ensue which only American force could quell. Unarmed as they were, they said, they would nevertheless rather bare their breasts to American machine guns than submit to a continuance of dictatorship. Refined ladies appeared and joined in these asserverations. If their sons and fathers had to die, as they undoubtedly would if some way were not found to prevent this Council of State election, then they also would die with them. A bit histrionic and *"tropical"* as the French say, but there it was."[3]

The nationalistic feeling among the whole Haitian people was so strong that candidates and partisans alike made it their duty to conduct the general elections in the utmost order to prove that the Haitian people, contrary to what President Borno had said, was fully qualified to elect their popular representatives and take back the nation's destiny in their own hands. "Nowhere," writes Bellegarde, "despite the complete abstention of the military, was there the slightest trouble between voters. Deputies and senators were chosen among the candidates who had most vehemently declared themselves against the continuation of the American regime in Haiti."[4]

Price-Mars was one of the victorious candidates, but only as the second Senator of the Northern Province; the first senator, Louis Zéphirin, a Cap-Haitian lawyer, was an overt partisan of Seymour Pradel, [5] who was also elected to the Senate along with Sténio Vincent.

On November 18, 1930 Price-Mars made a good showing at the National Assembly in the election of the President of the Republic with seven out of fifty votes on the first ballot of the Assembly as compared to five for Sannon, twelve for Pradel and 15 for Vincent. On the second ballot, Price-Mars had eleven votes, Pradel twelve and Vincent twenty-one. The latter, still leading on the third ballot, had twenty-five votes, Pradel twenty, and Price-Mars five. In spite of great pressure put on him in the Legislative Hall by his partners at the Coicou Clinic urging him to go over to Pradel, Price-Mars remained in the race. Vincent was elected on the fourth ballot with thirty votes. Pradel received nineteen votes. One blank vote was cast which everyone attributed to Price-Mars. One of those who had shown the greatest support for Price-Mars' candidacy at the National Assembly was a former student of his at the Lycée Pétion, Dumarsais Estimé who had been sent to the House of Representatives by the town of Verrettes in the Artibonite Province.

Although Price-Mars failed to secure the Presidency, he came out of the race with heightened prestige among his peers and particularly in the eyes of Haiti's intellectual youth. Despite the fact that at the end of the presidential election he chose not to vote for Vincent, he remained on friendly terms with the new President. Some of the President's former associates, however, formed a political cartel in the Senate, including Pradel, and initiated a bitter, often unreasonable opposition to the new Administration. But the new President who had purchased a house in Pétionville during the senatorial campaign, made several neighborly calls on the Price-Mars.

The Opposition was impatient with President Vincent for results from his foreign policy towards the United States. Vincent, in taking the helm of the Senate, discovered quickly that Washington was not at all disposed to remove the Military Occupation or to transfer to Haitian authority the agencies created under the Treaty still under American authority. However, on August 5, 1931, the Vincent Government succeeded in obtaining a diplomatic agreement with the United States which provided for the transfer to Haitian authority of three of the four Treaty agencies: Public Works, Sanitation, and the Technical Service of Agriculture. The fourth one, the Haitian military forces, would not be *Haitianized* until after President Franklin D. Roosevelt visited Haiti in July 1934.

During 1931, while the Vincent Government was registering its diplomatic success, Haitian Letters themselves registered a most important event, and Price-Mars a most significant tribute. Jacques

Roumain had published his novel *La Montagne ensorcelée* (The Bewitched Mountain) with a preface by Price-Mars who wrote:

> I thank the gods for having lifted the interdiction with which they had graced the mystery of their cult, thus allowing the curiosity of the profane to make works of art from it. It is to this state of mind that we owe today *The Bewitched Mountain* by Jacques Roumain. Turning his back on the usual mundane adultery, the coupling of concupiscence, the political masquerade which so stupidly retain the attention of our literature, the young novelist has evoked in beautiful pages the picturesque and dramatic life of our peasants. Of this life he has marvelously brought forth what makes both its charm and horror: faith. [6]

From the time he was elected to the Senate to that of his departure from the legislative chamber, Price-Mars, swept into the whirl of political life and social entertainment, did not have much time left to concentrate on scholarly production. He published here and there, however, in newspaper or reviews articles such as "Simple remarks of psychiatry on Voodoo trance" in 1930 in the *Annales de Médecine haitienne.* This was reproduced in the Paris *Revue de psychothérapie et de psychologie appliquée* in 1933. During the latter year he published at the Capital a booklet under the title *Christophe's sentiment of personal worth in regard to his role of Chief: Psychology of a Statesman.* This subject suited his thought and position as a statesman. Of the two other unsuccessful contenders for the Presidency, Price-Mars only remained in the limelight as leader of the Haitian intellectuals, venerated by his political and intellectual partisans for his elected office and moderate behavior. In contrast, Pradel had resumed his debonair way of life and used his Senate seat to bicker unproductively with President Vincent.

On July 5, 1934, Franklin D. Roosevelt landed at Cap-Haitien to pay an official vist to the Haitian Chief of State. It was there that he announced his decision to withdraw the U. S. Marines from Haiti. A month or so later on August 1, *La Garde d'Haiti* was transferred to Haitian authorities. In giving the command of the Haitian forces on that day to Colonel Démosthène Calixte, President Vincent said: "The country does not want to be deceived and humiliated another time." On August 21, as the leader of a nation drunk with joy and pride, President Vincent raised the Haitian flag over the Dessalines Barracks which the American forces had vacated earlier in the day to embark on a U. S. destroyer for their return home. President Vincent was the man of the hour.

Haiti's Constitution provided for a six-year term of office for the President. But the following year, claiming his desire to keep the nation on an even keel during the first years of its "new independence" and fearing a resumption of pre-Occupation domestic turmoil and political rivalries, Vincent decided to have his term extended through a plebiscite. Eleven Senators, including both Price-Mars and Pradel, rose in protest. Besides his two major successes, the official visit of the U. S. President and the ending of the foreign occupation, however, Vincent had devoted his efforts to social projects for the poor. He had instituted a land grant program, built low cost housing and opened dispensaries to combat diseases among the people. Thus his plebiscite went through like a knife through hot butter and, in light of the expressed will of the People, Vincent dismissed the eleven Senators, sending Price-Mars back to his scholarly preoccupations and his activities as a country doctor.

* * *

President Vincent's move was a perpetuation of the nearly unbroken tradition since Toussaint-Louverture of the Haitian Chief of State attempting to succeed himself in office. Some of Price-Mars' partisans who looked upon him as the logical successor of Vincent, saw Vincent's move as mulatto conspiracy to prevent the "Uncle" who had identified himself with Haiti's black masses, notwithstanding *A Stage of Haitian Evolution,* from taking over the leadership of his country.

From 1930 to 1935 Price-Mars exercised his predominance as *the* Mentor of Haitian thought and literature by writing five prefaces to the works of emerging writers.[7] Among others was his preface to a Haitian novel by a Northern writer, Jean-Baptiste Cinéas, *Le Drame de la Terre* (The Drama of the Earth).[8] Cinéas had dedicated his book "To the mountaineer, my Ancestor, who, along with his sensitive and honest soul has bequeathed me a feeling of contempt for hypocrisy and of horror for servitude and above all a passion for the land." In this connection, Price-Mars wrote:

> Poverty of all the peasants under the yoke of ignorance, hampered by superstition, loaded with prejudice, despised, deceived and derided by the Society of which they are the inescapable victims. Such are the elements of this *Drama of the Earth* by J. B. Cinéas. All the aspects of the struggle in which the rural man is engaged without any outlet other than death in poverty, is described with unequalled sensitiveness.

Then Price-Mars declared that the "silent resignation of those peasants stands as a terrible accusation against the collective selfishness of the élites with clever hands and sharp teeth.[7] In 1933, Emile Paultre won the Alliance Française Prize with his *Essai sur M. Price-Mars* and in the North, during the very year Price-Mars was dismissed from the Senate, Lafontant Jean heralded him as the "Oracle of Youth."[9] Price-Mars was not only consulted by young Haitian writers. Well established authors from the United States,

Latin America and Europe visited the Pétionville house to ask help in their research in the field of history and ethnology about Haiti. Despite his political defeat, Price-Mars continued as the center of Haitian intellectual life, returning to private life, a martyr to his friends and partisans. He joyfully took up his pen again and resumed work in the field of ethnology.

Compared to the days following his dismissal from the Lycée Pétion in 1922, things were much better for Price-Mars in 1935 following his exit from the Senate. He now had a family, the love and companionship of a courageous and understanding wife and the happiness of watching his daughter, Marie-Madeleine, born in 1932, grow in beauty as a marabout. Some of Price-Mars friends would jokingly say that she was his most beautiful "production" with black material.

By 1938, Black Consciousness, going beyond Indigenism to Africanism in literature and to the concept of a regenerated Haitian Society, saw the creation of *Les Griots,* a review started by a group of the same name.[10] In the realm of literature, Carl Brouard, previously of *La Revue Indigène,* and director of the new review, explained the inspiration and manner in contemporary Haitian literature which his review would reflect:

The Griots

> Far away in the mysterious land of Africa, when the griots pass by, men and women spit to show contempt because they are poets and sorcerers and people are afraid of mystery. Their wrists and necks covered with ouangas, and their eyes full of nostalgia, they go on, their steps sinking into the bush of the dream. They sing to love—a love red like the flamboyant flower, and to the strange immobility of death. The loas speak to them in dreams which are truer than reality for reality is only the shadow of the dream. When they beat their war drums the warriors dream of apotheosis; they are a caste apart. When they die, their cursed souls do not go to the gardens of Paradise and their remains, placed far away from the huts, become food for the jackals.[11]

As to the Griots' social convictions and design for the Haitian Society, Dr. François Duvalier and Lorimer Denis expounded their views in a "Declaration," in two parts. In the first part, the writers, following in Price-Mars' footsteps, affirmed that from the contact of African elements and European elements in Saint-Domingue were born not only a new ethnic variety, the mixed-blood, but also "un métissage culturel" affecting religion, tradition, customs and language. And still developing ideas that Price-Mars had expressed, particularly in *La Vocation de l'Elite,* the young writers commented:

> Independence came. The Haitian élite rejects the primordial factor to the exclusive advantage of the Gallo-Latin elements. This step, purely spiritual, has its impact in the politico-social field. Thus this

breakaway from the great Haitian ethnic base. As a consequence a moral disequilibrium resulting tragically in the American Occupation.

Noting that *La Revue Indigène* had started a spiritual reaction which *Ainsi Parla l'Oncle* eventually "crystallized," and that every effort had been made since Independence to suppress systematically the African heritage deemed of inferior quality in the literary as well as political-social domains, "our action," said the Griots, "should lead us to demand the revalorization of this raciological factor":

> We know indeed that biological equilibrium is a matter of time. But we know, too, that a mystique can do the work to a certain extent, and that is why the axis of our action has always been directed toward a methodical investigation of the bio-psychological elements of the Haitian man so as to attain a national doctrine which, anticipating the biological processes, would hasten the indispensable fusion for the full flowering of Haitian genius in all areas of human activity.

Like Price-Mars, they predicated their action upon "a total transformation of Haitian mentality."[12] At that very moment Price-Mars was deep in new investigations on the "bio-psychological elements of the make-up of the Haitian man," the result of which would provide the subject-matter of his fourth book, *Formation ethnique, Folk-lore et Culture du Peuple Haitien,* published in 1939, the year following the creation of *The Griots.*

As to the ethnic formation of the Haitian people, again with approximately the same arguments he used in his previous books, Price-Mars established that the Haitian people are "authentically" African and that four-fifths of Haiti's population are the descendants of slaves brought over from the regions of the Congo and Guinea. He depicted Haitian folklore as follows:

> Africa has given (the Haitian people) the structure of our beliefs and superstitions with animism as their background. The whole world has furnished inexhaustible sources for the building of our legends. France has given the style and the mould of some of our popular stories. Rural life, hard, simple and frugal, constitutes the setting. The painful and tragic memories of the slave trade, the horrors of slavery and vicissitudes of dispersion have furnished the characters. Then the creative imagination of the black, his taste for rhythm, his sense of lyricism have adorned the songs, cadenced the crambos, embellished the legends, in short, have built a folklore which is truly the mirror of our troubled, tossed and frustrated life which, despite all, remains full of optimism and is characterized by an infinite candor.[13]

On the question of Haitian culture, Price-Mars collided, head on, with Dantès Bellegarde whom he named as the defender of the thesis that the Haitian is "French, Catholic, Apostolic and Roman" as to his culture. At the same time, he agreed fully with the

Griots who viewed Haitian culture as a "métissage" (mixture) of cultures as a result of the fact that the one-fifth of the country's population representing the governing class is linked to Western culture, particularly French culture. "But," says Price-Mars, "the co-existence of the cultures on such a narrow territory as ours necessarily brings about facts of co-penetration and endomosis from the one and the other culture, producing as a consequence a cultural mélange." He noted that Dr. François Duvalier and Lorimer Denis have pointed out these facts about Haitian culture in a "fine communication" to the Society of Haitian History and Geography. The piece was reproduced in the *Revue anthropologique* of Paris, and again in the winter issue of the review *Les Griots, 1938:*

> It is because some people with considerable knowledge have wanted to minimize this phenomenon of métissage while nullifying the substratum constituted in that mixture by the larger mass that they have denied the existence of a Haitian culture. It is because others were afraid of establishing its results that they have preferred to seek refuge in a skeptical attitude . . . [14]

The fact that the educated Haitians speak French, he argued, does not rule out the existence of a Haitian culture. Merely because French is the official language of Haiti, the entire Haitian nation does not necessarily adopt the French intellectual process of thinking. France and Haiti differ in physical and human characteristics. They are influenced by completely different historical forces. Such an attitude tends to minimize the impact of Creole on the Haitian mind. Price-Mars' comment on Creole appeared in *Ainsi Parla l'Oncle*:

> The Creole language, for those who understand it well, is a tongue of great subtlety. Quality or defect, this characteristic comes less from the clarity of the sounds that it expresses than from the depth of the equivocations it insinuates by its implied thoughts, by an inflexion of the voice, and especially by the mimicry on the face of the person who speaks. This is perhaps why written Creole loses half the flavor of the spoken language; this is perhaps why Haitian folkore has not produced a written literature. The fact remains that in Creole the image bursts often from the mere repetition of an identical sound which, in creating an onomatopoeia, accentuates the musicality of the idiom . . . Besides, if additional proofs were needed to bring forth the cleverness of Creole it would suffice to mention such proverbs of disconcerting relevance, the application of which would not lack either flavor or interest . . . *"Parlé francè pa l'esprit et Nègre sott cé l'événement."* (To know how to speak French well does not mean being able to think well and the idiot is a danger.)[15]

Pursuing his thought on Haitian culture in *Formation ethnique,* Price-Mars observed:

> When we try to establish a parallelism between Haitian culture

and Congo-Guinean culture we become confused before the concordance and the similarity of their respective physiognomy: the same aptitudes of agricultural workers, the same technique with the hoe and the knife, the same habits with the predominance of the man in a polygamous family, patrilineal customs and the subordination of woman, the same animist beliefs and the same piety toward divinity with a fantastic power of religious assimilation and syncretic propensity, the same political organization with withdrawal of the individual in behalf of the State incarnated in the person of an all-powerful lord . . . [16]

To be sure, Price-Mars contemplates the absorption of the one-fifth by the four-fifths of the population or rather their fusion into a coherent whole. But he does not seem to be in a hurry as his young admirers of *Les Griots* seem to be to force a solution on the Haitian people. Obviously he is less determined at the time of writing *Formation ethnique* to force a fusion that he had been at the time he published his first book in which he said that if ever the Haitians should regain control of the destiny of their country, "one should not hesitate *to impose*" upon the country a system of education designed to change its general mentality. He now spoke of Haiti as "a field of sociological experimentation," borrowing the term from an eminent Haitian writer, Louis-Joseph Janvier, of the Delorme era. This field of sociological experimentation, Price-Mars declared:

> depends less on the formal will of men than on the insidious work of time for the only solution that is in conformity with our destiny as a nation and a historical race, that is to say the frank interpenetration of the elements of our ethnic formation in order to insure the success of our endeavor toward an ideal of order, harmony and stability.[17]

At this juncture, Price-Mars' moderation is that of a realistic statesman, a patriot, yet at the same time a shrewd politician. The historian, looking back, could hardly forget the recent past, and the poet, looking forward, could hardly fail to wonder if the future in the same brief span of time—two years—might not see the realization of his dream of the Presidency of the Republic.

On the one hand, Price-Mars certainly remembered the attempt in 1937 by some young army officers to overthrow President Vincent. One of them, who later joined *Les Griots,* was the mulatto poet, Arthur Bonhomme, co-author with Duvalier and Denis of *Les Tendances d'une Génération* for which Price-Mars had written a preface in 1934.[18] The conspirators wanted to put an end to the mulatto power which the American Occupation had established. They were all the more determined to overthrow Vincent as he had allowed the mulatto Colonel Durcé Armand, Chief of the Palace Guard, to take preponderance in the affairs of the Garde d'Haiti over its official Chief, Colonel Demosthène Calixte, a black. The young officers first undertook to assassinate Armand. But as they fired at him one afternoon from a passing automobile while he was on a café terrace, they only succeeded in inflicting a minor wound on his leg. Armand, who had the police directly under his influence, personally conducted the investigations that uncovered the would-be assassins. They were eventually arrested, tried and sentenced to various prison terms. No criminal charges were lodged against Calixte, but President Vincent removed him from the Garde d'Haiti and sent him to Europe as inspector of legations and consulates.

One of the many rumors that circulated throughout the country after the failure of the conspiracy was that Calixte, a Northerner aware of his intellectual shortcomings, was thinking of placing Price-Mars, instead of himself, in the National Palace. By the time Price-Mars published *Formation ethnique* his chances of getting to the National Palace in 1941 were slim, barring a miracle, for Armand had become the most powerful man on Haiti's political scene. But as the Haitian politicians, hoping against hope, usually say in such situations, "Mon cher, il y a toujours des impondérables!" Perhaps Price-Mars realized that the mulatto élite would again have the decisive hand in selecting the next President in 1941 and was himself thinking of the possible emergence of those "imponderables" when he wrote the following dedication to *Formation ethnique:* "To my wife and children, daily witnesses of my life full of unshakable sympathy for all Haitians, my brothers in guilt and in hope."

As President Vincent approached the end of his eleven years in office, he found himself in the midst of a tug-of-war within the Palace. Many of his closest collaborators had come to believe that they had become presidential timber and wanted to succeed him. But Vincent wanted to remain in power, even dreaming of a Presidency for Life as the "Second Liberator" of the country. As Vincent played one candidate in his entourage off the other, the tug-of-war eventually reached the streets, providing an opportunity to a candidate outside the Palace. Price-Mars stood as the most prominent leader of the Opposition. At the last minute, however, as a result of long premeditation and engineering, Elie Lescot entered the race with two strong supports: Washington, where he was serving as Haitian Minister and, General Raphael Leonidas Trujillo, President of the Dominican Republic, where Lescot had also served as Haitian Minister for many years prior to his transfer to Washington. Thus, in Haitian parlance, Vincent "*sauté gaguè,*" that is to say, he gave up the fight for his dream. But it was not until he had secured Colonel Armand's agreement on Lescot that Vincent undertook to arrange things in behalf of the latter. A month or so before the presidential election, Vincent named Lescot Senator to enable him to participate personally in the proceedings of the National Assembly.

In April 1941, on election day, the whole capital knew before the National Assembly opened its doors that Lescot would be elected or, rather, was in fact the new President of the Republic. However, Price-Mars presented himself before the Assembly as the candidate of the Opposition—the lone contender, only to watch the legislators elect Lescot by a vote of 56 to 2. No sooner was Lescot elected than Washington made a loan of five million dollars to Haiti which Lescot had negotiated on behalf of the Vincent Government as Minister to Washington. The State Department had postponed disbursement, however, pending the outcome of the general election in Port-au-Prince. Lescot's relations with the U. S. were the most cordial that had ever existed between the two republics. It lasted until the death of President Roosevelt. Each one called the other "my friend" and seemed to mean it in a true spirit of friendship and respect.

Soon after he went to the National Palace, President Lescot offered Price-Mars, leader of the Opposition, a seat in the Senate.[19] Price-Mars accepted the offer and Lescot "named" him back to his old seat of "Senator of the Northern Province." In the resentful and indignant eyes of some of his political partisans and intellectual friends—Price-Mars' acceptance of that post was a colossal defeat. Politically, in their eyes, Price-Mars was dead.

Fourteen

To The Unknown Black

The title, "Monsieur le Sénateur," which Price-Mars acquired this time by Presidential appointment, added little or nothing to his prestige. For the practical politicians in government circles, it merely reflected perfunctory deference, for he no longer ranked as potential leader. On the other hand, "Dr. Price-Mars," with a half century of hard work, personal integrity, distinguished intellectual achievement and indefatigable love for his "good people of Haiti" behind him, still enjoyed the esteem of his countrymen. Even those who deplored his acceptance of Lescot's offer, remained attached to the man. They knew that there were extenuating circumstances in the case of a scholar and country doctor. Books do not feed an author in Haiti, neither do the honoraria Price-Mars might have received from his peasant patients. In this connection, he wrote in the first anniversary edition of *La Relève*:

> In a country where the finest things have the worst fate, where more than 50,000 people pretend to be devoted to works of the mind, where the budget of public instruction exceeds several million gourdes annually, how can one explain . . . that not one publishing house is able to survive on professional activity alone, not one newspaper, not one magazine is able to cover expenses and continue the work of social action—the sole justification for their existence? This is such an anomaly that one could lose his mind in attempting to explain it.[1]

Admittedly, the Pétionville general store which Madame Price-Mars owned helped to prevent daily anxiety from destroying the scholar's ability to think and write about intellectual subjects. In 1939, four years after he had been expelled from the Senate, he had published his fourth book, *Formation ethnique.*

On coming to power in 1941, Elie Lescot had brought a new atmosphere to the National Palace. Although he had been an important member of the Vincent Government, he had not been involved in the daily game of local politics, having served for the most part in diplomatic posts abroad. And there had been no political campaign on his part for the Presidency of the Republic. However, after he became a Senator and everyone realized that he was Vincent's choice for the Presidency, he had let it be known that he would refuse to continue old enmities of the Vincent Government. Thus he had welcomed Jacques Roumain into his Administration.[2]

Price-Mars and Roumain immediately renewed their old scholarly association and in no time the latter succeeded, with governmental and municipal help, in creating a Bureau-Museum of Ethnology, while the former established and directed an Institute of Ethnology. Roumain and Madame Suzanne Sylvain-Comhaire, among others, taught courses there. At the inauguration of the Institute in November 1941, and as an introduction to a course on Africology, Price-Mars lectured on "Black Africa and her Peoples." The following year he published a booklet on *The Haitian Contribution to the Struggle in the Americas for Human Liberty.*

The development of closer relations between Haiti and the United States brought about the founding of a Haitian American Institute in Port-au-Prince. Evidently the name of "Dr. Price-Mars" had lost none of its luster, for North American and Haitian members of the new organization selected him as its director. In that capacity he was invited by the State Department in Washington to make an extended tour of the United States in 1943. In Washington he met Dantès Bellegarde who was then a visiting professor at Howard University, and the two old friends, in the company of two eminent Spanish-speaking ethnologists, Fernando Ortiz of Cuba and Fernando Romero of Peru, requested the American Council of Learned Societies to sponsor an Afro-American review to publish studies in English, Spanish and Portuguese. The subject was the Negro in the New World. Unfortunately, the project never materialized.

In 1942, Price-Mars lost his enthusiastic collaborator, Jacques Roumain, whom President Lescot had appointed as Haitian Chargé d'Affaires in Mexico. Perhaps the President made this move after being informed that Roumain, who had never renounced his political creed, had again taken up communist activities. The fact remains that about this time young leftist writers began to attack the Government from the underground for what they called "the assassination of Haitian land by the SHADA" (the Haitian-American Society for Agricultural Development). SHADA was established with the proceeds of a loan from the United States which was granted to alleviate Haiti's economic difficulties caused by the war which had closed its traditional European markets. SHADA undertook to produce sisal and the latex of a newly discovered weed named cryptostegia, that was used in the U.S.A. in the making of synthetic rubber. To produce these materials on a large scale, the Lescot Government had expropriated the lands of a great number of peasants.

Opposition intensified in 1944 when Lescot fell prey to the Haitian Chiefs of State syndrome. After serving only three years of his initial mandate, he persuaded the Haitian Legislative Chambers to re-elect him for a new seven-year term. On the pretext that elections would jeopardize Haiti's war effort, he also decreed that legislators would retain their seats for four additional years. No sooner had this deal between the National Palace and the Legislative Chambers been made than an ominous event occurred in Port-au-Prince. A week or so before May 15, when Lescot was scheduled to take the oath of office, a conspiracy to assassinate him was discovered. Again it was hatched in the Haitian Army, but this time not by its officers. The enlisted men, most of them former peasants and practically illiterate, intended to place one of their sergeants in the National Palace, taking their inspiration perhaps from the Batista saga of nearby Cuba.

The execution of the conspirators did not make the Presidency any safer for President Lescot who was finally overthrown in January 1946 following a student strike. He was then accused of having made himself solely President of the Mulattoes. The Republic came under the rule of a Military Junta made up of Colonel Franck Lavaud, Major Paul Magloire and Major Antoine Levelt whom President Lescot had asked to take over the Government to avoid bloodshed as he prepared to leave the National Palace. The Junta ruled the country until the following August when Dumarsais Estimé was elected President of the Republic.

Few Haitians were surprised when the new President, a former student and long time admirer of Price-Mars, appointed him Minister of Foreign Affairs and subsequently Minister of National Education. Price-Mars remained at those posts until April 1947 when he was sent to the Dominican Republic as Haitian Ambassador. While serving in Ciudad Trujillo, he published his fifth book, *Jean-Pierre Boyer Bazelais et le Drame de Miragoâne* (1948).

In this book Price-Mars reflects apprehensively on Governmental instability and revolutions to which he refers in his preface as "the eternal story of the man who believes he can solve the problems of collective life with fire and sword." Realizing no doubt that his presidential ambitions have definitely gone with the wind, he philosophizes:

> ... among the dominant aspirations of the public man in Haiti, that of becoming Chief of State is one of the most peremptory, attractive, and also the most deceptive in existence. By a fatality which springs from the very conditions of public life in this country, the political leader's popularity crystallizes in his person all the wishes and passions of those who see in him the virtual realization of their dreams of conquering power. Whether he wishes or not, the presidential candidacy is the ransom paid to the multitude by the man who has risen from the ranks. This is the

chief stumbling-block to effective action and it often marks the beginning of his calvary.[4]

As Price-Mars himself indicated, most of the material presented in the volume had already been published. It consists of letters, a day-by-day record of the life, military preparations and action, as well as the administrative processes of the Liberals who had landed at Miragoâne in an attempt to overthrow General Salomon, then President of Haiti and leader of the National Party. But these papers, Price-Mars tells us, contain a valuable lesson for "apprentice statesmen" who try to import foreign institutions that may not be immediately adaptable on the Haitian scene. Boyer Bazelais wanted to introduce English parliamentary liberalism which was difficult, "if not impossible to apply in a social milieu still unready for such an experience, the success of which depended on conditions and qualities foreign to it." The Haitian people was then "in a certain state of infantilism" and is still "an inarticulate people," as the Americans have described them. And Price-Mars exclaimed:

> Ah! I see very well how dramatically the problem of government has presented itself in the past and is still presenting itself before the conscience of the minority that is in power or aspiring to capture it.[5]

He concluded that the Liberals' venture failed because it lacked the support of an "organized electorate, that is to say, the consensus of a community conscious of its rights and duties." He ended his comments with this crucial question: *"But where was, where is the Haitian people, in all such undertakings?"*

Once again Price-Mars was smelling the future in the wind. At that moment, the country was experiencing the same collective psychosis which had led to armed conflict in the past between Nationals and Liberals as a result of the color syndrome. President Estimé had met the color problem from the beginning of his Administration. He had tried to help the Blacks gain economic power so as to create a Black middle class to counterbalance the power of the Mulatto bourgeoisie in the political field. But he had not accomplished much for the great Black peasant mass.

As Minister of National Education in the Cabinet of a Black President who had himself served in the same post under Vincent, Price-Mars was frustrated to see that nothing was being attempted to remove the rural people from their "state of infantilism" through public instruction. Perhaps for this reason Price Mars requested transfer to the Dominican Republic post which had interested him for quite some time.[6] Indeed he had published several articles in the *Société haitienne d'Histoire et de géographie* about the Dominican Republic. Whatever plan he may have had in mind for "social transformation" of rural Haiti would certainly have required substantial financial appropriations for its implementation. However, President Estimé had made Haiti's economic independence his first priority. He achieved this in 1947 by paying off the American loan after two years of budgetary restraint in other governmental projects.

To increase Haiti's revenues from tourism, immediately after paying the American debt, the President started on the gigantic project of an International Exposition to commemorate the two hundredth anniversary of the founding of Port-au-Prince. Opposition to that project came from one of the members of the defunct Military Junta, Colonel Paul Magloire, a Black from the Northern Province. As all Port-au-Prince knew, Magloire was waiting to succeed Estimé in the National Palace. He, too, had in mind a grandiose project: a celebration of the 150th anniversary of Haiti's independence in 1954.

While President Estimé was holding with the hare and running with the hounds on the color question,* Magloire had more or less openly associated himself with the mulatto élite who were accusing the National Palace of permitting Voodoo right in the capital. One of the President's uncles was rumored to be the principal promoter of the African cult in a fashionable section of Port-au-Prince.

The International Exposition was a great success, attracting participants from Latin-America and most of the Western powers. The Vatican built a replica of the Sistine Chapel at the "Cité Dumarsais Estimé," as the Exposition grounds were called. The success of the Exposition, payment of the American loan, and Estimé's no less successful maneuver in the local field on behalf of the black middle class, had made the President a giant in the eyes of the Blacks throughout the country as he approached the end of his term in 1950. Succumbing to the traditional malady endemic to Haitian Chiefs of State, as so many had before, Estimé decided to capitalize on the record of his Administration and declared himself a candidate for re-election despite the fact that the 1946 Constitution forbade immediate re-election of the incumbent president. Prompted no doubt by Colonel Magloire, the Legislative Chambers refused to accede to Estimé's wishes. The President then called on the people to demonstrate their wishes in the matter. The result was pandemonium. On May 9th the common people of the capital turned out in an avalanche of men and women who surrounded the National Palace and acclaimed the President. That evening Colonel Magloire allegedly visited the Government Printing establishment and carried off the decree signed by President Estimé dissolving the Legislative

---

*Considering the power of the Mulattoes, the man in the street approved this policy on his part and had nicknamed Estimé "Roulé deux bords," which means to pass alternatively from one side to the other, while persevering toward one's goal.

Chambers. The next morning, instead of seeing his decree in print, the President saw two young mulatto officers, friends of Magloire, invade his living quarters at the National Palace. Armed with machine guns, they forced Estimé to write out his letter of resignation from the Presidency.

At that time Price-Mars was at the United Nations as the Head of the Haitian Delegation to the World Organization, having been sent there by President Estimé in 1949. The latter's affection and veneration for the "Uncle" had prompted him to make Price-Mars the outstanding beneficiary of his Government by assigning him to the highest posts possible. In a sense, those assignments could be considered as reparation for the neglect of past governments which had never even considered Price-Mars for such posts.[7] Needless to say, Price-Mars was distressed by the news of Estimé's ouster for the event would probably cause his own retirement from public life at the age of seventy-four.

*   *   *

Colonel Magloire restored to power the same Military Junta which had taken the reins after the overthrow of President Lescot. Whereas he had remained more or less in the background the first time to help build by foreign governments, this time he presented himself overtly as the leader of the group and a candidate for the Presidency. Eventually he was elected Chief Executive by direct popular vote and took the oath of office on December 6, 1950. Price-Mars returned home in January 1951 and in November lectured at the Alliance Française on the subject of "Folklore and Patriotism."

While Estimé had tried belatedly to make the common people the bulwark of his Administration[8] and had come close to creating a "black mystique" among the black intellectuals, President Magloire openly made himself the friend and protector of the élite. Price-Mars was particularly incensed by the charge that Estimé had enfranchised Voodoo in the nation's capital. The "Uncle" went so far as to shower anathema on the élite in his talk "Folklore and Patriotism":

> Ah! you do not want to hear Voodoo mentioned; your ears are offended by the raucous sound of the drums; the dynamic, rhythmic crisscross of the Voodoo dances confuses your vision and your conception of choreography; your academism is revolted by the syncopated beat of the chant; you feel nothing but shame and scorn for this form of barbarism and you call on the Penal Code to help stop this scandal that clashes so violently with the degree of civilization which you pride yourself on having attained.
>
> So be it!
>
> Beware, however, lest all these grievances be used someday as charges that the people shall level against you at the fateful hour

when you shall be called to account. For, in fact, if you and the people are two distinct and irreconcilable entities, then the question of deciding to whom this land belongs can only be settled by force.

I should hope that victory will not be on your side because, even now, the economic basis on which our material civilization rests is crumbling under your feet.

We must realize that all of us belong to the same Haitian community that has emerged from the infamy of slavery. The social separation timidly started during colonial days has only widened since the time you and I replaced the former masters to enjoy all the privileges of domination through wealth and authority. So the people has a right to ask us: What have you done during the last 150 years to raise our intellectual and moral status? What have you done for the people of this country, since 80 percent [of the population] is still illiterate.[9]

Two years later Price-Mars was still bitter about the racial issue when he published the two volumes of his book on *La République d'Haiti et la République Dominicaine.* It was from that book that we borrowed the title of this chapter which appeared as its frontal caption. Telling the story of the whole island from its discovery on December 6, 1492, the author writes: "The central character of this great tragedy is the Black Man who, for four hundred years has been engaged here in a ferocious battle with the entire world to bring it to recognize his status as a Man."

Price-Mars could not help feeling enraged by the claim of the Dominicans that they belonged to the Caucasian Race. One of their writers, Pena Battle, in the 1940's ferociously attacked Haiti about her Voodoo, pleading for the preservation of the biological integrity of the Dominicans against the intrusions of the Haitians who are themselves definitely of African race.[10] This psychological problem has kept Haitians and Dominicans on a war footing ever since the latter were brought under Toussaint-Louverture's rule in 1801. And Price-Mars now undertakes to destroy the myth of Dominican racial superiority with the combined help of history, geography and ethnology. Taking advantage of the "Album del Oro," published by the Dominican Government in 1935, which produced statistical charts concerning demographic information on the Dominican people. Price-Mars had this to say:

From the beginning of the formation of our nationality to where we have arrived in our life as free men in 1953, we have devoted one hundred and fifty years of struggle, effort, anguish, and sacrifices of all kinds to defend the existence and preserve its integrity against all forms of imperialism. It seems to us that in this crucial adventure we have not proved unworthy of ourselves and of humanity . . .

Does one need to reaffirm here that the ancestors who successfully revolted against the suffering and the degradation inflicted on human nature have transmitted to their sons the strength and the privileges of an indestructible power of human creation and continuity?

Let the intellectuals on the Ozama River believe that the Dominican community is made up of the Caucasian race, *métissée* or autochthonous. The scorn they show for the most elementary notions of ethnology indicates a specific tendency of their mentality. Their whole attitude in that instance is tinged with emotional subjectivity. In this respect one might say that they illustrate the Mussolini joke, namely that the notion of race is a matter of feeling.[11]

Price-Mars was seventy-seven years of age when he produced the five hundred and sixty-five pages of *La République d'Haïti et la République Dominicaine*. He had worked on the book for a long time. After reading the book one of his students at the Lycée Pétion remembered "more than one page he had made us the first to know as mere history notes from his research and meditations."[12] But we are told by Henock Trouillot that those notes and other materials that previously appeared in the *Revue de la Société haitienne d'histoire et de géographie* "had been revised, completed and provided with new documentation, more solid and more relevant [documentation] which presented them in a fresh perspective."[13] This underscores the amount of work Price-Mars had done to prepare the final version of his work, in which he demonstrated the same vigor of thought, the same erudition, the same thoroughness in his research as well as the same attention to his style. This book contributed much to inspire his admirers—both in Haiti and abroad, to create around him the aura of glory—the glory he dreamed about as a youth and actually enjoyed in 1956 on his eightieth birthday, when *Témoignages sur la vie et l'oeuvre du Dr. Jean Price-Mars* was published in Port-au-Prince with contributions from sixty-six writers, Haitian and foreign. Among those from abroad were President Léopold Sédar Senghor, of Senegal and W. E. Burghardt DuBois, of the United States, to name only the two most prominent soldiers on the ramparts of "Négritude."

Meanwhile, in 1954, Colonel Magloire, having obtained from the Haitian Legislature the rank of Major General, presided over the ceremonies of the 150th Anniversary of the Independence of Haiti in a resplendent military outfit. Yet, as he approached the end of his presidential term all the acclamations he had orchestrated on that National Day vanished in thin air. He found it necessary at one time to defend himself in an official speech about "his whiskey drinking" at the National Palace, which was being lampooned in the popular Creole songs of the country. Eventually on December 6, 1956, the year of the publication of *Témoignages*, the General informed the nation that he would remain at the National Palace. His brothers-in-arms were by that time completely disillusioned with his six years performance in the Presidency of the Republic—to say nothing of the common people who knew him only as "Cançon Fè" meaning in Creole "Iron Pants," as he liked to be called by his friends to intimidate the man in the street. The ranking officers of the Haitian Army thus turned thumbs down on him and called on Joseph Nemours Pierre-Louis, President of the Haitian Supreme Court, to form and lead a provisional government. Like Dumarsais Estimé, the new President from the Northern Province, was a great admirer of Price-Mars. Thus, as expected, a month later he called Price-Mars out of retirement, naming him Rector (President) of the University of Haiti.

In the fall of the same year, 1956, Price-Mars once more went to his beloved Paris to find that another great tribute was awaiting him at the Sorbonne. He went there as the Delegate from Haiti to participate in the First Congress of Black writers and Black artists. At that time Léopold Sédar Senghor was representing Senegal in France's National Assembly. As one of the foremost poets of *Négritude,* he took the initiative of asking his colleagues at the Congress to interrupt its proceedings and to join with him in celebrating the jubilee of Price-Mars, for 1956 was the fiftieth anniversary of Price-Mars's lecture on "The Prejudice of Races." In the course of the Congress Price-Mars was elected president of the newly created Société Africaine de Culture.

Price-Mars returned to Haiti to become in December Foreign Minister once again. In February 1957 President Pierre-Louis sent him back to Paris as Haitian Ambassador to France. Soon after that Haiti entered a period of political turmoil which brought about the end of the provisional government as the result of a fierce political competition among the many candidates for the Presidency. Finally another former student of Price-Mars at the Lycée Pétion, Dr. François Duvalier, was elected by the National Assembly on September 22, 1957.

It goes without saying that the new President did not recall Price-Mars from Paris. He remained there as the central personality of the "Monde Noir." And in 1959, as Black intellectuals around the world prepared for the Second Congress of Black writers and Black artists, he published his seventh book, *De Saint-Domingue à Haiti.* He wrote in his foreward:

> At this moment when Black Africa is confronted by a new destiny in the political, economic and social transformation which the present evolution of all the peoples on the earth reveals, it seemed opportune to record what the Haitian people have accomplished culturally in 155 years of independence. However fragmentary and incomplete the essays in this volume may be, they at least indicate that Haiti has endeavored to make her contribution to the flowering of Western civilization.[14]

That same year he presided over the second annual meeting of the Congress of Black Writers and Black Artists in Rome. His new book corrected the defects of the earlier *Stage of Haitian Evolution,* presented analysis of Haitian literature and art as well as included a chapter on "Haiti's position and French culture in the Americas." By that time folkloric dances, "primitive" painting and wood-carving from Haiti had won the praise of intellectuals, artist and buyers. In Washington, Madame Lina Mathon's dance group had been invited by the *Washington Post* and was acclaimed at Constitution Hall in 1940 and 1941. The following year the Marcelin brothers had won the Latin American Novel Prize with their *Canapé Vert,* and two years later Jacques Roumain's *Gouverneurs de la Rosée* had appeared[15] Selden Rodman had popularized Haitian painting in his magnificent book, *Renaissance in Haiti: Popular Painters in the Black Republic* (1948). Referring to all this with understandable pride, Price-Mars commented:

> But what is this rhythm that comes again and again into my pen and onto my lips so persistently? What is the meaning of this new aspect of Haitian art? To what does this renewal of Haitian literature correspond? How can one explain this flowering of our arts and literature if not by the American intervention into our lives. This is the point of departure of a new ideology which has brought about the contrast between our conception of yesterday and that of today in regard to art, literature and culture in the ethnographic sense of the term. It has forced us to revise our peculiar Haitian values and Black values in general, and to see that they are none other than the essence and substance of man, different yet similar to himself here as elsewhere, everywhere on the planet, tied to the same destiny and playing the same role in the oppressive tragedy of life.[16]

It would seem that Price-Mars produced the best specimen of his literary style.[17] For in the year of its publication, *De Saint-Domingue à Haiti* was awarded the French Academy's prize for the French language which the Academy extended to Price-Mars' previous works as well. Indeed Price-Mars had achieved the unity of of his two Haitian cultural heritages. Dantès Bellegarde probably smiled, not scornfully but joyously, on reading Price-Mars' reply to the rhetorical question: In what language did Haiti speak to an astounded world after she had gained her independence?

> Would you believe it? Well, to proclaim *urbi et orbi* her right to dispose freely of her destiny, she found that no other instrument was more appropriate for promulgating her gospel than this beautiful French language, universally used and appreciated. She used it with pride. Thus, it was in French that she wrote the constitutive Acts of her Nationality. Moreover, she deliberately and resolutely adopted the same institutions that had brought down all the Bastilles in 1789; and she proudly paid homage to the

principles she had inscribed on the flags of her victorious armies. In doing so, she wanted to proclaim that she was the eldest daughter of the French Revolution.[18]

President Duvalier recalled Price-Mars later that year and had the Haitian Legislature grant the "Uncle" a pension equal to that of a Chief of State.[19] *Présence Africaine* published his eighth book, *Silhouettes de Nègres et de Négrophiles,* which contains a number of biographies, among them one on Dr. George Washington Carver. This he wrote at the suggestion of this biographer.[20] One also finds in the book a study of Toussaint-Louverture, Price-Mars' ever present inspiration as the authentic Black man, replacing the artificial one white people had created in their own minds and even forced the Blacks the world over to adopt. The "Uncle" was still fighting Toussaint's battle, confident that his voice would resurrect the spirit of the Black Titan which would in turn stimulate all Blacks to continue the struggle until justice is eventually achieved.

For the subject of his next book, Price-Mars selected his early benefactor, Vilbrun Guillaume Sam.[21] He hoped to exonerate the memory of the man who had loved him as a child, had taken an interest in his education, had welcomed him under his roof and eventually called for his help at the National Palace. Price-Mars reminded his readers that the real culprit in the massacre of July 27, 1915, which resulted in the American Occupation, was not Vilbrun, but Charles Oscar, Military Commander of Port-au-Prince, known by many to be a man of deranged mentality. It was General Oscar who ordered the executions. But Price-Mars seemed to forget that it was Vilbrun who ordered the political prisoners held in the Government jail despite a no-cause judgment on their behalf.

The following year, at the age of eighty-six, Price-Mars published *De la Préhistoire d'Afrique à l'histoire d'Haiti,* a work of some 217 pages which was to be his last printed volume. Two years later Price-Mars lost his beloved wife, Clara. She died at the moment he needed her most, for in 1964 he had begun to lose his sight. She had not only graced his home and enshrined him in her affection, but had also been a most sensitive collaborator. One of his foreign friends recorded this testimony:

> During my stay in Haiti I had the exceptional good luck to reside in Pétionville not very far from the home of Dr. Price-Mars, who honored me with his friendship . . . How many times on his shaded villa porch we discussed innumerable problems: history, diplomacy, ethnology, folklore . . . He examined each problem with a great sense of the human and, above all, without the slightest resentment or racial or color prejudice . . . Often . . . his charming wife would enter with a smile and join the visitors, bringing a touch of charm to the arid conversation . . . Dry theories were suddenly illustrated by touching episodes from the life of Kenscoff peasants, to which she could add Creole proverbs.[22]

Price-Mars was almost completely blind in 1966. Nevertheless, he accepted an invitation from President Senghor and went to Dakar as the guest of the Senegalese Government to attend the First World Festival of Negro Arts. There he was greeted by the African President as "The Father of Négritude," and went about being led by Marie-Madeleine. This was the last significant honor he received while still alive.[23]

Until the end of his life, he usually got up at five a.m., took his bath and dressed, always wearing a tie for he expected friends to come by. He lived not for study alone, but for friendship too. While waiting he listened to the world news on the powerful radio in his den. According to his son, Louis, the day before his death he was talking about some work he wanted to do and about a biography of Anténor Firmin he had completed and hoped to publish soon.[24] The "Uncle" died on Saturday, March 1, 1969. He left no last word for posterity having passed away in his sleep. He left the name Price-Mars which by itself was a manifesto to all those who believed as he did.

* * *

Price-Mars lived long enough to see his words become action at home and abroad. In Haiti, his thoughts, particularly those in *Ainsi Parla l'Oncle,* had caused a literary, spiritual and social revolution. Abroad, Stokely Carmichael was drawn to Haitian history to rediscover Toussaint-Louverture, as the young black militant once told an American reporter, to serve as his inspiration in his Black Power crusade in the United States and the Caribbean where he was born. "The Caribbean Black Power movement," wrote a *Time* magazine contributor," can be traced to the writing of Haiti's Jean Price-Mars in the 1920's. Long before Senegal's Poet-President Léopold Senghor had defined his concept of *Négritude,* Price-Mars was writing of the black man's need to accept his African heritage and to use it as a cultural resource, a theme echoed today by Martiniquan poet and dramatist, Aimé Césaire. Accordingly, many of the Caribbean's contemporary radicals, like their counterparts in the U.S., talk about a spiritual return to Africa.[25]

Price-Mars was ninety-three years old when he died. He lived through several Haitis as well as several worlds. Curiously enough, he was born in the shadow of Cormiers where Dessalines, the Founder of the Haition nation was born, and he died in Pétionville, a city named after Alexandre Pétion who had established the Republican form of government in the newly born independent State. He had witnessed countless revolutions and civil wars as well as the loss of Haiti's sovereignty to the United States, and had lived to see the Haitians retake to themselves the destiny of their country.

Jean Price-Mars and Family

Back Row: *Raymond Mars, Marie-Madeleine Price-Mars, Elizabeth Scott, Dr. Louis Mars, Maurice Mars*
Front Row: *Louis Henry Mars, Mme Louis Mars, Dr. Jean Price-Mars, Mme Jean Price-Mars, Emmeline Mars*

Because he was a patriot and never a politician in the usual pejorative sense of the word, the succeeding phases of his long life have been related to the problems of the existence and the programs of the "Fatherland" with an intensity bordering on hallucination.

These problems and events, combined with the spiritual inspiration Price-Mars had received from his birthplace, were to stimulate his intellectual growth to the height where the merged strength of his lucid mind and his passionate heart brought about the captivating blossoming of his "Black" thoughts on the universal vine of humanism. They helped to strengthen the stamen of his moral conscience whose rectitude at times may have seemed to waver under pressures of necessity or threats of violence, but which regained full force at critical moments in the life of his nation.

In 1956, René Piquion, one of Price-Mars' ardent partisans in the presidential campaign of 1930, wrote in a newspaper article that some of Price-Mars' young followers had blamed him for having failed to exploit the color question to his advantage in the presidential campaign and election of 1930. They obviously felt that Price-Mars would have won the presidency had he done so. A decade later in 1966, Piquion again expressed this opinion in a book he published on *Négritude*.[26]

Price-Mars did not respond to this criticism until 1967. At that time, the color question had become extremely acute for the whole nation as President Duvalier was developing the "mystique" he had announced in his "Declaration" published in *The Griots*.

The notorious activities of the so-called *Tontons Macoutes* had rendered the political and social climate the more explosive because some of the Duvalier's fanatical Black followers would interpret the coincidence of the date of Duvalier's election to the Presidency and the date of the "Fire" during the Presidency of Salomon, September 22, as a command from Salomon's unsatisfied soul that Mulatto Power be eliminated from Haiti even at the cost of continuing devastation.

At such a conjuncture, Price-Mars was to consistently challenge the status quo from the strength of his honest conscience to tell the "unvarnished truth" he had vowed to speak when was in his twenties? Thus spoke "Uncle":

> In order to go to the North to start campaigning I had to resign myself to sell at a low price the horse I used to visit my rural patients, $60. Some devoted, generous friends whose names I have promised not to divulge put a Dodge car at my disposal. It was in such conditions that I went to fight the senatorial battle in the North. Running for the Presidency constituted a real defiance of destiny. For my senatorial status had not increased my financial status. The lack of money that characterizes my life was thus the essential cause of my presidential failure of 1930. I could not help

any of my most zealous partisans to be elected either to the Senate or the House so they might participate in the National Assembly for the election of the Chief of State. If to this major infirmity some secondary causes were added, none, however, constituted what some people have called my inability to raise "the color question" as a tactic that might have helped me gain power. Not only would such a maneuver have been unworthy of my whole life which I have tried with great effort to maintain as righteous, laborious and honest, but I would feel ashamed for lowering myself to the level of those contemptible politicians who are always ready to change their opinions and their feelings in accordance with the circumstances, provided their baser instincts and their ambitions are satisfied.[27]

Price-Mars entered political life not as a politician of the kind he described in his reply to Piquion. He sought the Presidency of the Republic not as a man thirsty for power merely to use it to dominate his fellow-citizens and satisfy personal resentments. He sought power with a healthy mind and prompted by a generous heart to use it in the interest of his "good people of Haiti." And what he dreamed of accomplishing had always been to cure the Haitian people of their detrimental class hatred and color antagonism and to transform them into *one* community—a stable, decent and progressive community of concerned and harmonious partners, remembering perhaps Aristotle's saying that "Friendship is the greatest good of states."

Price-Mars' advocacy of "Black consciousness" never meant hating another person on account of his race or skin color. For he felt at all times an indestructible bond of solidarity between himself and all Haitians. Under a mystical guidance, he had lived a long life of reaching out to all peoples to bring them closer together. His "Black consciousness" primarily meant, as he illustrated with his own life, working unceasingly to carve one's own "black marble" in one's own way to contribute something worthwhile to one's own society and that of the larger world community. For the freedom to do so, he was ready to fight at any moment, and he fought fiercely with his pen on behalf of Haiti and the Black race for sixty-three years. By the time of death, due in large measure to his work, the white man's disparaging and dishonest image of the Negro had been destroyed in the minds of all Black people.

Jean Price Mars

Footnotes

Chapter One

[1] Salnave had come from exile in the Dominican Republic to lead the revolution that eventually overthrew President Fabre Geffrard.

[2] General Boisrond-Canal became the leader of the moderate wing of the Liberal Party the following year as he went to the National Palace as President. He was no reformist or moralist as was Boyer-Bazelais, the titular head of that party in the Haitian parliament. As President of the Republic, Boisrond-Canal usually expressed his philosophy of government through two Creole words, "Laissez grainin" (Let things work themselves out) whenever he was faced with problems requiring strong intervention on his part against governmental abuses.

[3] Dantès Bellegarde, *La Nation haitienne,* J. de Gigord, Editeur, Paris, 1938, p. 134.

[4] Hannibal Price had been elected to the House by the people of Jacmel, a prosperous city of the Western Province, on the southern coast of the island. Jacmel had been the scene of the fiercely fought color war of 1800, between Toussaint-Louverture and the mulatto general André Rigaud, with Dessalines on the side of Toussaint, both Black and former slaves, and Pétion on the side of Rigaud, both mulattoes and freemen.

[5] During the 1820's, the idea of returning the American Negroes to Africa had taken root in the U. S. following the founding of the American Colonization Society in 1817. President Boyer intervened to try to divert some of the Blacks to Haiti to replace manpower lost in the war between Toussaint and Rigaud and the war for Haitian independence. He hoped thus to promote agricultural development in Haiti with skilled artisans from the U. S. He felt that the Negroes "groaning in the United States, under the weight of prejudice and misery, should be disposed to come to Haiti and partake with [her] citizens the benefits of a liberal constitution and a paternal government." (Quoted in Rayford Logan, *The Diplomatic Relations...,* p. 217). To provide the necessary funds for the transportation of American Negroes to Haiti, Boyer sent an agent in New York City 50,000 pounds of coffee to be sold in the U. S.

[6] Cf. Mrs. Harold K. Heneise's letter to the writer of this biography from the Séminaire Théologique Baptiste d'Haiti in Cap-Haitian, dated November 6, 1969.

[7] *La Relève,* Vol. 3, December 1934, p. 2. In another work, much later, Price-Mars wrote the name "Godart" with a final "d" instead of a "t".

[8] Ibidem, p. 4.

[9] Today Grégoire is remembered for his abolitionist activities and for his famous volume, *De la Littérature des Nègres,* published in Paris in 1808.

[10] Price-Mars, *Silhouettes de Nègres et de Négrophiles,* Paris: Présence Africaine, 1960, p. 204.

[11] Thomas Madiou, *Histoire d'Haiti,* Port-au-Prince, Imp. Edmond Chenet, 1922, Vol. 1, p. 252.

[12] Price-Mars, *Silhouettes de Nègres et de Négrophiles,* Paris: Présence Africaine, 1960, pp. 44-45.

[13] *Ibid.,* p. 46.

[14] *La Relève,* op. cit. p. 11.

[15] James Leyburn, *The Haitian People,* New Haven: Yale University Press, 1941, p. 295.

[16] Price-Mars, *Ainsi parla l'oncle,* Compiègne, 1928, p. 166.

[17] President Geffrard also brought to Haiti a number of American Negroes, as President Boyer had done in the 1820's and for the same purpose.

[18] *La Relève,* op. cit., p. 17.

Chapter Two

[1] The lad was then called Ti-Price (pronounced *Tee Preece* in the French manner.) "TI" is the unavoidable prefix standing for *petit* (small), which is often added to Christian names of children in Haiti.

[2] Emmanuel Lamaute, *Le vieux Port-au-Prince,* Port-au-Prince: Imp. de la Compagnie Lithographique d'Haiti, 1939, p. 90.

[3] *La Relève,* op. cit., p. 3.

[4] *La Relève,* op. cit., p. 5.

[5] President Salomon was a black, the brother of a senator who had been executed by the Geffrard Government. The President, a well-educated man, had also been a senator. Ostracized from the political scene, he had been kept in exile for twenty years as Haiti's diplomatic representative in Paris and London, and had returned home to be the candidate of the National Party after the resignation of Boisrond-Canal.

[6] *La Relève,* op. cit., p. 5

[7] René Piquion, *Manuel de Négritude,* Port-au-Prince: Eds. Henri Deschamps, n.d., p. 163.

[8] S. Rouzier, *Dictionnaire géographique et administratif universel d'Haiti,* Vo. 1-2 (A-Ha) under the headline "Grande Rivière du Nord," p. 60.

[9] *La Relève,* op. cit., p. 5.

[10] Practices dating back to colonial times when such leaders of slave revolts as Mackandal, Bookman, Hyacinthe, and others claimed to be unvulnerable under the protection of African gods. Toussaint-Louverture, though an overtly practicing Catholic himself, is suspected of having had such belief from the fact that after he became a soldier he always had his head covered with a handkerchief which he never removed in public even while attending mass.

[11] An octoroon, she looked like a white person. In King Christophe's court, one of Eléomont's forebears, a Jean-Pierre Gaou Mars, was an excellent harness-maker, though he bore the title of Baron. (Cf. Emile Paultre, *Essai sur M. Price-Mars,* Port-au-Prince, 1966, p. 33.)

[12] *La Relève,* op. cit., p. 5.

[13] Firmin, born in Cap-Haitien, had campaigned unsuccessfully in 1879 for election to the House of Representatives. At this time, however, he was riding the crest of popular acclaim gained three years earlier with the publication in Paris of his monumental work of some 650 pages, *On the Equality of Human Races.*

[14] Anténor Firmin, *De l'Egalité des races humaines,* as quoted in Pradel Pompilus and Frères de l'Instruction Chrétienne's *Manuel Illustré de la Littérature Haitienne,*

Editions Henri Deschamps, Port-au-Prince, 1961, pp. 192-193.

[15]*La Relève,* op. cit., p. 4.

[16]Emile Paultre, op. cit., p. 30.

[17]C. Texier, *Au Pays des Généraux,* Paris: Calmann Lévy, 1891, p. 283.

[18]Ludwell Le Montague, *Haiti and the United States, 1714-1938,* Duke University Press, Durham, North Carolina, 1940, p. 150.

[19]Rayford W. Logan, *The Diplomatic Relations of the United States with Haiti,* The University of North Carolina Press, Chapel Hill, 1941, p. 433.

[20]Montague, op. cit., p. 150.

[21]Logan, op. cit., p. 448.

The World, New York, Monday, January 25, 1892, p. 3.

[23]By a former British Minister to Haiti, Sir Spencer St. John.

[24]Price-Mars, *Lettre ouverte au Dr. René Piquion,* Les Editions des Antilles, Port-au-Prince, 1967, p. 8.

[25]Emmanuel Lamaute, op. cit., p. 89.

[26]Referring precisely to that time, the Haitian author of *Le vieux Port-au-Prince* writes: "If one knows that right in the city the *houngans* were consulted for the mildest cases of cold or any discomfort, one will easily understand the frequency of child mortality, particularly among the poor." (Ibid., p. 90)

[27]Emile Paultre, op. cit., p. 34.

Chapter Three

[1]Price-Mars, *Vilbrun Guillaume Sam, ce méconnu,* Port-au-Prince, 1961.

[2]At the time Price-Mars was born, Vilbrun was stationed at Grande Rivière, serving in the Army as secretary to Seide Télémaque.

[3]Firmin, *Letters from St. Thomas,* 1910. (This was Firmin's last political writing in which he admonished the Haitians never to abandon their Latin culture for Anglo-Saxon culture.)

[4]*La Relève,* op. cit., p. 12.

[5]Ibid.

[6]Ibid., p. 13.

[7]Dantès Bellegarde, *Ecrivains Haitiens,* Port-au-Prince, 1947, p. 283.

[8]Quoted in Thomas Madiou, op. cit., Vol. III, p. 150.

[9]Price-Mars, "Son Ideal," in *La Ronde,* 1900.

[10]Price-Mars, "Les Corbeaux," in the Haitian magazine *L'Essor,* December 1912.

[11]Ibid.

[12]The immediate cause of his departure will be discussed at the beginning of Chapter IV.

[13]Ludwell Lee Montague, op. cit., p. 179.

[14]Dantès Bellegarde, "Un Haitien Parle . . . " in *Cahiers d'Haiti,* Port-au-Prince, 1943, Vol. I, No. 1, p. 35.

[15]*Rehabilitation of the Black Race by the Republic of Haiti,* appeared in Port-au-Prince. The author had this to say in its avant-propos: "I felt the need of raising my voice to defend my country so viciously slandered, to show and prove to other peoples that the words they have heard about Haiti are words of hatred and not words of History, and more less those of philanthropy." Price who had died in exile in

Brooklyn, New York, 1893, had come back to haunt the minds of Haitian youth with this challenge, contained in his book: "This nation certainly has a mission from Heaven to discharge in the world, which it cannot betray without incurring God's wrath. This mission is the complete destruction of racial prejudice by making the progress of Haiti unmistakable." p. 155.

[16] Léon Gontran Damas, "Price-Mars, le père du Haitianisme," in *Présence Africaine*, Paris, June-September, 1960, p. 168.

Chapter Four

[1] This had also happened to President Geffrard after the incident of July 6, 1861, when he bowed before the armed threat of Spanish Admiral Rubalcava. Public opinion urged him to adopt the same attitude his predecessor, Emperor Faustin, had taken a decade or so earlier when French Admiral Duquesne came to demand payments on a French loan. The Emperor dismissed the threat by his courageous retort to the Frenchman: "I shall repel force with force." (Cf. Dantès Bellegarde, *La Nation Haitienne*, p. 122).

[2] As quoted in Price-Mars, *Une Etape de l'Evolution Haitienne*, Imp. "La Presse," Port-au-Prince, 1929, p. 195. Beauvais Lespinasse is the author of *History of the Freemen of Saint-Domingue*, Paris, 1882.

[3] Manigat's name had figured in the New York conspiracy to overthrow President Hyppolite. On taking office, President Tirésias had named him to the Legation in Paris to put the Atlantic Ocean between them, rather than to have him in Jamaica, only seventy miles away.

[4] J. Montague Simson, *Six Months in Port-au-Prince and my experience*, Philadelphia; G. S. Ferguson Co., 1905, p. 45.

[5] Robert Cornevin, "L'Oncle n'est plus (1876-1969), champion de la négritude" in *France-Eurafrique*, No. 205, Vol. 21, April 1969, p. 3.

[6] J. C. Dorsainvil, *Manuel d'Histoire d'Haiti*, Port-au-Prince, 1934, p. 330.

[7] General Boisrond-Canal could not have forgotten his bitter experience with the "liberals" under the leadership of Boyer-Bazelais, the same "liberals" who now called themselves "Firministes."

[8] The feud between General Nord and Firmin dated back to December 22, 1867, when General Nord betrayed Salnave's revolution against Geffrard and attempted to take Cap-Haitien by force. He was met by the youth of the city, led by Anténor Firmin, who was then only seventeen years of age. They forced the assailants to withdraw after Firmin had single-handedly seized their cannon from under the General's nose. Firmin rode in triumph on this cannon through the streets of Cap-Haitien. He later married Salnave's daughter.

[9] Price-Mars, *La Relève*, Vol. 3, December 1934, p. 14.

[10] Ibid.

[11] Almost the first move made by the new President was to put on trial ex-President Tirésias and members of his government, among them Vilbrun, who had not gone into exile. Vilbrun was convicted later in the Consolidation trial and sentenced to life imprisonment at hard labor, but remained in prison only a short while.

[12] Price-Mars, *La Vocation de l'Elite*, Port-au-Prince, 1919, pp. 198-200.

[13] Hannibal Price, *De la Réhabilitation de la Race Noire par la République d'Haiti*, Port-au-Prince, 1900, p. vii.

[14] Douglass Papers, Cedar Hill, Anacostia, Washington, D. C.

[15] Ibid.

[16] Demosthènes and Lycurgue Sam, his sons; L.B. St. Victor and General Vilbrun Guillaume. The latter, who had been his last Minister of War, was a natural son of Vilbrun Guillaume Sam, who was himself a brother of Augustin Simon Sam, father of Tirésias, and a brother as well of Adelina Simon Sam, mother of Price-Mars' grandmother.

[17] J. Montague Simpson, op. cit., p. 45.

[18] Pouget may have told Price-Mars this anecdote: On December 6, 1897, the day of the *Affaire Lüders*, he, Pouget, was acting as Chargé d'Affaires in Berlin. Pouget was then twenty-eight years old and, like Pierre Fréderique in Port-au-Prince, was seeing red in Berlin. He requested and obtained an audience with the German Emperor, but as he was leaving for the Imperial Palace, he received a cable from home: the Haitian Government was informing the Legation that it had met the German demands. Pouget had intended to go to the Imperial Palace to kill the Kaiser.

[19] The year before, Jacques-Nicolas Léger, then Haitian Minister in Washington, published an article in the *North American Review*, in which he painted a very bright picture of Haitian progress and prosperity. His article prompted this comment by J. Montague Simpson: "Despite what Mr. Léger may assert to the contrary, there is a great deal of voodooism in Haiti, education is backward and the mass of the people entirely illiterate."(Op. cit., p. 7.)

[20] Price-Mars, *La Vocation de l'Elite*, pp. 177-178. It was in 1903 that W. E. B. DuBois published *The Souls of Black Folk*, which contained a straightforward criticism of the Tuskegee philosophy and a statement of DuBois' own aims of higher training for Negroes. This spear-headed Negro opposition to what soon afterward came to be called the "Washington Program."

[21] Price-Mars, Ibid., p. 179.

[22] Price-Mars, Ibid., p. 178.

[23] Fleury Féquière, *L'Education haitienne*, Port-au-Prince, 1906. As quoted in Lélia J. Lhérisson, *Manuel de Littérature Haitienne*, Port-au-Prince, 1955, pp. 264-266.

[24] Price-Mars, *La Vocation de l'Elite*, p. 179.

[25] Ibid., p. 180.

[26] Ibid., p. 165.

[27] Ibid., pp. 180-182.

[28] Ibid., p. 186.

[29] Dantès Bellegarde, "Hommage à Price-Mars," in *Témoignages sur la vie et l'oeuvre du Dr. Jean Price-Mars*, Port-au-Prince, 1956, p. 7.

[30] In addition to his medical degree, he had also obtained a Doctorate in Law from the University of Paris.

[31] Simpson, op. cit., p. 105.

[32] Ibid., p. 29.

Chapter Five

[1] Price-Mars, *La Vocation de l'Elite*, p. 185.

[2] Price-Mars, *Une Etape de l'évolution haitienne*, Port-au-Prince, Imp. "La Presse," 1929, p. 54.

[3] Frédéric Marcelin, *Autour de deux romans*, Paris, 1903, p. 120.

[4] Ibid., p. 119.

⁵J. Montague Simpson, op. cit., pp. 142-143.

⁶Ibid., p. 151.

⁷*La Relève,* Vol. VI, No. 11, May 1938, p. 13.

⁸Antoine Bervin, *Louis-Edouard Pouget,* Société d'Editions et de Librairie, Port-au-Prince, 1946, p. 137.

⁹Ibid., p. 145.

¹⁰Ibid., pp. 169-170.

¹¹Price-Mars, *La Vocation de l'Elite,* p. 192.

¹²All these types, except the quadroon, were to be found in Price-Mars' own family. His godmother, Arthemise Lacoste, was an octoroon, the product of a quadroon and a white.

¹³Price-Mars, *La Vocation de l'Elite,* p. 209.

¹⁴Jean-Jumeau had been a sort of proconsul under President Salomon in the Department of the Artibonite where Gonaives is located.

¹⁵J. C. Dorsainvil, op. cit., p. 335.

¹⁶As quoted in Pompilus et al., op. cit., p. 504.

¹⁷Hannibal Price, op. cit., p. 141.

¹⁸Delorme had already played an outstanding part on Haiti's political scene before he became the leader of the National Party in 1876, which was to help Salomon gain power three years later. He had been the intellectual torchbearer of the revolution of 1865 which overthrew Geffrard and brought Salnave to the Presidency. The latter who was a Mulatto had made himself the leader of the common people, hence his nickname "Black Salnave," and took Delorme in his Cabinet as Minister of Foreign Affairs and Public Instruction. Delorme became a literary giant five years later with the publication of his monumental book, *The Theoreticians in Power,* in which he argued that in a Democracy, "the more a man rises by his intelligence and his heart, the more he becomes qualified to lead beneficially in that system." However, he was to meet with the scorn of the capital's intellectuals in 1877, when they began to refer to him as an "old bonze" after the publication of his novel *Le Damné* whose plot takes place during the Renaissance in Italy and Switzerland. In another book, published four years before, *Diverses Reflexions sur Haiti,* Delorme discussed such subjects as railroad and paper money, which were precisely the issues before the Antoine Simon Government. But the author insisted in his work that agricultural development should be the primary concern and was, as he put it, "the vital question, the true question, the unique question that is to be promoted in Haiti."

¹⁹Taine was also the author of other books, including *Philosophy of Art,* which Price-Mars may have consulted while preparing his lecture on "Esthetics and Races."

²⁰*La Relève,* op. cit., p. 15.

²¹Ibid., p. 16.

Chapter Six

¹J. C. Dorsainvil, op. cit., p. 339.

²The name *cacos* came from the Dominican Republic and signified peasants in revolt.

³J. C. Dorsainvil, op. cit., p. 340.

⁴Edner Brutus, *Instruction publique en Haiti,* Port-au-Prince: Imp. de l'Etat, 1948, pp. 366-367.

Footnotes

⁵Price-Mars' Report in the *Official Bulletin of the Department of Public Instruction*, No. 2, December 1912-January 1913.

⁶Price-Mars, *La Vocation de l'Elite*, p. 69.

⁷Henock Trouillot, *La Pensée du Dr. Jean Price-Mars*, Edition Spéciale, *Revue de la Société haitienne d'histoire, de géographie et de géologie*, Port-au-Prince, July-October 1956, pp. 20-21. Mr. Trouillot was Secretary-General of that review.

⁸Price-Mars, *Jean-Pierre Boyer Bazelais et le drame de Miragoâne*, Port-au-Prince: Imp. de l'Etat, 1948, pp. 29-30.

⁹Price-Mars, *Vilbrun Guillaume Sam, ce méconnu*, p. 174.

¹⁰Ibid., p. 64.

¹¹Ibid., p. 61.

¹²Ibid., p. 63.

¹³Ibid., p. 63.

¹⁴Ibid., p. 65.

Chapter Seven

¹Price-Mars, "La Réforme de l'Enseignement Primaire," in *Haiti littéraire et scientifique*, Port-au-Prince, July 5, 1912.

²For five years from the time he became a Deputy in 1905, Price-Mars served on the School Supervisory Committee of Grande Rivière du Nord (County).

³Price-Mars, "La Réforme de l'Enseignement Primaire," in *Haiti Littéraire et scientifique*, Port-au-Prince, July 5, 1912.

⁴Ibid.

⁵Ibid., September 5, 1912.

⁶Quoted by Henock Trouillot in *Revue de la Société Haitienne d'Histoire, de Géographie et de Géologie*, July-October 1956, p. 25.

⁷Ibid., p. 26.

⁸Price-Mars, *Haiti littéraire et scientifique*, September 5, 1912.

⁹Price-Mars, *Vilbrun* . . ., p. 68.

¹⁰Ibid., p. 70.

¹¹Solon Méos, *L'Affaire Lüders*, Imp. J. Verrollot, 1898, op. cit., pp. 233-234.

¹²Dantès Bellegarde, *La Nation Haitienne*, op. cit., p. 156.

¹³After taking the oath of office, President Vilbrun moved from the Dessalines Barracks to a large brick house known as the Laroche residence on the Champ-de-Mars. The National Palace was on the east side of the park and General Oscar lived on the opposite side.

¹⁴Price-Mars, *Vilbrun*. . . , pp. 58-59.

Chapter Eight

¹Hogar Nicolas, *L'Occupation américaine d'Haiti*, Madrid, 1955, p. 141.

²Arthur C. Millspaugh, *Haiti under American control, 1915-1930*, Boston, 1930, p. 38.

³Paultre, op. cit., p. 53.

⁴Price-Mars, *La Vocation de l'Elite,* p. 1 (Preface).
⁵Ibid., p. 14.
⁶Ibid., p. 15.

⁷Price-Mars was referring to the indemnity of 150 million francs that France had demanded from President Boyer in 1825 as the price for recognizing Haiti as an independent State. Although the indemnity was later reduced to 60 million, it had nevertheless burdened the Haitian budget for fifty-five years before it was liquidated.

⁸Ibid., p. 36.
⁹Ibid., pp. 39-40.
¹⁰Ibid., p. 50.

¹¹Anténor Firmin had quoted the same writer in his *Letters from St. Thomas.* From an article Sir Harry Johnston had published in the London Times (April 1909), he extracted this passage: "Annually some large sums of money are appropriated in the Haitian budget for the maintenance of schools in all the communes of Haiti. This appropriation, I am sorry to say, constitutes one of the most cruel pranks played on the Haitian people by their government. In the general budget, superbly printed each year in Port-au-Prince, there is under Department of Public Instruction, a series of provisions for primary, secondary and higher education, with a detail and perfection worthy of Switzerland and Germany. However, a large part of this organization exists only on paper, and the funds appropriated for this splendid purpose find their way into the pockets of functionaires of the government or have never left the treasury...There exist some very good schools at Port-au-Prince and at the eleven or twelve chief-cities on the coasts of Haiti. I doubt that there are rural schools, in spite of the fact that 500 of them are indicated in the budget, or if there are some of them, they only serve to provide some meager means of existence to some absolutely incompetent persons. The serious offense is that about 2,500,000 out of 3,000,000 Haitians cannot read nor write and are as ignorant as the wild native of Africa."

¹²Edner Brutus, op. cit., pp. 369-370.

¹³Bonamy, a mulatto, had been a School Inspector and Director of the Lycée Pétion before becoming Minister of Public Instruction under Nord Alexis in 1903. He had served as President of a Ministerial Commission that produced a School Reorganization Plan in 1906, which Nord Alexis ignored.

¹⁴Price-Mars, *La Vocation de l'Elite,* pp. 61-62.
¹⁵Ibid., p. 63.
¹⁶Ibid., p. 88.
¹⁷Haitian currency unit worth about U. S. $.20.
¹⁸Op. cit., pp. 89-90.

Chapter Nine

¹Letter of August 26, 1915. Library of Congress, Lejeune papers.
²Price-Mars, *La Vocation de l'Elite,* p. 74.
³Ibid., p. 98.
⁴Ibid., p. 96.
⁵Ibid., pp. 103-104.
⁶Ibid., p. 79.

Footnotes

⁷Ibid., pp. 124-125.

⁸As quoted in Henock Trouillot, *Les Origines sociales de la littérature haitienne*, Port-au-Prince, Imp. N. A. Theodore, 1962, p. 295.

⁹A. C. Millspaugh, "Our Haitian Problem," in *Foreign Affairs*, July 1929, Vol. 7, pp. 557-558.

¹⁰Justin J. Kenol, In *Témoignages sur la vie et l'oeuvre du Dr. Jean Price-Mars*, Port-au-Prince, 1956, pp. 84-85.

¹¹Price-Mars, *La Vocation de l'Elite*, pp. 160-161.

¹²Bellegarde, *Témoignages sur la vie et l'oeuvre du Dr. Jean Price-Mars*, Port-au-Prince, 1956, p. 8.

¹³Emile Paultre, op. cit., (2nd ed.), 1966, p. 38.

¹⁴Price-Mars, *La Vocation de l'Elite*, p. 85.

¹⁵Ibid., p. 87.

¹⁶Ibid., pp. 141-142.

¹⁷Ibid., p. 142.

¹⁸Ibid., pp. 69-70.

¹⁹Ibid., p. 72.

²⁰Ibid., p. 158.

²¹Laleau was twenty-nine years of age when he began to write his novel. It was not published until 1932.

²²Price-Mars, *La Vocation de l'Elite*, p. 83.

²³Colonel Frederic May Wise, *A Marine Tells It to You*, J. H. Sears & Company, Inc., New York, 1929, pp. 311-314.

²⁴Price-Mars, *La Vocation de l'Elite*, p. 40(n).

²⁵Price-Mars, *Une Etape de l'évolution haitienne*, Port-au-Prince, Imp. "La Presse," 1929, pp. 113-114.

²⁶André Fréderique, "Mon Hommage d'Anniversaire au Dr. Price-Mars," in *Témoignages sur la vie et l'oeuvre du Dr. Jean Price-Mars*, p. 24.

Chapter Ten

¹Dantès Bellegarde, *La Résistance Haitienne*, Montreal, 1937, p. 67.

²James Weldon Johnson, "The Truth about Haiti," in *Crisis* (September 1920), p. 224.

³*Crisis*, May 1921, p. 18.

⁴James W. Johnson, *Along This Way*, The Viking Press, New York, 1933, p. 347.

⁵Ibid.

⁶Price-Mars, *La Vocation de l'Elite*, p. 78.

⁷As quoted in Dantès Bellegarde, *La Résistance Haitienne*, p. 105.

⁸Sténio Vincent was President of the Haitian Senate in 1917 when the Marines disbanded it. Percevel Thoby was a prominent lawyer of Port-au-Prince.

⁹Courtilien Charles, "Price-Mars et Pétionville," in *Haiti-Journal*, April 11, 1932.

¹⁰James Weldon Johnson, op. cit., p. 347.

¹¹Price-Mars, *Ainsi parla l'oncle*, Imp. de Compiègne, 1928, p. 220.

¹²Ibid., p. 221.
¹³Ibid., p. 236.
¹⁴Both Estimé and Duvalier became President of Haiti, respectively in 1946 and 1957.
¹⁵*La Relève*, Vol. I, July 1932, pp. 7-8.
¹⁶Colonel May Wise, op. cit., p. 30.
¹⁷Ibid., p. 304.
¹⁸Ibid., p. 313.
¹⁹Ibid., p. 307.
²⁰Ibid., pp. 307-308.
²¹Dantès Bellegarde, *La Résistance Haitienne*, p. 69.
²²Price-Mars, *Une Etape de l'évolution haitienne*, Imp. "La Presse," Port-au-Prince, 1929, pp. 128-129.
²³Ibid., p. 134.
²⁴Ibid., pp. 134-135. (The African precepts were quoted from a book by the Catholic Bishop Leroy, entitled *The Religion of the Primitives* in which the author made the following comment which Price-Mars also quoted: "It is therefore in many parts, by numerous parcels and "in quite different ways"—(multisque modis)—such as spoken words, visions, dreams, inspirations, internal enlightenment, natural intelligence, fortified and directed—that Revelation or rather the Revelations could have been made, and not only to the direct ancestors of the Hebrew people but to all the children of Adam and Eve who had a soul to save, so that all of them had at least the necessary means to obtain salvation: For it is certain that God wishes salvation for all human beings." Ibid., p. 132.)
²⁵Ibid., p. 128.
²⁶Ibid., pp. 146-147.
²⁷Price-Mars, *La Vocation de l'Elite*, p. 80.
²⁸Ibid., p. 81.
²⁹A *marabou* is a very dark person with dark eyes and long straight hair; a *griffe* is a brown skin person with brown eyes and kinky hair; a *chabine* is a light brown skinned person with light brown eyes and reddish hair.
³⁰Ibid., pp. 151-152.
³¹Ibid., p. 152.

Chapter Eleven

¹As quoted in Henock Trouillot, *Les origines sociales de la littérature haitienne*, pp. 352-353.
²Price-Mars, *Ainsi parla l'oncle*, preface, p. 2.
³As quoted in Franck Fouché, *Guide pour l'étude de la littérature haitienne*, Eds. Panorama, Port-au-Prince, 1964, pp. 97-98.
⁴*Autour de deux romans*, p. 120.
⁵Franck Fouché, op. cit., p. 96.
⁶Sylvain died a few months later.
⁷Emile Roumer. He became the review's editor after Normil's death in 1929. The review then published an anthology of the verses of its members and ceased to appear.

Footnotes

⁸Franck Fouché, op. cit., p. 99.

⁹Jacques C. Antoine, "Literature: De Toussaint à Jacques Roumain," in Mercer Cook, *Introduction to Haiti*, Pan American Union, Washington, D. C., 1951, p. 107.

¹⁰Price-Mars, *Ainsi parla l'oncle*, preface, p. 1.

¹¹Ibid., preface, p. 3.

¹²Ibid., p. 3.

¹³Ibid., p. 11.

¹⁴Ibid., p. 25.

¹⁵Ibid., pp. 164-165.

¹⁶Ibid., p. 165.

¹⁷It is claimed that the Virgin Mary appeared to someone there; a church was built at the spot where the miracle took place. The hamlet whose name means "Happiness-city" is near a waterfall which is the residence of the Voodoo loa "Master of the Water" as any other spring or body of land water.

¹⁸Ibid., p. 14. (The author translated the last Creole sentence: "I am the servant of these gentlemen.")

¹⁹Price-Mars, "On the 'Negro Renaissance' in the United States," as reproduced in *La Relève*, Vol. I, July 1, 1932, p. 15.

²⁰Ibid., pp. 16-17.

²¹Ibid., p. 20.

²²Ibid., pp. 13-14.

²³Dr. J. C. Dorsainvil, *Quelques vues politiques et morales (Questions haitiennes)*, Imp. Modele, Port-au-Prince, 1934, p. 71.

²⁴Price-Mars, *Ainsi parla l'oncle*, p. 191.

²⁵Ibid., p. 193.

²⁶Ibid., p. 192.

²⁷Published in 1906.

²⁸"Cabinet ministers and other people in high places in the Administration were enthusiastically calling for a third term for Borno at the National Palace, seemingly with the approval of the President."

²⁹*Témoignages sur la vie et l'oeuvre du Dr. Jean Price-Mars*, p. 3.

Chapter Twelve

¹*La Relève*, Vol. II, December 1, 1933, p. 24.

²Ibid., pp. 27-28.

³Ibid., p. 28.

⁴Ibid., January 1934, p. 54.

⁵As political tension increased in the capital the U. S. Marines were alerted throughout the country. On December 6, a group of peasants on their way to the city of Les Cayes to sell their produce there were met on the road at a place called Marchaterre by a contingent of U. S. Marines who, thinking it a surprise attack, fired into the group killing several and wounding many.

⁶Mendel Doctrine.

⁷Price-Mars, *Une Etape de l'évolution haitienne*, Imp. "La Presse," Port-au-Prince, 1929, pp. 25-26.

8. Ibid., p. 30.
9. Ibid., p. 31.
10. Ibid., p. 33.
11. Ibid., pp. 109-110.
12. *Témoignages sur la vie et l'oeuvre du Dr. Jean Price-Mars,* pp. 73-74.
13. Price-Mars, *La Vocation de l'Elite,* pp. 85-86.
14. Ibid., p. 86.
15. This book appeared in New York a few months before *A Stage of Haitian Evolution.*
16. Dantès Bellegarde, *La Résistance Haitienne,* p. 151.
17. Bellegarde, *La Nation Haitienne,* pp. 311-312.
18. Richard A. Loederer, author of *Voodoo Fire in Haiti,* 1935.
19. Ibid., p. 346.
20. Ibid., p. 65.
21. French economist (1806-1882); a traditionalist and conservative writer who advocated a strong organization of family, religion and property.
22. Ibid., pp. 77-78.
23. Ibid., pp. 62-63.
24. Ibid., p. 68. (A bachelor all his life, Pradel still enjoyed the title of "Prince of Haitian youth" which his peers of *La Ronde* had conferred on him at the turn of the century. He had been an ardent equestrian and fencer, but at that time practiced mostly tennis both with people of his age and younger members of the élite who liked his debonair style of life.)
25. Ibid., preface, pp. vii-viii.
26. Ibid., p. 87.
27. Ibid., p. 111.
28. W. B. Seabrook, *Magic Island,* Harcourt, Brace & Co., New York, 1929, pp. 138-141.
29. Price-Mars, *A Stage of Haitian evolution,* p. 185.
30. Ibid., pp. 185-186.
31. Ibid., p. 188.
32. Ibid., pp. 193-194.
33. Ibid., p. 202.
34. Price-Mars, "Ce que peut attendre le pays du Service Technique d'agriculture," in *La Relève,* Vol. II, January 1934, p. 53.

Chapter Thirteen

1. Jacques Roumain, "La poésie comme arme," in *Cahiers d'Haiti,* November 1944, pp. 39-40. This article first appeared in English under the title "Is Poetry Dead?" in *New Masses,* New York, issue of January 7, 1941, pp. 22-23.
2. Mr. Bellegarde was then very active in the *National League for Constitutional Action* which was created soon after President Borno announced officially on May 15, 1929 that he would not be a candidate for re-election. The League demanded the re-establishment of the Senate and House of Representatives. About the same time Roumain had organized the *The Patriotic Haitian Youth's League* of which he was

elected president. Mayard was a former Minister of the Interior under Dartiguenave and was particularly remembered for having said, "The Occupation is expanding in all its beauty." Moravia, editor of the newspaper *Le Temps* had been arrested several times and was at one time Haitian Consul General in New York. The various sectors of the Opposition had joined hands to enhance their chances of getting rid of the Borno-Russell régime.

[3] Henry Prather Fletcher, "Quo Vadis, Haiti?" in *Foreign Affairs,* July 1930, Vol. 8, p. 543.

[4] Dantès Bellegarde, *La Résistance Haitienne,* p. 171.

[5] Pradel was very popular in the North for having fought at the town of Limbé in behalf of Firmin. And Zéphirin had escaped from death in the Vilbrun Guillaume Massacre at the Port-au-Prince prison in 1915, but had lost one of his eyes there from a gun shot.

[6] Price-Mars, Preface to Jacques Roumain, *La Montagne ensorcelée,* Collection Indigène, Port-au-Prince, "La Presse," 1931.

[7] The fine works were: Jacques Roumain, *La Montagne ensorcelée;* Jean-Baptiste Cinéas, *Le Drame de la Terre;* Mme. Virgile Valcin, *La Blanche Negresse,* 1934; Dr. François Duvalier et al., *Les Tendances d'une Génération,* 1934; Maurice Casséus, *Viejo,* 1935.

[8] Jean-Baptiste Cinéas, *Le Drame de la Terre,* Imp. Adventiste, Cap-Haitien, 1933 (Preface).

[9] The "Oracle" was not only consulted by young Haitian writers. Well established authors from the United States, Latin America and Europe visited the Pétionville house to ask help in their research in the field of history and ethnology about Haiti.

[10] Their ideas and principles came from both Price-Mars and Dr. J. C. Dorsainvil, author of *Vodou et névrose,* 1913; *Une explication philologique du Vodou,* 1924; *Quelques vues politiques et morales (Questions haitiennes),* 1934. The leader of the original group was Louis Diaquoi, an ardent admirer of Price-Mars to whom he devoted a series of articles in the newspaper *National Action* under the title "Art and Science at the service of Action." He died unexpectedly in 1932 at the age of twenty-three.

[11] St. Louis et Lubin, *Panorama de la poésie haitienne,* Port-au-Prince, Ed. Henri Deschamps, 1950, p. 358.

[12] As reproduced in Pompilus, op. cit., pp. 586-588.

[13] Price-Mars, *Formation ethnique, Folk-lore et Culture du Peuple Haitien,* V. Valcin, Port-au-Prince, 1939, p. 44.

[14] Ibid., p. 117.

[15] Price-Mars, *Ainsi parla l'oncle,* p. 17.

[16] Price-Mars, *Formation ethnique, Folk-lore et Culture du Peuple Haitien,* p. 138.

[17] Ibid., p. 48.

[18] In his contribution to the book Bonhomme spoke of Indian influence in Haitian culture, if only psychological. In his preface for the book and again in his own *Formation ethnique,* Price-Mars denied the survival of any such influence in Haiti. But Suzanne Sylvain-Comhaire, Georges Sylvain's daughter, who has specialized in the field of ethnography expressed a contrary opinion and has even brought to light from her own investigations a number of Haitian popular stories of Indian origin or Indian influence, saying: "One is ashamed of researching one's Indian line of descent because in the public's eye this would be tantamount to negating or minimizing one's African origin." Sylvain-Comhaire, "Influences indigènes dans le folklore haitien," in *La Relève,* Vol. VI, January 1938, p. 7.

[19]The 1935 Plebiscite, beside furnishing Vincent the means for the "dismissal" of Price-Mars and his other ten colleagues, had remolded the Senate much into the shape of the Council of State under Dartiguenave and Borno, of pitiful and bitter memory.

Chapter Fourteen

[1]Price-Mars, "Vive La Relève!" in *La Relève,* Vol. II, July 1933, pp. 4-5. Edited by Jacques C. Antoine, *La Relève* lasted six years; in 1970 it was reprinted by Kraus Reprint and presented in six clothbound volumes for redistribution throughout the world.

[2]Roumain had created the Haitian Communist Party in 1934, and soon after was arrested and convicted to three years in prison for subversive activities. Released before the end of his prison term, he voluntarily went into exile in Europe, then in New York until 1941, when he returned to Haiti after the election of Lescot to the Presidency.

[3]The Head of the State Department's cultural division was Richard Pattee, an ardent admirer of Price-Mars. Several outstanding black writers and artists from the United States were either sent by Washington or invited by the Lescot Government, among them, W.E.B. DuBois, Alain Locke, Rayford Logan, Marian Anderson, Katherine Dunham, Todd Duncan, etc. Mercer Cook came to Haiti in 1943 as Supervisor of an English-Teaching Project and spent 22 months in the country. While there he also gathered material for a book, *Education in Haiti,* which was published in 1948.

[4]Price-Mars, *Jean-Pierre Boyer Bazelais et le Drame de Miragoâne,* Imp. de l'Etat, Port-au-Prince, 1948, pp. 27-28.

[5]Ibid., p. 23.

[6]Price-Mars had published several articles in the *Société d'Histoire et de géographie* about the Dominican Republic such as "L'unité politique d'Haiti s'est-elle opérée en 1822 par la violence ou par le libre ralliement des Dominicains à la République d'Haiti," October 1937; "La Diplomatie haitienne et l'Indépendance dominicaine, 1858-1867," January 1939.

[7]Estimé also took an interest in Price-Mars' son. When he named Price-Mars Foreign Minister in his first Cabinet in 1946, he appointed Louis Mars, then a medical doctor, to replace his father as director of the Institute of Ethnology, which had just become part of the University of Haiti.

[8]Thus applying the "lesson" that Price-Mars had taught in his book on Boyer Bazelais.

[9]The talk was published soon after in the form of a booklet under the same title, *Folklore et Patriotisme,* Les Presses Libres, 1951, pp. 18-19.

[10]Manual A. Pena Battle, "Al Sentido de una politica," a speech delivered on November 16, 1931.

[11]Price-Mars, *La République d'Haiti et la République Dominicaine,* Port-au-Prince, Imp. Held, S.A., Lausanne, 1953, pp. 326-327.

[12]Frédéric Kebreau, "Jean Price-Mars, professeur," in *Témoignages sur la vie et l'oeuvre du Dr. Jean Price-Mars,* p. 37.

[13]Henock Trouillot, *La Pensée du Dr. Price-Mars,* p. 90.

[14]Price-Mars, *De Saint-Domingue à Haiti,* Paris: Présence Africaine, 1959, p. 7.

[15]In 1944, Roumain was preparing to publish another novel when he died. The book, *Gouverneurs de la Rosée* (Masters of the Dew), which appeared a month or so after his death, depicts the triumph of collective effort on the part of the Haitian

peasants over resignation, despair and discord in the community; it was immediately translated into English by Mercer Cook who as still in Haiti. Since, the novel has been translated into sixteen other languages and is considered not only Roumain's masterpiece, but the Haitian masterpiece in the novel genre.

[16]Price-Mars, *De Saint-Domingue à Haiti*, pp. 101-102.

[17]The very year of its publication *De Saint-Domingue à Haiti* was awarded the French Academy's prize for the French language, which the Academy extended to Price-Mars' previous works.

[18]Price-Mars, *De Saint-Domingue à Haiti*, p. 160.

[19]Duvalier replaced the "Uncle" by his son Dr. Louis Mars at the Haitian embassy in Paris. He had already named his old Lycée Pétion schoolmate Foreign Minister and Ambassador to the United States.

[20]Jacques C. Antoine, "Education in Haiti," in *The Negro History Bulletin*, Vol. XII, January 1949, p. 95: "I remember telling him that our youth needed inspiration of that sort if it was to awaken to its duty toward the community, and to create a happier and more decent life for all. Dr. Mars wrote a magnificent article about Carver which appeared in the January 1945 issue of *Cahiers d'Haiti* that I was then editing in Port-au-Prince."

[21]As previously mentioned, *Vilbrun Guillaume Sam, ce méconnu* appeared in 1961. The year before marked the one hundredth anniversary of the late President's birth, as established by his birth certificate at Grande Rivière du Nord.

[22]Raoul Aglion, "Hommage au Dr. Price-Mars," in *Témoignages sur la vie et l'oeuvre du Dr. Jean Price-Mars*, pp. 21-22. Mr. Aglion, a Frenchman, spent several years in Haiti as Head of the United Nations Technical Assistance Mission to the country.

[23]Price-Mars was made a Doctor *Honoris Causa* by the University of Dakar and received many other tributes in the form of decorations such as Médaille de Vermeil de l'Union Latine, Médaille de Bronze de l'Ordre Cubain "Unidad por America," Chevalier de l'Ordre National de L'Education, Chevalier de l'Ordre National de la Santé Publique, Commandeur de l'Ordre "El Sol del Peru," Médaille de 1ère Classe de l'Ordre Vénézuelien Francisco de Miranda, Etoile de 1ère Classe de l'Ordre Souverain et Militaire de Malte, Commandeur de la Légion d'Honneur, Grand-Croix Chevalier de Mérite de l'Ordre Hospitalier Militaire de St. Lazare de Jérusalem, Chevalier de l'Ordre de la Courtoisie française as well as Grand-Croix de l'Ordre National "Honneur et Mérite" of Haiti. In 1970 the Senegalese Government issued a postage stamp bearing Price-Mars' likeness; the Government of Cameroun also did so during the same year.

[25]*Time*, New York, August 3, 1970, p. 27.

[26]René Piquion, *Manuel de Négritude*, p. 168.

[27]Price Mars, *Lettre Ouverte au Dr René Piquion: Le Préjugé de couleur est il la question sociale?* Les Editions des Antilles, S. A., Port-au-Prince, 1967, pp. 22-23.

Bibliography

Bellegarde, Dantès. *La Résistance haitienne.* Montréal: Ed. Beauchemin, 1937.

――――――. *La Nation haitienne.* Paris: J. de Gigord, 1938.

――――――. *Ecrivains haitiens.* Port-au-Prince: Ed. H. Deschamps, 1947.

Bervin, Antoine. *Louis Edouard Pouget.* Port-au-Prince: Société d'Editions et de Librairie, 1946.

Bobo, Rosalvo. *A propos du Centenaire.* Cap-Haitien: La Conscience, 1903.

Brierre, Jean F. *Au coeur de la Citadelle.* Port-au-Prince, 1929.

――――――. *A la Croix de Marchaterre.* Port-au-Prince, 1929.

――――――. *Le Drapeau de demain.* Port-au-Prince: Imp. Haitienne, 1931.

Brutus, Edner. *Instruction Publique en Haiti.* Port-au-Prince: Imp. de l'Etat, 1938.

Casséus, Maurice. *Viejo.* Port-au-Prince: Ed. La Presse, n.d.

Charles, Courtilien. "Price-Mars et Pétionville," in *Haiti-Journal* (11 April 1932).

Cinéas, J. B. *Le Drame de la terre.* Cap-Haitien: Imp. Adventiste, 1933.

Coicou, Massillon. *Passions.* Paris: Lib. des Mathurins, 1903.

Cook, Mercer. *Introduction to Haiti.* Washington, D. C.: Pan American Union, 1951.

Dorsainvil, Dr. J. C. *Manuel d'histoire d'Haiti.* Port-au-Prince: Ed. H. Deschamps, 1934.

――――――. *Quelques vues politiques et morales (Questions Haitiennes).* Port-au-Prince: Imp. Modèle, 1934.

――――――. *Vodou et Névrose.* Port-au-Prince: Imp. La Presse, 1931.

――――――. *Une explication philologique du Vodou.* Port-au-Prince: Imp. V. Pierre-Noel, 1924.

Delorme, Demesvar. *Les théoriciens au pouvoir. Causeries historiques.* Paris: Plon, 1870.

――――――. *Le Damné.* Paris: Challamel, 1877.

―――――――. *Diverses réflexions sur Haiti.* Paris (?), 1873.

Du Bois, William Edward Burghardt. *The Souls of Black Folk.* Chicago, 1903.

Féquière, Fleury. *L'éducation haitienne.* Port-au-Prince: Imp. de l'Abeille, 1906.

Firmin, Anténor. *De l'égalité des races humaines.* Paris: F. Pichon, 1885.

―――――――. *Lettres de Saint-Thomas.* Paris: V. Giard & E. Brière, 1910.

―――――――. *Roosevelt. Président des Etats Unis et la République d'Haiti.* N.Y.: Hamilton Bank Note & Publishing d'Haiti, 1905.

Fouché, Franck. *Guide pour l'étude de la littérature haitienne.* Port-au-Prince: Editions Panorama, 1964.

Innocent, Antoine. *Mimola.* Port-au-Prince, 1906.

Johnson, James Weldon. *Along This Way.* New York: The Viking Press, 1933.

―――――――. "The Truth about Haiti," in *Crisis* (September 1920).

Kébreau, Fréderic. "Jean Price Mars, professeur," in *Témoignages sur la vie et l'oeuvre du Dr Price Mars.* Port-au-Prince: Imp. de l'Etat, 1956.

Kénol, Justin K. *Témoignages sur la vie et l'oeuvre du Dr Jean Price Mars.* Port-au-Prince: Imp. de l'Etat, 1956.

Lamaute, Emmanuel. *Le Vieux Port-au-Prince.* Port-au-Prince: Imp. de la Compagnie Lithographique d'Haiti, 1939.

Laleau, Léon. *La Flèche au coeur.* Paris: Les Editions Parville, 1926.

―――――――. *Le Choc.* Port-au-Prince: Imp. La Presse, 1932.

Le Bon, Gustave. *The Psychology of Peoples.* New York: Stechert Reprint, 1924.

Lespinasse, Beauvais. *Histoire des Affranchis de Saint Domingue.* Paris: Kugelmann, 1882.

Leyburn, James. *The Haitian People.* New Haven: Yale University Press, 1941.

Logan, Rayford W. *The Diplomatic Relations of the United States with Haiti.* Chapel Hill: The University of North Carolina Press, 1941.

Lubin, Maurice A. and Carlos Saint Louis. *Panorama de la poèsie haitienne.* Port-au-Prince: Ed. Henri Deschamps, 1950.

Madiou, Thomas. *Histoire d'Haiti. Vol. 1.* Port-au-Prince: Imp. Edmond Chenet, 1922.

Marcelin, Frédéric. *Autour de deux romans.* 1902.

Ménos, Solon. *L'affaire Lüders.* 2nd ed. Port-au-Prince: Imp. Verrollot, 1898.

Montague, Ludwell Lee. *Haiti and the United States, 1714-1938.* Durham: Duke University Press, 1940.

Millspaugh, Arthur C. *Haiti under American Control, 1915-1930.* Boston, 1930.

Nicolas, Hogar. *L'Occupation américaine d'Haiti.* Madrid, 1955.

Paultre, Emile. *Essai sur M. Price-Mars.* Port-au-Prince, 1966.

Pena, Manual A. Battle. *Al sentido de una politica.* Speech. November 16, 1942, delivered in S. Domingo.

Piquion, René. *Manuel de Négritude.* Port-au-Prince: Ed. Henri Deschamps, n.d.

Pompilus, Pradel & Frères de l'Instruction Chrétienne. *Manuel illustré de la Littérature Haitienne.* Port-au-Prince: Ed. Henri Deschamps, 1961.

Price-Mars, Dr Jean. *Ainsi parla l'Oncle.* Paris: Imp. de Compiègne, 1928.

_____. *La Contribution haitienne à la lutte dans les Amérique pour la liberté humaine,* no details.

_____. *De Saint Domingue à Haiti.* Paris: Présence Africaine, 1959.

_____. *Folklore et Patriotisme.* Port-au-Prince: Imp. Les Presses Libres, 1951.

_____. *Formation ethnique Folklore et culture du peuple haitien.* Port-au-Prince: Imp. V. Valcin, 1939.

_____. *Jean-Pierre Boyer-Bazelais et le drame de Miragoâne.* Port-au-Prince: Imp. de l'Etat, 1948.

_____. *Lettre ouverte au Dr René Piquion: Le Préjugé de couleur est-il la question sociale?* Port-au-Prince: Les Editions des Antilles, 1967.

_____. *La République d'Haiti et la République Dominicaine.* Port-au-Prince: Imp. de l'Etat, 1953.

———. *La Vocation de l'èlite.* Port-au-Prince: Imp. Ed. Chenet, 1919.

———. *Silhouettes de nègres et de négrophiles.* Paris: Présence Africaine, 1960.

———. *Une étape de l'evolution haitienne.* Port-au-Prince: Imp. La Presse, 1929.

———. *Vilbrun Guillaume, ce méconnu.* Port-au-Prince: Imp. de l'Etat, 1961.

Rouzier, Séméxant. *Dictionnaire Géographique et administratif universel d'Haiti.* Vols. 1 and 2. Paris: Imp. de Charles Blot, 1892.

Roumain, Jacques. *La Montagne ensorcelée* (collection indigène). Port-au-Prince: Imp. La Presse, 1931.

———. *Gouverneurs de la rosée.* Port-au-Prince: Imp. de l'Etat, 1944.

Seabrook, W. B. *Magic Island.* New York: Harcourt, Brace & Co., 1929.

Simpson, J. Montague. *Six Months in Port-au-Prince and My Experience.* Philadelphia: G. S. Ferguson Co., 1905.

Sylvain, Georges. *Confidences et Mélancolies.* Paris: Ateliers Haitiens, 1901.

Texier, C. *Au pays des Généraux.* Paris: Calman Lévy, 1891.

Trouillot, Hénock. *Les origines sociales de la littérature Haitienne.* Port-au-Prince: Imp. N. A. Théodore, 1962.

Wise, Colonel Frederic May. *A Marine Tells It to You.* New York: J. H. Sears & Company, Inc., 1929.

Magazine Articles

Antoine, Jacques C., "Education in Haiti," in *The Negro History Bulletin,* Vol. XII (January 1949), p. 93.

Bellegarde, Dantès, "Un Haitien parle" in *Les Cahiers d'Haiti,* Vol. 1, No. 1, 1943, p. 35.

Cornevin, Robert, "L'oncle n'est plus (1876-1969), champion de la Négritude," in *France-Eurafrique,* Vol. 21, No. 205 (April 1969), p. 3.

Carmichael, Stokely, "The Caribbean Black Power Movement," in *Time* (August 3, 1970), p. 27.

Charles, Courtilien, "Price-Mars et Pétionville," in *Haiti-Journal* (April 11, 1932), p. 1.

Damas, Léon G., "Price-Mars, le père du Haitianisme," in *Présence Africaine,* Paris (June-September 1960), p. 168.

Fletcher, Henry Prather, "Quo Vadis, Haiti," in *Foreign Affairs,* Vol. 8 (July 1930), p. 543.

Frédérique, André, "Mon hommage d'Anniversaire au Dr. Price Mars," in *Témoignages.* Port-au-Prince: Imp. de l'Etat, 1956.

Johnson, James Weldon, "The Truth about Haiti," in *Crisis* (September 1920), p. 224.

Millspaugh, Arthur C., "Our Haitian problem," in *Foreign Affairs,* Vol. 7 (July 1929).

Price-Mars, Dr. Jean, "Ce que peut attendre le pays du Service Technique," in *La Reléve,* (Vol. 2, January 1934).

_____. "Les Corbeaux," in *L'Essor* (December 1912).

_____. "L'éducation des enfants retardés," in *L'Essor* (April 1914).

_____. "La Négro-Renaissance aux Etats-Unis," in *La Relève,* Vol. 1 (July 1, 1932).

_____. "Rapport du Jean Price-Mars," in *Bulletin officiel du Département de l'Instruction Publique* (December 1912-January 1913).

_____. "La Réforme de l'Enseignement Primaire," in *Haiti Littéraire et Scientifique,* (July 5, 1912).

_____. "Vive la Relève," in *La Reléve,* Vol. II (July 1933), pp. 4-5.

_____. *Une étape de l'évolution haitienne.* Port-au-Prince: Imp. La Presse, 1929.

Roumain, Jacques, "La Poèsie comme arme," in *Cahiers d'Haiti* (November 1944), pp. 39-40.

Trouillot, Hénock, "La Pensée du Dr Jean Price-Mars," in *Revue de la Société Haitienne d'histoire et de Géographie* (special edition), Port-au-Prince (July-October 1956).

Unpublished Letters and Papers

Mrs. Harold K. Heneise's letter of the Seminaire Théologique Baptiste, Cap-Haitien, November 6, 1969.

Douglass Papers, Cedar Hill, Anacostia, Washington, D. C.

Lejeune Papers, U. S. Library of Congress, Washington, D. C.

Booker T. Washington Papers, U. S. Library of Congress, Washington, D. C.

INDEX

A

(The) Act of Independence, 16, 42
Alexis, General Nord, 41, 42, 43, 47, 48, 54, 56, 58, 59, 60, 65, 66, 67, 69
L'Alliance Française, 48, 50, 57, 59, 61, 67, 97, 156, 170
Annales de Médecine Haitienne, 169
Archer, Stephen, 122
Aristotle, 191
Armand, Colonel Durcé, 174, 175
Association for the Celebration of the Centennial of Haiti's Independence, 40
Audain, Dr. Léon, 27, 28, 29, 32, 33, 43, 55, 56, 125;
Some unpublished fragments of our contemporary history, 43
Audain, Dr. Louis, 27
Auguste, General Tancrède, 70, 71, 73, 76, 78, 79, 82, 158

B

Baptist religion, 11, 24
Barnett, Major-General, 99, 119
Bassett, Ebenezer D. C., (article) "Should Haiti be Annexed?", 45
Battle, Manuel A. Pena, 183
Bellegarde, Dantès, 30, 46, 54, 55, 85, 112, 113, 121, 155, 166, 167, 172, 178, 186;
photograph, 52
Bellegarde, Windsor, 30, 32, 48
Blanton, Edward A. Jr., 59
Blot, Fénelon Louis (stepfather of Jean Price-Mars), 19, 20, 22
Blot, Probus (stepbrother of Jean Price-Mars), 30, 41, 86
Bonhomme, Arthur, 174
Bonhomme, Duvalier, Denis, *Les Tendances d'une Génération,* 174
Bobo, Dr. Rosalvo, 67, 87, 88, 89, 93, 97;
A Propos du Centenaire, 42, 46
Boisrond-Canal, General, 10, 19, 22, 41
Bonamy, Auguste, 112, 122
Borno, Louis, 93, 112, 122, 123, 125, 126, 131, 133, 147, 153, 154, 156, 157, 158, 166, 167
Bourget, Paul, *A Cruel Enigma,* 32
Boyer-Bazelais, Jean-Pierre, 10, 11, 16, 19, 22, 54, 59, 60, 64, 151, 156, 180
Brierre, Jean F., 166;
preface, 3
poems, *The Flag of Tomorrow; In the Heart of the Citadel; Poem to the Marchaterre Cross,* 166
Brouard, Carl, 134, 171
Brown, Philips Marshall, 154
Bureau-Museum of Ethnology, 178

C

Calixte, Colonel Démosthènes, 169, 174, 175
Canapé Vert, 186
Caperton, Admiral William B., 93, 95
Cap-Haitien's Secondary School for Girls, 71-72
Carmichael, Stokely, 188
Carteron, Pierre, 65, 66

Carver, Dr. George Washington, 187
Catholic primary schools, 82, 83
Catholic religion, 11, 16, 20, 24, 59, 124, 131, 138, 139
Central School of Agriculture, 147, 148, 153
Césaire, Aimé (of Martinique), 124, 188
Chanlatte, Juste, 31, 56
Charles, Courtilien, 123
Chavannes, Jean-Baptiste, 12, 13
(The) Chicago Defender, 120
Christophe, King Henry, 22, 43, 156
Cinéas, Jean-Baptiste, *Le Drame de la Terre,* 170
Codio, General Joseph Misaël, 86
Coicou Clinic, 125
Coicou, Jules, 65
Coicou, Massillon, 40, 65
poem,
Complaintes d'esclaves, 124-125
Collège de France, 35, 41
Commercial Court of Cap-Haitien, 11
Committee of Public Safety, 9
Commune Grande-Rivière-du-Nord, 9, 11, 15, 19, 21, 23, 24, 29, 43, 48, 68, 72, 73, 83, 89, 124
map, 118
Conan, Archbishop J., 82
The Constitution of 1918, 111
Courrier Haitien, 158
Crisis, 104, 119, 120

D

Dalbémar, Jean-Joseph, 40, 45
Dalencourt, Dr. François, 155
Dalmas, Louis, 59
Dartiguenave, Sudre, 93, 96, 112, 119, 120, 121, 122, 154, 158,
Déjean, Léon, 154
Delorme, Démesvar, 10, 67-68, 140, 142, 144, 151
Les Théoriciens au Pouvoir, 35-36
Denis, Lorimer, 171, 173
Deschanel, Paul, 156
Dessalines, Jean-Jacques, 17, 42, 56, 77, 78, 79, 96, 155, 188
Domingue, General Michel, 9, 10, 11
The Dominican Republic, 18, 69, 180, 183
Dorsainvil, J. C., 41, 69, 70, 83
Dorsinville, Hénoc, 81
Dorval, Maurice, 31, 32, 33, 34-35
Douglass, Frederick, 26, 45, 50, 94
My Bondage and My Freedom, 45
Dreyfus, Captain Alfred, 32
Drice, Mirabeau, 27, 30, 32
Dubois, Elie, 17
Dubois, W. E. Burghardt, 141, 184
Dufailly, Paul, 31
Durand, Oswald, 57, 79
poem,
"L'Epopée des Aieux," 79
Duvalier, François, 125, 171,

173, 185, 187, 190
Duvivier, Ulrick, 86, 87, 101

E

Ecole Elie Dubois, 51
Ecole Normale Supérieure, 30
emancipation of the slaves, 13
L'Essor, 73, 79, 81, 84, 94, 123, 148, 158
Estimé Dumarsais, 125, 181, 182, 185

F

Féquière, Fleury, 48, 51, 60
   Haitian Education, 48, 50
Finot, Jean, *The Prejudice of Races*, 51
Firmin, Anténor, 22, 23, 26, 27, 30, 33, 37, 39, 40, 41, 51, 54, 55, 59, 67, 69, 140, 144, 151, 188
   photograph, 52
   De l'égalité des races humaines, 142
   "Political Testament," 35
   Mr. Roosevelt and Haiti, 47
(The) First World Festival of Negro Arts, 188
Fisk University, 49
Flaubert, Gustave, *St. Antoine's Temptation*, 76
Fletcher, Henry P., 167
Forbes, Cameron, 166
The Forbes Commission, 167
Frédérique, Pierre, 37, 59, 67
Freemasonry, 20
(The) French Cable Company, 30
(the) French Revolution, 53, 150

Fuller, Mr. Paul, 88, 89

G

Gabriel, Camille, 43, 48
La Garde d'Haiti, 169
Geffrard, General Nicolas, 16, 17
(President) Geffrard's Concordat of 1860, 16
Germany, 37, 40, 87
Gérôme, Pétion, 31
Gherardi, Admiral Bancroft, 25, 26, 39
Gobineau, "Essay on the Inequality of the Human Races," 37
Godart (ancestor of Jean Price-Mars), 13
Godart, Marie Elizabeth P. (grandmother of Jean Price-Mars), 9, 12, 19, 20, 22, 23, 24, 27, 30, 68, 89-90
Goering, Consul Dr. Heinrich, 40
Grant, President Ulysses S., 18
Grégoire, Henri, 12, 13
Les Griots, 171, 172, 173, 174, 190
Guérin, Elie, 158
Guerrier, General Philippe, 24
Guignebert, Professor, 94
Guilbaud, Tertulien, 70, 71, 73, 82, 84, 88, 93, 100, 101
   Fatherland, 70

H

Haiti, *map*, x
Haiti Integrale, 158
Haiti médicale, 83
Haiti or the Black Republic (by

Sir Spencer St. John, former British Minister to Haiti), 26
Haitian-American Convention of September 16, 1915, 96
Haitian-American Society for Agricultural Development (SHADA), 178
Haitian Council of State, 93
Haiti littéraire et scientifique, 70
Haitian National School of Law, 40, 82
Haitian Society of History, Geography and Geology, 75
Haitian Society of Legislation, 55
Harding, U. S. Senator Warren (later U. S. President), 120, 121
Henri Grégoire Collége, 21, 23, 29, 143
(The New York) Herald, 26
(The New York) Herald Tribune, 166
Hickey, Captain B. F., 127, 137
Hoover, U. S. President Herbert, 154, 166
Howard University, 49, 178
Hurel, Jules, *De New-York à la Nouvelle-Orleans,* 50
Hyppolite, General Florvil, 22, 23, 25, 26, 27, 71

I

L'Impartial, 37
International Exposition to commemorate the two hundredth anniversary of the founding of Port-au-Prince, 181
Innocent, Antoine, *Mimola,* 143

J

Janvier, Louis-Joseph, 87, 174
Jean-Gilles, General Turenne, 65
Jaurès, Jean, 32, 33, 115
Jean, Lafontant, 170
Jean-Gilles, General Turenne, 65
Jean-Jumeau, General, 65
Jefferson, Thomas, 35
La Jeune Haiti, 27, 30
Johnson, Sir Harry, *The Negro in the New World,* 100
Johnson, James Weldon, 98, 119, 120, 121
  Self-Government, 120
  Along This Way, 120, 122
Jolibois, Joseph, Jr., 158
Le Journal des Etudiants, 27, 29

K

Knapp, Admiral, 120, 127
Kenol, Justin J., 112
  Témoignages sur la vie et l'oeuvre du Dr. Jean Price-Mars, 184

L

Lacoste, Mrs. Arthemise, 22
La Fontaine, *Fables,* 21, 143
Laleau, Léon,
  Le Choc, 115, 158
  La Flèche au Coeur, 130
  photograph 165
Lamartine, Alphonse de (French poet), 135
Lavaud, Colonel Franck, 179
(The) League of Haitian Youth,

Index

130, 131

Le Bon, Gustave, 56, 81, 94, 107 114, 115, 149
editor, *Bibliothèque de Philosophie Scientifique*, 35
Psychological Laws of the Evolution of Peoples, 35, 36 37, 45, 51, 54, 94
Psychology of Education, 114

Lechaud, Thomas, 125

Leconte, President Cincinnatus, 40, 69, 70, 76, 77, 79, 81, 86, 99, 100, 101, 113, 123, 131

Légitime, President François, 22

Lejeune, General J. A., 107

Léona Affaire, 138

Lescot, President Elie, 175, 176, 177, 178, 179, 182

Lespinasse, Beauvais, 39

Levelt, Major Antoine, 179

Leyburn, James, *The Haitian People*, 15

Lhérisson, Justin, 27

Liberal Party, 10, 54, 60, 64, 65, 151

Lilavois, Alexandre and Drossaint, 122

Lincoln, Abraham, The Emancipation Proclamation, 44
The Second Inaugural Address, 141

Louisiana Purchase Centennial Exposition in 1904, 43-44, 55

Lüders Affaire (Emile Lüders), 37, 39, 87

Lycée Pétion, 23, 24, 29, 112, 113, 116, 121, 125, 171, 185

M

Magloire, Auguste and Clément, 156

Magloire, Major Paul, 179, 181, 182, 184

Mahan, Alfred T., *The Influence of Sea Power Upon History, 1660-1873*, 25

Manigat, General François, 26, 39

Manigat, M., 21

Marcelin, Frédéric, 57, 58, 108, 110, 134, 136
Autour de deux romans, 134
Thémistocle-Epaminondas Labasterre, 57
La Vengeance de Mama, 57

Marcelin brothers, *Canapé Vert*, 186

Marchaterre (rural village in Haiti), 148, 167

Marius, Vice President Septimus, 10, 11

Mars, Jean-Baptiste, 14

Mars, Jean Eléomont (father of Jean Price-Mars), 9, 10, 11, 19, 20, 21, 22, 23

Mathon, Etienne, 84

Madame Lina Mathon's dance group, 186

(Le) Matin, 142, 156

Mayard, Constantin, 166

Mayo, Admiral Henry T., 120

(The) Mayo Commission, 120, 126, 127

McCormick Committee (U. S.), 98

Ménos, Solon, 87
L'affaire Lüders, 87
Michel, Fortuna Delcour (mother of Jean Price-Mars), 10, 19
Military Hospital in Port-au-Prince, 27, 28, 33
Millspaugh, Arthur C., 111, 112
Môle Saint-Nicolas, 25, 27, 39, 46, 87
(Le) Moniteur, 70, 101
Mon Repos, 25
(The) Monroe Doctrine, 37
Montaigne, *Essays,* 64
Moravia, Charles, 166
Moton, Dr. Robert R., 131

N

(The) Nation, 120
(The) National Association for the Advancement of Colored People, 99, 119
(The) National City Bank of New York, 122
National Lycée, 71
National Party, 10, 64, 65, 151
(The) National Progressive Party, 147
National School of Medicine, 27, 29
négritude, 27, 44, 56, 58, 63, 94, 95, 100, 108, 109-110, 116, 124, 132, 140-141, 144, 165, 166, 171, 172-173, 183, 184, 185, 187, 188, 190, 191
Niles, Mrs. Blair, 162
Black Haiti, 152

Nord, Jean-Joseph, 40
Northern Caribbean Sea, *map,* 2
La Nouvelle Ronde, 134, 135

O

Ogé, Vincent, 12
Official Bulletin, 54, 55
Oreste, Michel, 60, 82, 84, 85, 86
Ortiz, Fernando, 178
Oscar, General Charles, 87, 89, 187

P

"Pan" (nickname given to Marie Godart by her grandson, Jean Price-Mars), 12, 14
Parisiana Theatre, 95, 96
Paul, Edmond, 64, 67, 151
Paul, Thomas, 11
Paultre, Emile, *Essai sur M. Price-Mars,* 170
Pellé *Affaire,* 17, 126, 138
Péralte, Charlemagne, 111, 115, 116, 130
Pérez, Clara, 167
Pétion, Alexandre, 10, 56, 77, 78, 101, 156, 188
Petit, Georges J., 158
(Le) Petit Impartial, 158
Pierre-Louis, President Joseph Nemours, 185
Pierrot, General Jean-Louis, 43
Piquion, René, 190, 191
Plebiscite of February 1929, 147

Index

Polverel, French Commissioner, 13
Polyclinique-Péan, 33, 125
Port-au-Prince, *photograph*, 91
Pouget, Louis-Edouard, 48, 60, 61
Powell, William F., 37, 59, 69
Pradel, Seymour, 27, 85, 113, 157, 167, 168, 170
(La) Presse, 142
Price, Hannibal, 11, 23, 26, 38, (note), 39, 45, 46, 51, 67, 140
The Rehabilitation of the Black Race by the Republic of Haiti, 26-27, 38, 44
Price-Mars, Madame Clara, 177, 187
Price-Mars, Jean
 Books,
  Ainsi parla l'oncle (Thus Spoke Uncle), 58, 136, 137, 139-140, 142, 143, 144, 147, 151, 152, 155, 156, 172, 173, 188
  Christophe's sentiment of personal worth in regard to his role of Chief: Psychology of a Statesman (booklet), 169
  Formation ethnique, Folk-lore et Culture du Peuple Haïtien, 172, 173, 174, 175, 177
  The Haitian Contribution to the Struggle in the Americas for Human Liberty (booklet), 178
  Jean-Pierre Boyer Bazelais et le Drame de Miragoâne, 179
  Les Fêtes de Cormiers, 42
  On the "Negro Renaissance" in the United States, 141
  De la Préhistoire d'Afrique à l'histoire d'Haïti, 187
  La République d'Haïti et La République Dominicaine (The Republic of Haiti and Dominican Republic), 40, 183, 184
  De Saint-Domingue à Haïti, 185, 186
  Silhouettes de Nègres et de Nègrophiles, 187
  A Stage of Evolution of the Haitian People, 149, 151, 152, 153, 154, 155, 157, 158, 162, 165, 170, 186
  La Vocation de l'Elite, 144, 171
 Prose poem,
  "The Mutilated Victories," 73-75, 153
 Articles,
  "Les Corbeaux," 32, 33, 34
  "Pan," 12, 14
  "The Reform of Primary Education," 70
  "Simple remarks of psychiatry on Voodoo trance," 169
  "Son Idéal" (His Ideal), 31, 32, 108
  "Black Africa and her People," 178
  "Economic and Political Denomination of the Elite," 96, 103
  "The Equality of Human Races, according to a recent work by Jean Finot," 48
  "Esthetics and Races," 61
  "The First of the Blacks," 97-98
  "The Postulate of a Social Education," 95
  "The Prejudice of Races," 102
  "The Religious Sentiment and Phenomenon among the Blacks of Saint-Domingue," 127-128, 160
  "La Vocation de l'Elite," 101, 104, 114, 115, 121, 124, 130

"The Woman of Tomorrow," 108
Speech,
"The Art of Reading as a Discipline of General Education," 112-113, 114
photographs, viii, 192, 189(family)
Price-Mars, Louis (son of Jean Price-Mars), 112, 125, 188
Price-Mars, Marie-Madeleine (daughter of Jean Price-Mars), 171, 188
Primavera Club, 123, 125, 134, 135, 140

R

racial inequality, 25, 36-37, 54, 61-62, 81, 107, 115, 149-150, 152, 161, 162, 165
(La) Relève, 177
Renan, Ernst, 14
retarded school-age children, 94
Revue anthropologique, 173
Revue de psychothérapie et de psychologie appliquée, 169
(La) Revue Indigène, 135, 139, 158, 171, 172
Revue littéraire et scientifique, 81
Riché, General Jean-Baptiste, 24
Rodin, Auguste, 34
Rodman, Selden, Renaissance in Haiti Popular Painters In the Black Republic (1948), 186
Romero, Fernando, 178
(La) Ronde, 30
Roosevelt, President Franklin Delano, 163, 168, 169, 176

Roosevelt, President Theodore, 48, 163
Roumain, Jacques, 135, 158, 165, 166, 168-169, 178
Gouverneurs de la rosée, 186
La Montagne ensorcelée, 169
photograph, 159
Roumer, Emile, Poèmes d'Haiti et de France, 135
Roy, Eugène, 122, 166
Ruan, Addison T., 112
Rubalcava, Spanish Admiral, 17
rural people, 16, 19, 85, 95, 96, 97, 100, 101, 102, 103, 116, 123, 125, 127, 128, 169, 180
Rural Code, 98
Russell, Colonel John H., 119, 133, 165

S

Saint-Domingue, 12, 14, 53, 63, 128, 137, 149, 150, 152
St. John, Sir Spencer, Haiti or the Black Republic, 26
Saint-Méry, Moreau de, 63, 150
Description of the Island of Saint-Domingue, 128
Salnave, Sylvain, 9, 78
Salomon, General Louis-Félicité, 19, 22, 65, 180, 190
Sam, General Vilbrun Guillaume 29, 43, 76, 77, 78, 79, 81, 85, 86, 87, 88, 89, 94, 96, 99, 101, 116, 153, 187
Sam, General Tirésias Simon, 9, 19, 23, 27, 29, 33, 37, 39, 40, 47, 69, 71, 99
Sannon, Pauléus, 30, 32, 47, 61, 66, 112, 120, 121, 122, 125, 128, 129, 168

Index

School of Political Science, 41
Seabrook, W. B., *Magic Island,* 152, 160, 161-162
Seligman, Mr. Herbert, 119
Senghor, President Léopold Sédar (of Senegal), 124, 144, 184, 185, 188
SHADA, *see* Haitian-American Society for Agricultural Development, 178
Simon, General Antoine, 66, 69
Simpson, J. Montague, 48, 55
Société Africaine de Culture, 185
Société haitienne d'Histoire et de géographie, 180, 184
Society of the Friends of the Blacks, 12
Society of Haitian History and Geography, 125, 127
smallpox epidemic of 1881-1883, 19
Sonthonax, French Commissioner, 13
Sorbonne, 35, 41, 124
Sylvain-Comhaire, Madame Suzanne, 178
Sylvain, Georges, 72, 120, 126, 133, 135, 143, 156, 158
Cric Crac, 143
Sylvain, Normil, 135

T

Taine, Hippolyte, 153
Voyage to Italy, 67
Télémaque, General Séide, 9, 22, 43
Témoignages sur la vie et l'oeuvre du Dr. Jean Price-Mars (by Justin K. Kenol), 184
Texier, C., *Au Pays des Généraux,* 25
Théodore, Davilmar, 86, 87
Thoby-Marcelin, Philippe, 134, 136
Time (magazine), 188
Tontons Macoutes, 190
Toussaint-Louverture, 97, 101, 150, 153, 155, 170, 183, 187, 188
Treaty with the United States in 1915, 110
(La) Trouée, 135
Trouillot, Ernst, 151, 152
Trouillot, Henock, 75, 184
Trujillo, Raphael Leonidas, 175
Tuskegee Institute, 46, 48, 49, 50, 56, 131

U

Union Patriotique, 99, 120, 121, 123, 135
(The) United States of America, 18, 25, 37, 87, 88, 89, 93, 96-97, 98-100, 105, 107, 111, 112, 116, 119, 120, 121, 126, 127, 133, 154, 160, 169, 174, 176
Universal Exposition of French art and industry, 34

V

(The) Vatican, 181
Vieux, Antonio, 134
Vilaire, M. Etzer, 72, 130
Vilmenay, Thomas A., 60
Vincent, President Sténio, 167,

168, 169, 170, 174, 175

Voodoo, 16, 17, 19, 20, 21, 84, 124, 126, 127, 128, 129, 130, 137, 138, 139, 144, 155, 161, 169, 181, 182, 183

W

Waller, Colonel Littleton W. T., 107
Waring, Samuel, 11
Washington, Booker T., 46, 49, 50, 56
Up from Slavery, 49

The Washington Post, 186
Williams, Mr. W. T. B., 131
Wilson, President Woodrow, 93, 111, 120
Wise, Colonel May, 126, 127
A Marine Tells It To You, 116
women, 50, 63, 108-109, 110, 160

Z

Zamor, Oreste, 86, 87, 88, 89
Zéphirin, Louis, 168

Jean Price-Mars and Haiti

—The Author—

Jacques C. Antoine, now resident in Buenos Aires, served at one time as the Haitian Ambassador to the United States, as well as an official of his government in Haiti. Antoine's parents were from Cayes and he did all studies in Haiti, including his law degree. Antoine's study of Price-Mars offers the reader an historical picture of Haiti spanning almost one hundred years as it was lived through by Price-Mars in his many roles—politician, diplomat, ethnologist, teacher, philosopher and moralist. The author, Antoine, was for many years Professor of Literature at Howard University in Washington, D. C.

Jean Price-Mars on:

His birthplace, Grande Rivière du Nord in Haiti: . . . the mountains, nearby and faraway, present to the eyes the dazzling colors of their garments which change capriciously with the play of light . . .

On the Haitian elite: . . . Ah! yes, we are ready to spend thousands of gourdes to set up clubs for play and pastime, ... but we are unable to support a good literary magazine, to create clinics, night schools, or to establish a good college where . . . , we might offer a better education to our elite of tomorrow.

On noting the similarities of the Voodoo and Catholic religions: Don't the Catholic, and the Voodoo worshipper believe in the existence of a supreme God? . . . Don't they both believe in supernatural beings—saints, angels and demons . . . . Isn't it a fact that both have found almost the same term—mystery—to envelop their ignorance of any phenomena that seem unexplainable to them? Moreover, are they not both obsessed by the fear of Satan?

LC No : 80-80888; ISBN: 0-914478-55-9 (Case); –56-7 (Paperback)

Some of Our New Books From the Caribbean:

Caribbean Writers: A Bio-Bibliographical Critical Encyclopedia *Herdeck, Lubin, Figueroa, Figueroa, et al.*

Harlem, Haiti and Havana: A Comparative Study of Langston Hughes, Nicolás Guillén & Jacques Roumain *Martha Cobb*

Black Shack Alley (Jospeh Zobel's *La rue cases-nègres*), Trans. by Keith Q. Warner

The Lonely Londoners, A Brighter Sun and Ways of Sunlight (novel and two volumes of short stories) *Sam Selvon*

Three Continents Press, Inc.   Washington, D. C.   3CP

LIBRARY OF DAVIDSON COLLEGE